# Teach Yourself
# VISUALLY™
## HTML and CSS

Visual™

by Mike and Linda Wooldridge

WILEY

Wiley Publishing, Inc.

# Teach Yourself Visually™
# HTML and CSS

Published by
**Wiley Publishing, Inc.**
10475 Crosspoint Boulevard
Indianapolis, IN 46256
www.wiley.com

Published simultaneously in Canada

*Library of Congress Control Number: 2008927916*

ISBN: 978-0-470-28588-6
Manufactured in the United States of America
10 9 8 7 6 5 4 3 2 1

## Trademark Acknowledgments

## Contact Us

For general information on our other products and services contact our Customer Care Department within the U.S. at 800-762-2974, outside the U.S. at 317-572-3993 or fax 317-572-4002.

For technical support please visit www.wiley.com/techsupport.

## Permissions

Wiley Publishing, Inc.

**Sales**

Contact Wiley
at (800) 762-2974 or
fax (317) 572-4002.

# Praise for Visual Books

*"Like a lot of other people, I understand things best when I see them visually. Your books really make learning easy and life more fun."*

John T. Frey (Cadillac, MI)

*"I have quite a few of your Visual books and have been very pleased with all of them. I love the way the lessons are presented!"*

Mary Jane Newman (Yorba Linda, CA)

*"I just purchased my third Visual book (my first two are dog-eared now!), and, once again, your product has surpassed my expectations.*

Tracey Moore (Memphis, TN)

*"I am an avid fan of your Visual books. If I need to learn anything, I just buy one of your books and learn the topic in no time. Wonders! I have even trained my friends to give me Visual books as gifts."*

Illona Bergstrom (Aventura, FL)

*"Thank you for making it so clear. I appreciate it. I will buy many more Visual books."*

J.P. Sangdong (North York, Ontario, Canada)

*"I have several books from the Visual series and have always found them to be valuable resources."*

Stephen P. Miller (Ballston Spa, NY)

*"Thank you for the wonderful books you produce. It wasn't until I was an adult that I discovered how I learn – visually. Nothing compares to Visual books. I love the simple layout. I can just grab a book and use it at my computer, lesson by lesson. And I understand the material! You really know the way I think and learn. Thanks so much!"*

Stacey Han (Avondale, AZ)

*"I absolutely admire your company's work. Your books are terrific. The format is perfect, especially for visual learners like me. Keep them coming!"*

Frederick A. Taylor, Jr. (New Port Richey, FL)

*"I have several of your Visual books and they are the best I have ever used."*

Stanley Clark (Crawfordville, FL)

*"I bought my first Teach Yourself VISUALLY book last month. Wow. Now I want to learn everything in this easy format!"*

Tom Vial (New York, NY)

*"Thank you, thank you, thank you...for making it so easy for me to break into this high-tech world. I now own four of your books. I recommend them to anyone who is a beginner like myself."*

Gay O'Donnell (Calgary, Alberta, Canada)

*"I write to extend my thanks and appreciation for your books. They are clear, easy to follow, and straight to the point. Keep up the good work! I bought several of your books and they are just right! No regrets! I will always buy your books because they are the best."*

Seward Kollie (Dakar, Senegal)

*"Compliments to the chef!! Your books are extraordinary! Or, simply put, extra-ordinary, meaning way above the rest! THANK YOU THANK YOU THANK YOU! I buy them for friends, family, and colleagues."*

Christine J. Manfrin (Castle Rock, CO)

*"What fantastic teaching books you have produced! Congratulations to you and your staff. You deserve the Nobel Prize in Education in the Software category. Thanks for helping me understand computers."*

Bruno Tonon (Melbourne, Australia)

*"Over time, I have bought a number of your 'Read Less - Learn More' books. For me, they are THE way to learn anything easily. I learn easiest using your method of teaching."*

José A. Mazón (Cuba, NY)

*"I am an avid purchaser and reader of the Visual series, and they are the greatest computer books I've seen. The Visual books are perfect for people like myself who enjoy the computer, but want to know how to use it more efficiently. Your books have definitely given me a greater understanding of my computer, and have taught me to use it more effectively. Thank you very much for the hard work, effort, and dedication that you put into this series."*

Alex Diaz (Las Vegas, NV)

# Credits

**Project Editor**
Jade L. Williams

**Acquisitions Editor**
Jody Lefevere

**Copy Editor**
Kim Heusel

**Technical Editor**
Namir Shammas

**Editorial Manager**
Robyn Siesky

**Business Manager**
Amy Knies

**Sr. Marketing Manager**
Sandy Smith

**Editorial Assistant**
Laura Sinise

**Manufacturing**
Allan Conley
Linda Cook
Paul Gilchrist
Jennifer Guynn

**Book Design**
Kathie Rickard

**Production Coordinator**
Lynsey Stanford

**Layout**
Andrea Hornberger
Jennifer Mayberry

**Illustrators**
Ronda David-Burroughs
Cheryl Grubbs

**Screen Artist**
Jill A. Proll

**Proofreader**
Lynda D'Arcangelo

**Quality Control**
Jessica Kramer

**Indexer**
Sherry Massey

**Vice President and Executive Group Publisher**
Richard Swadley

**Vice President and Publisher**
Barry Pruett

**Composition Director**
Debbie Stailey

## About the Authors

**Mike Wooldridge** is a user-interface designer based in the San Francisco Bay Area. He has been building Web sites with HTML since 1995.

**Linda Wooldridge** is a former senior editor at ***Macworld***. She is the coauthor of ***Teach Yourself Visually Photoshop Elements 6*** and other books in the Visual series.

## Authors' Acknowledgements

Mike and Linda thank Jody Lefevere for assigning them the book, Jade Williams for managing the project, Namir Shammas for his technical editing, Kim Heusel for his copyediting, and Ronda David-Burroughs and Cheryl Grubbs for their artistic creations. Mike and Linda dedicate the book to their eight-year-old son, who enjoys surfing the Web and blogging.

# Table of Contents

# chapter 3   Adding Text

# chapter 4   Formatting Text

# Table of Contents

**chapter 5** Adding Images

**chapter 6** Adding Links

# chapter 7  Working with Tables

# Table of Contents

chapter **9**    Creating Forms

## chapter 10 Creating Style Sheets

## chapter 11 Formatting Text with Style Sheets

# Table of Contents

## chapter 14  Adding Multimedia and Extra Touches

## chapter 15  Publishing Your Web Pages

# Getting Familiar with HTML and Web Page Basics

Are you interested in building your own Web pages? This chapter introduces you to HTML, the language used to create Web pages. It also explains the basics behind HTML editors and Web browsers, which you use to design and view your Web content.

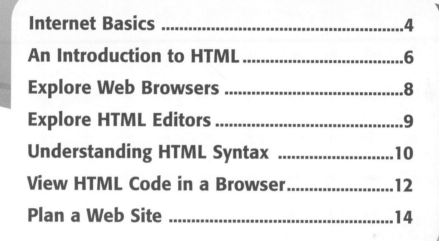

# Internet Basics

The Internet is a worldwide collection of interconnected computer networks that enables businesses, organizations, governments, and individuals to communicate in a variety of ways. One of the most popular ways users communicate on the Internet is by publishing and interacting with Web pages. You can also use the Internet to send and receive e-mail, chat with other users, and transfer files between computers.

**The Internet began as a military research project in the late 1960s. In 2007, the number of Internet users around the globe topped 1.2 billion.**

## Types of Connections

Users connect to the Internet through a variety of methods. A relatively inexpensive but slow way to connect is with dialup service, which involves using a modem and a phone line. Faster ways to connect include DSL (digital subscriber line), cable modem, satellite, and ISDN (integrated services digital network). Networks include special wireless transmitters that allow computers to access the Internet wirelessly. Companies that help you connect to the Internet are known as *Internet service providers*, or ISPs.

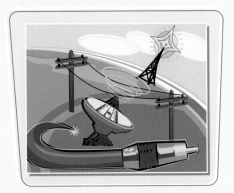

## Connection Speeds

Connection speeds play an important part in a user's Internet experience because slower connections result in slower file transfers and Web page viewing. Dialup connections offer the slowest access to the Internet at up to 56 kilobits per second, or Kbps, followed by ISDN connections at 64 to 128 Kbps. DSL usually offers connection speeds of up to 3 megabits per second, or Mbps, while cable modems can achieve speeds of up to 6 Mbps. A Web page that takes about 20 seconds to download via dialup can take less than a second using a cable modem.

## Communication Standards

The Internet infrastructure relies on a variety of protocols that dictate how computers and networks talk to each other. For example, *Transmission Control Protocol/Internet Protocol*, or TCP/IP, is a set of rules that control how Internet messages flow between computers. *HyperText Transfer Protocol*, or HTTP, is a set of rules that determine how browsers should request Web pages and how server computers should deliver them. Having agreed-upon protocols allows seamless communication among the many different types of computers that connect to the Internet.

## The World Wide Web

The World Wide Web is a giant collection of documents, or pages, stored on computers around the globe. Commonly called *the Web*, this collection of pages represents a wealth of text, images, audio, and video available to anyone with a computer and an Internet connection. Web pages are stored on servers, which are Internet-connected computers running software that allows them to serve up information to other computers. When you place a text file, image, or other document in a special Web directory on a server, that information is available for other Web users to view. Chapter 15 talks about how to transfer information to a Web server.

## URLs and Links

Every page on the Web has a unique address called a URL, which is short for *Uniform Resource Locator*. A URL looks like this:

http://www.example.com/index.html

If you know a page's URL, you can type it into a Web browser to view that page over the Internet. You can also view pages by way of *hyperlinks*, or simply *links*, which are clickable words or images on Web pages. Every link on a Web page is associated with a URL that leads to another page on the Internet. Users can jump from one Web page to another by clicking links. Chapter 6 discusses how to create links with HTML.

## Browsers

A Web browser is software that allows you to view and interact with Web pages. When you type a URL or click a link in a Web browser, the browser retrieves the appropriate page from a server on the Internet and displays that page. Microsoft Internet Explorer, Mozilla Firefox, and Apple Safari are the three most popular browsers in use today. Each program has evolved through a number of versions, with newer versions supporting more recent Web features. As you build your pages using HTML code, remember that different browsers may display your pages slightly differently depending on the version.

# An Introduction to HTML

You build Web pages using HTML, which is short for *HyperText Markup Language*. HTML documents are made up of text content and special codes known as *tags* that tell Web browsers how to display the content. HTML documents are identified by their .html or .htm file extensions.

**For the most part, HTML is platform independent, which means you can view Web pages on any computer operating system, including Windows, Mac, and Linux.**

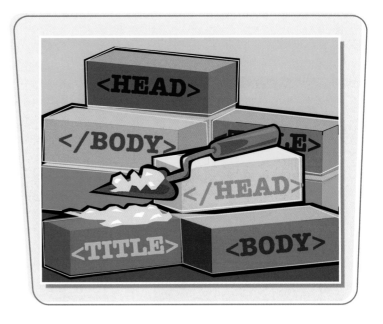

## HTML Tags

HTML consists of text interspersed with special instructions known as *tags*. Surrounded by brackets, < >, HTML tags tell a browser how to organize and present text, images, and other Web page content. Many tags are written using an opening tag and a closing tag that surround content that appears on the page. When writing HTML tags, you can use upper- or lowercase letters. To make the coding easy to distinguish from other text in the page, you can type tag names in uppercase. For details, see the section "Understanding HTML Syntax."

## Rendering HTML

When a browser displays a Web page, it retrieves the HTML file for that page from a server, parses the HTML tags to determine how the content should be formatted, and renders the page. The HTML tags tell the browser what images, video, audio, and other content need to be downloaded and integrated into the page. The HTML may also tell the browser to download style sheets and interactive scripts to further enhance the page. To view the HTML underlying a Web page, see the section "View HTML Code in a Browser."

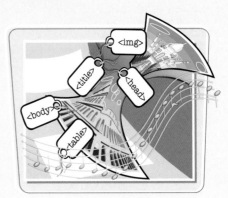

## HTML Standards

The World Wide Web Consortium, or W3C, is the primary group guiding the evolution of the HTML language. The W3C is made up of hundreds of companies and organizations including Web industry leaders such as Microsoft, Apple, and Google. The standards developed by the W3C give developers of Web servers and browsers a set of common guidelines with which to develop their products. You can visit the W3C's Web site at www.w3.org.

## HTML Versions

The most recent version of HTML is 4.01. Version 4.01 includes rules for using more than 90 HTML tags, most of which are covered in this book. It improves on previous versions by adding better support for multimedia, scripting, and style sheets. Support for style sheets is especially important because it allows developers to apply more precise formatting to Web pages. It also allows developers to keep complex styling information separate from the rest of the HTML. Style sheets are covered in Chapters 10, 11, and 12.

## XHTML

XHTML, or *Extensible HyperText Markup Language*, is an alternative language for coding Web pages that conforms to the stricter standards of XML, or *Extensible Markup Language*. XHTML is tag-based and uses many of the same tags as in HTML. However, in XHTML, all tags must be closed, tag names and attributes must be coded in lowercase, and attribute values for tags must be surrounded by quotes. Most modern browsers can read both HTML and XHTML. Although XHTML is not covered in this book, you can read more about it at the W3C site at www.w3.org.

## Next Generation of HTML

As this book is being published, the W3C is developing the specification for HTML 5, the next version of HTML. This version will introduce features to help Web designers more easily create and maintain the dynamic pages seen in many of today's Web sites. HTML 5 will include tags for defining headers, footers, and navigation sections, along with tags for adding interactive elements such as editable and sortable tables. For more information, see www.whatwg.org/html5.

# Explore Web Browsers

A Web browser is software that can retrieve HTML documents from the Web, parse the HTML instructions, and display the resulting Web pages. You can also use a browser to display HTML documents you save locally on your computer. When coding your HTML, you can use a Web browser to test your work.

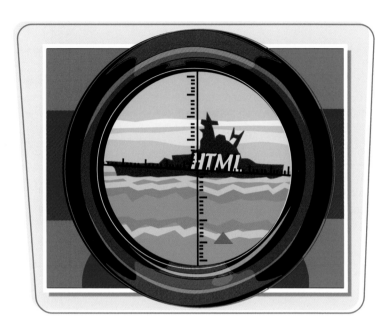

## Finding a Browser

Most computer operating systems come with a Web browser already installed. Microsoft Windows Vista computers include the Internet Explorer browser, while Apple Mac computers include the Safari browser. (The examples in this book use Internet Explorer.) Mozilla Firefox is another Web browser that has become increasingly popular in recent years. You can learn more about Firefox and download it free at www.mozilla.com/firefox. For more information about the Web browsers in use today, see the Wikipedia at http://wikipedia.org/wiki/Web_browser.

## Browser Discrepancies

There are many Web browsers in use today, and numerous versions of each. While most of them interpret HTML essentially the same way, slight differences in interpretation mean that not all of them display Web pages exactly the same way. Also, some more recent browser versions recognize newer HTML features that older browsers do not. You can avoid surprises by writing clean, well-formed HTML code and testing your pages in different browsers as you work. The Wikipedia offers a detailed comparison of Web browser features at http://wikipedia.org/wiki/Comparison_of_web_browsers.

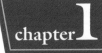

Because HTML documents are plain-text documents, you can use any text-editing program to code HTML and create a Web page. You can also use a variety of Web-specific coding environments that will write your HTML code, validate it, and upload it to a Web server.

## Simple Text Editors

Simple text editors, also called plain-text editors, are easy to find. Microsoft Windows Vista comes with Notepad, while Apple Mac computers come with TextEdit. Simple text editors offer no-frills word processing and are often the best choice when you are learning to write HTML. This book uses the Windows WordPad and Notepad text editors in its examples. The Wikipedia has a list of free and commercial text editors at http://wikipedia.org/wiki/List_of_text_editors.

## HTML Editors

HTML editors, such as Adobe Dreamweaver and Microsoft Expression, are dedicated programs for writing HTML code and managing Web pages. These programs can shield you from having to write HTML code by offering a graphical environment for building Web pages as well as a text-based environment. Most HTML editors will also color your HTML tags for easier viewing, validate your code, and help you upload finished pages to a server.

## Word Processing Programs

You can also use word processing programs, such as Microsoft Word, to write HTML. In Word, you can select HTML as the file type when you save a document, and the program automatically adds the appropriate HTML tags. However, commercial word processors tend to store lots of extra information with your HTML, which can make it a challenge to edit the files in other editors.

# Understanding HTML Syntax

HTML is a language for describing Web page content. HTML rules, or *syntax*, govern the way in which code is written. Learning the right way to write your code can save you time and confusion later.

## Writing HTML

In HTML, tags determine how page content is organized and formatted. Tags consist of words or abbreviations surrounded by angle brackets, < >. Tags can be written using upper- or lowercase letters. You can type tag names in uppercase to distinguish the code from other text. This HTML code creates a paragraph in your page:

```
<P>Hello, world!</P>
```

## Tag Structure

Certain structural HTML tags identify different parts of your HTML document. For example, the <BODY> and </BODY> tags surround the main body content that appears in the browser window. Many tags, such as the paragraph tags (<P> and </P>), are written using an opening tag and a closing tag while others, such as the image tag (<IMG>), stand alone. Closing tags must always include a slash (/) before the tag name.

## Attributes and Values

You can assign specific attributes to each HTML tag to customize its behavior. Most attributes work by setting a numeric or descriptive value. For example, you can set a paragraph's alignment on the page using the ALIGN attribute along with a type of alignment: left, right, or center. The code for creating a centered paragraph looks like this:

```
<P ALIGN="center">My centered text.</P>
```

Attributes always go inside the opening HTML tag, and it is good form to enclose attribute values in quotation marks.

## Entities

You can add special characters to a page, such as a copyright symbol or a fraction, by using special codes called *entities*. Entities represent characters not readily available on the keyboard. All entities are preceded by an ampersand (&) and followed by a semicolon (;). For example, the following code adds a copyright symbol to your page:

```
&copy;
```

For more about entities and special characters, see Chapter 3.

## Avoiding Syntax Errors

To avoid HTML errors, always take the time to proofread your code. Most HTML editors have features that highlight bad syntax. Make sure your tags have brackets, your closing tags include a slash, and your attribute values are surrounded by quotation marks. Multiple HTML tags should be properly nested, meaning your closing tags should be in the reverse order of the opening tags. For example:

```
<P ALIGN="center"><B>My text.</B></P>
```

To help make your HTML readable, consider using new lines to type code instead of running everything together on one long line. Doing so will not affect how your page is displayed, because Web browsers ignore extra white space.

# View HTML Code in a Browser

You can view the HTML code for any Web page that you have loaded into your Web browser. Viewing HTML from different Web sites is a good way to learn how to write your own code and can spawn new ideas for your own pages. You can also save a Web page locally for use as a template or to study later.

**In Microsoft Windows Vista, Internet Explorer opens the HTML code in the Notepad text editor. To view an HTML page that you have saved locally, see Chapter 2.**

---

## View HTML Code in a Browser

### VIEW THE SOURCE CODE

1. Open a Web page in your browser window.

2. Click **View**.

3. Click **Source**.

A Notepad window appears displaying the HTML source code for the page.

4. Click the Close button () when finished.

The window closes.

## SAVE THE SOURCE CODE

**1** In the Notepad window that displays the source code, click **File**.

**2** Click **Save As**.

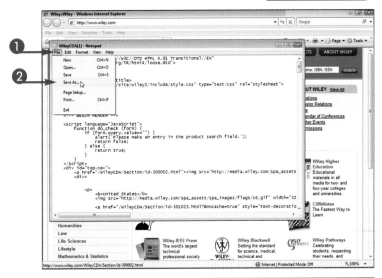

The Save As dialog box appears.

**3** Click here to navigate to the folder where you want to store the page.

**4** Type a name for the page.

HTML pages should have an .html or .htm file extension.

**5** Click **Save**.

Notepad saves the page.

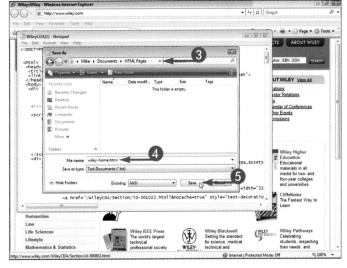

**TIPS**

### Will the HTML documents that I save to my computer work when I open them in a browser?

Possibly. It depends on how the HTML is coded. In addition to the HTML, you may have to download images, style sheets, scripts, and other external content separately, and then edit the HTML so that the page references them correctly. For more about referencing content, see Chapter 6.

### How else can I save a Web page in my browser?

In Internet Explorer, you can click **File** and then **Save As**. The browser gives you several ways to save your page. "Complete" saves the HTML and embedded content, "HTML only" saves just the HTML, and "Web Archive" saves the HTML and other content as a single file.

A Web site is a group of related Web pages, all hyperlinked together and hosted on a server. Before you start writing the HTML to create a site's pages, it is a good idea to do some planning.

### Know Your Audience

It is important to understand the audience that will visit the pages on your Web site. It is important to know their technical ability so that you can use language they are comfortable with. It is also important to know their interests so that you can present imagery and other content that will keep them interested and at your site. You can conduct interviews with potential users early on to get ideas for your site designs. You can also have users test out your site after it launches to get feedback on how to improve it.

### Plan a Home Page

The home page is usually the first page a visitor sees when visiting a Web site, so it is important that it concisely communicate the site's purpose and what information users can expect to find. It should also include prominent links to the other important pages on your site. Optimally, users should be able to see all of this information without having to scroll in their browser window. Clear communication is important on all of your site's pages, but especially on the home page.

## Site Map

A useful tool for planning your site's overall structure is a *site map*, which represents your Web pages as boxes and the hyperlinks as arrows. The home page of a site is usually placed at the top of a site map. A site map gives you an overview of the pages you need to build and also shows the navigational structure. You should arrange your pages so that important content is easy to get to from the home page. You can sketch your site map using pencil and paper or using software such as Microsoft Visio, which has tools specifically made for creating site maps.

## Linear Structure

A linear site layout moves the user through your content in a step-by-step fashion, like pages in a book. Linear layouts are good for presenting sequential instructions or a narrative story. In a linear layout, each Web page usually links to the next page and the previous page. The site map of a linear site will have the pages arranged one after the other in a line.

## Hierarchical Structure

A hierarchical layout resembles a pyramid, with the home page at the top and other pages fanning out from there. A hierarchical site map looks like a company's organizational chart or a family tree. Hierarchical layouts are appropriate for sites with categorized content, such as online merchants. Each branch in such a site represents a product category with the for-sale items at the end of the branches.

## Gathering Content

After you plan the pages and structure of your site, you need to gather the content. For simple sites, this may involve writing text and shooting digital photos. More complex sites may require recording audio and video, creating illustrations, and programming interactive media. You can organize all of this content into your Web pages using HTML.

# Creating Your First HTML Page

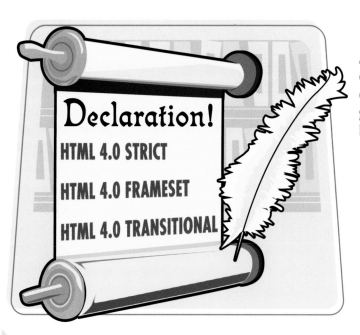

Are you ready to begin creating a Web page? This chapter shows you how to get started with a basic HTML document.

# Understanding HTML Document Structure

Although Web pages can differ widely in terms of content and layout, all pages have certain HTML tags that give them the same basic structure. Understanding this structure helps you begin to build your own HTML pages.

## HTML Tags

The <HTML> and </HTML> tags at the beginning and end of a text document identify it as HTML code. When a browser encounters these tags, it knows that anything within the two tags defines a Web page. Older Web browsers expect to see the HTML tags; with the latest version of HTML and newer versions of browsers, the tags are not always necessary, but adding them is good form.

## Document Type Declaration

You can add a DOCTYPE declaration to specify which tags a browser can expect to see in your HTML document. In HTML 4.01, there are three document types: HTML 4.01 Transitional, HTML 4.01 Strict, and HTML 4.01 Frameset. The transitional type is the most inclusive, incorporating both current tags and older tags that have been phased out, or *deprecated*. The strict type is more pared down and excludes deprecated tags. The frameset type is the same as the transitional type but includes all the tags necessary to make frames on a page. For more about frames, see Chapter 8.

## Document Header

You use the header of an HTML document to add descriptive and accessory information to your Web page. The document header tags, `<HEAD>` and `</HEAD>`, immediately follow the opening `<HTML>` tag. The document header contains information that does not appear in the browser window, including title information, metadata, scripts, and style sheets. For more about scripts, see Chapter 13. For more about style sheets, see Chapter 10.

## Document Title

You can add a title to your HTML document to help people and search engines identify your Web page. For example, if you are building a Web page for a business, you might want to include the company's name and specialization in the title. Most Web browsers display the title in the browser window's title bar. The `<TITLE>` and `</TITLE>` tags define a page title and appear inside the document header. It is good form to keep the title to fewer than 64 characters in length.

## Metadata

Metadata means "data about data." On a Web page, metadata can include author information, the type of editor used to create the page, a description of the content, relevant keywords, and copyright information. Search engines often use metadata when trying to categorize a page. You place metadata inside the document header.

## Body

The visible content that makes up your Web page, including paragraphs, lists, tables, and images, lives in the body of your HTML document. The body of the document is identified by the `<BODY>` and `</BODY>` tags. The body of a document comes after the header of a document. Most of the HTML tags covered in this book belong inside the body of the document and determine how its content is formatted. To learn how to begin formatting body text, see Chapter 3.

# Start an HTML Document

You can start an HTML document using a text editor, HTML editor, or word processing program. You use sets of HTML tags to define the basic structure of your page.

**The** <HTML>, <HEAD>, **and** <TITLE> **tags are basic elements that appear at the beginning of all HTML documents.**

## Start an HTML Document

① Open an editor or word processing program.

**Note:** *The examples in this book use both Windows Notepad and WordPad. See Chapter 1 to learn more about editors.*

② Type **<HTML>**.

This tag declares the document as HTML.

③ Press **Enter**.

④ Type **<HEAD>**.

This tag defines where the title, metadata, and other descriptive information appear.

**Note:** *For more about adding metadata to a Web page, see the section "Add Metadata."*

⑤ Press **Enter**.

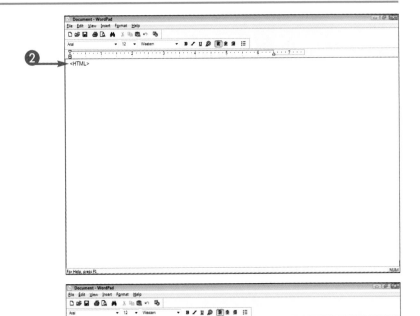

**6** Type `<TITLE>`.

**7** Type title text for your page.

Title text describes the contents of the page and appears in the title bar of the Web browser.

**8** Type `</TITLE>`.

**9** Press Enter.

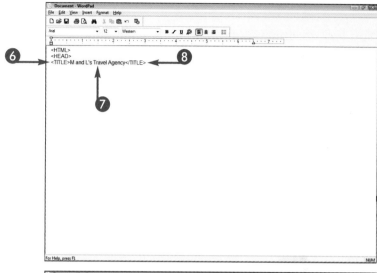

**10** Type `</HEAD>`.

This tag completes the document header information for the page.

**11** Press Enter.

**Note:** *You do not need to press* Enter *each time you start a new tag or add a closing tag. However, placing tags on their own lines can help make your code more readable.*

**Note:** *Browsers ignore extra white space in the code when rendering Web pages.*

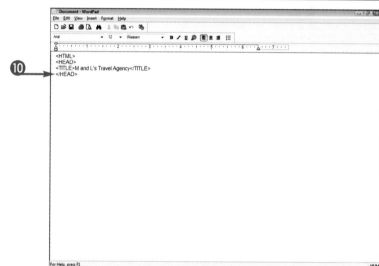

**TIPS**

**Which should I add first to my HTML document, the HTML tags or the page content?**
It is usually easier to start your HTML document by typing the basic structural tags, which include the `<HTML>`, `<HEAD>`, and `<BODY>` tags. These tags appear in all HTML documents, and typing them first helps ensure they have valid syntax and are in the correct order. After you add the basic structural tags, you can add the body content and additional HTML tags to format that content.

**Does it matter if I type my tags in uppercase, lowercase, or mixed case?**
No. The current HTML standard allows for different cases in your HTML text. However, it is good form to format your HTML tags consistently. Also, typing tags in all uppercase letters can make it easier to distinguish HTML code from the page content and to identify errors in your code.

continued 21

You can use the body tags,
<BODY> and </BODY>, to define
the content in your Web page.
Page content can include lines of
text, bulleted and numbered
lists, tables, forms, and more.

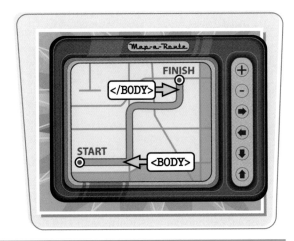

⑫ Type **<BODY>**.

This tag marks the beginning of
the actual content of your Web
page.

⑬ Press Enter.

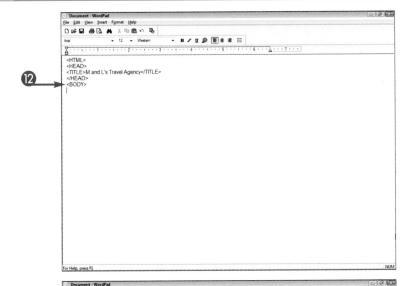

⑭ Type the body text you want to
appear on the page.

Body text is the content that
appears in the browser window.
For practice, you can type a
simple paragraph for the body
text.

⑮ Press Enter.

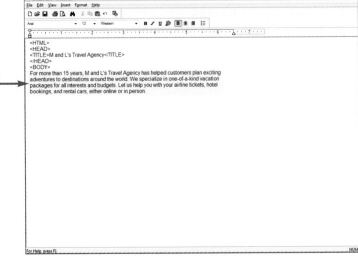

⑯ Type **</BODY>**.

This tag closes the body portion of the page.

⑰ Press **Enter**.

⑱ Type **</HTML>**.

This tag ends the HTML code of your document.

You can save your document and view the page in a Web browser.

**Note:** *To learn how to save a file, see the section "Save an HTML Document." To learn how to view the results of your HTML coding, see the section "View an HTML Page."*

### How do I turn on WordPad's text wrapping?

It can be annoying when the HTML code in WordPad scrolls off the right side of the screen. You can turn on the text-wrapping feature to keep your code in view at all times.

❶ In WordPad, click **View**.

❷ Click **Options**.

The Options dialog box appears.

❸ Click the **Text** tab.

❹ Select the **Wrap to window** option (◎ changes to ◉).

❺ Click **OK**.

WordPad activates text wrapping.

# Save an HTML Document

You can save your Web page as an HTML file so that users can view it in a Web browser. When saving a Web page, you can use either the .html or .htm file extension.

When naming a Web page, it is best not to use spaces and to keep the characters limited to letters, numbers, hyphens (-), and underscores (_). If you are creating a home page for a Web site, it is common to name the page index.html or default.htm.

## Save an HTML Document

**1** Click **File**.

**Note:** Your text editor may have a different command name for saving files. See your program's documentation for more information.

**2** Click **Save**.

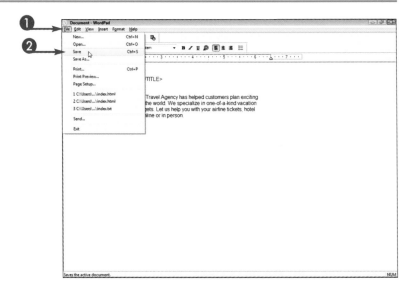

The Save As dialog box appears.

**3** Click here to navigate to the folder or drive where you want to store the file.

**4** Click here and select **Text Document**.

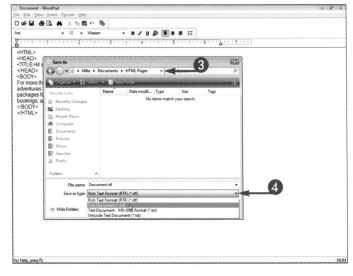

⑤ Type a name for the file, followed by **.html** or **.htm**.

⑥ Click **Save**.

A dialog box may appear alerting you that all the formatting will be removed.

⑦ Click **Yes**.

The editor saves the file.

**TIPS**

### What is the difference between the .html and .htm extensions?

The shorter .htm extension is left over from the early, pre-Windows days, when file names could have only three-character file extensions. Some Windows-based programs still default to the .htm extension. Today's computers can handle longer file names and extensions, so the three-character limit is no longer an issue. While Web browsers and servers can read either extension, you probably want to opt for .html because it is more universally used.

### What makes a good file name for a Web page?

When naming a file, it is a good idea to keep the name simple so that you can easily remember it and locate it again later. In addition, because you need to type file names when creating hyperlinks, it is best to use a name that relates to the pages you are designing. For example, if you are creating a page that lists contact information for your company, the file name for that page might be contact.html. It is also a good idea to keep your Web page files in one folder and give the folder a name that clearly identifies the content, such as My Web Pages.

# View an HTML Page

After you create and save an HTML document, you can view it in your Web browser. Your Web browser can view HTML pages that you have saved on your computer as well as pages on the Internet.

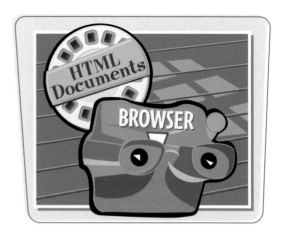

## View an HTML Page

① Open your Web browser.

This example uses the Internet Explorer browser.

② Click **File**.

③ Click **Open**.

The Open dialog box appears.

④ Click **Browse**.

**5** Click here to navigate to the folder or drive in which your HTML document is stored.

**6** Click the file name.

**7** Click **Open**.

● The Open dialog box displays the path and name of the file.

**8** In the Open dialog box, click **OK**.

The Web browser displays the page.

● The title information appears here.

● The body information appears here.

● The location of the HTML file appears here.

If you make changes to the HTML of the page that is displayed in the browser, you can click [refresh icon] to refresh the page and view the changes.

**TIPS**

**Does it matter what browser I use to view the pages I'm building?**

No. All popular Web browsers are set up to view HTML pages that you have saved on your computer, also known as *offline pages*. You may need to follow a slightly different set of steps to open an offline HTML document in a browser other than Internet Explorer, such as Mozilla Firefox. Be sure to consult your browser's documentation for more information.

**What happens if I cannot view my page?**

If you do not see any content for your page, you need to double-check your HTML code for errors. Make sure your document uses correctly paired start and end tags, and proofread your HTML code to make sure everything is correct. Also make sure you named your page with an .html or .htm extension.

# Add a Document Declaration

You can use a document declaration at the top of your Web page to declare which type of HTML tags the browser can expect to see. You can use one of three types: HTML 4.01 Transitional, HTML 4.01 Strict, or HTML 4.01 Frameset.

**The transitional version of HTML is the most inclusive. It has all the standard structural elements as well as older tags that have been phased out of the current standard. The strict type includes only currently sanctioned tags. The frameset type is the same as the transitional type but includes additional tags for creating frames.**

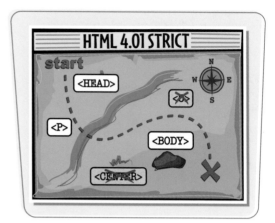

Add a Document Declaration

① Open the HTML document you want to edit.

② Position your cursor before the `<HTML>` tag and press Enter to insert a new line.

③ Type the DOCTYPE declaration.

● To specify HTML 4.01 Transitional, type:

```
<!DOCTYPE HTML PUBLIC
"-//W3C//
DTD HTML 4.01
Transitional//EN"
"http://
www.w3.org/TR/REC-
html4/loose.dtd">
```

You may need to press Enter to continue the coding on a new line.

● To specify HTML 4.01 Strict, type:

```
<!DOCTYPE HTML PUBLIC "-
//W3C//
DTD HTML 4.01 Strict//EN"
"http://
www.w3.org/TR/REC-html4/
strict.dtd">
```

● To specify HTML 4.01 Frameset, type:

```
<!DOCTYPE HTML PUBLIC "-
//W3C//
DTD HTML 4.01
Frameset//EN" "http://
www.w3.org/TR/REC-html4/
frameset.dtd">
```

The declaration statement is complete.

### Do I have to include a document declaration?

Most popular browsers can display your page without a DOCTYPE declaration. However, if you are using a validation tool to check your page for proper form, the tool may require that you include a declaration so that it knows what type of HTML it should validate your page against. Including a document declaration is also considered good form.

### Which version of HTML should I use?

All Web browsers support HTML Transitional. However, professional developers are moving toward HTML Strict and using it with Cascading Style Sheets (CSS) to control page formatting. Many of the deprecated tags in HTML have been replaced by formatting rules that you apply with CSS. If your page uses frames, then you need to use HTML Frameset because it allows you to add frames to a page. Deciding which version to use really depends on what Web page elements you plan to use and what type of coding you are familiar with.

# Add Metadata

You can add metadata to your page to include extra descriptive information that does not appear in the browser window. Metadata can include a page description, author and copyright information, keywords, and more. What you insert in metadata tags can help search engines categorize your page.

**You define metadata in the document header using the <META> tag.**

## Add Metadata

### ADD AN AUTHOR NAME

**1** Click between the <HEAD> and </HEAD> tags and press Enter to start a new line.

In this example, the metadata appears below the <TITLE> tags.

**2** Type **<META NAME= "author"** followed by a space.

**3** Type **CONTENT="My Name">,** replacing *My Name* with your name.

**4** Press Enter.

### ADD A PAGE DESCRIPTION

**5** Type **<META NAME= "description"** and a blank space.

**6** Type **CONTENT="Page Description">,** replacing *Page Description* with your own page description.

**7** Press Enter.

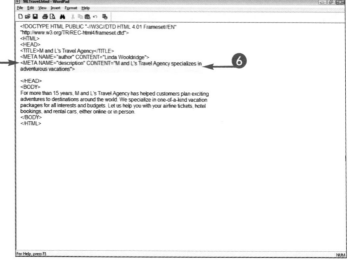

## SPECIFY KEYWORDS

⑧ Type **<META NAME= "keywords"** and a space.

⑨ Type **CONTENT="My Keywords">**, replacing *My Keywords* with a keyword.

For multiple keywords, use a comma followed by a space to separate the keywords.

⑩ Press Enter.

## ADD A COPYRIGHT

⑪ Type **<META NAME= "copyright"** and a space.

⑫ Type **CONTENT="2008">**, replacing *2008* with your own numbers or copyright information.

⑬ Press Enter.

The metadata is now a part of the HTML document.

### How do I add the name of the program I used to design my page to the metadata information?

To specify an authoring program, type **<META NAME="generator" CONTENT="Program Name">**. Substitute the name of your program for the text *Program Name*.

### Who can view my metadata?

The only way users can see your metadata information is if they view the HTML code for the page. To view the HTML code of any page in your browser window, click **View** and then **Source**. This opens a text-editor window displaying the HTML used to create the page. Any metadata assigned to the document appears at the top inside the <HEAD> and </HEAD> tags.

# Adding Text

TACOS....$1.25

25

ENSALADA..

BURRITOS...$1.95

RICE.......$1.25

Are you ready to begin building your Web page by adding text? This chapter shows you how to add different types of text elements to a document.

# Create a New Paragraph

You can use paragraph tags to start new paragraphs in an HTML document. In a word processing program, you press Enter or Return to separate blocks of text. Web browsers do not read these line breaks. Instead, you must insert a `<P>` tag in your HTML any time you want to start a new paragraph in your Web page.

**Paragraphs are left-aligned by default, but you can choose a different alignment using the align tags. See the section "Change Paragraph Alignment" to learn more.**

## Create a New Paragraph

① Type **<P>** to start a new paragraph.

② Type your text.

③ Type **</P>** at the end of the paragraph.

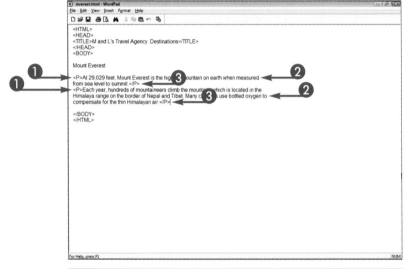

When displayed in a Web browser, the text appears as a paragraph with extra space above and below it.

**Note:** *To create paragraphs that are indented at the sides, see the section "Add Block Quotes."*

# Change Paragraph Alignment

You can control the horizontal positioning, or alignment, of your paragraphs using the ALIGN attribute. You can choose to align a paragraph to the left, right, or center, or justify the text so it is aligned on both the left and the right. Paragraphs are left-aligned by default.

**You can use the ALIGN attribute within numerous tag elements, including headings and lists. For example, you can center a heading or right-align a bulleted list.**

## Change Paragraph Alignment

① Click inside the <P> tag in which you want to change the alignment.

② Type a space and then **ALIGN="?"**, replacing *?* with **Left**, **Center**, **Right**, or **Justify**.

*Note: You can type HTML commands in upper- or lowercase letters, or a combination of the two.*

When displayed in a Web browser, the text aligns as specified.

● In this example, the line of text is centered on the page.

*Note: To control the width of a paragraph using style sheets, see Chapter 12 for more information.*

# Add a
# Line Break

You can use the line break tag, <BR>, to control where your text breaks. Web browsers normally wrap text automatically; when a line of text reaches the right side of the browser window, it breaks and continues on the next line. You can insert a line break to instruct the browser to break the text and go to a new line.

**You can also use the <BR> tag to add blank lines between paragraphs. This is useful if you want to add extra space above or below a block of text or a heading.**

① Type **<BR>** in front of the line of text that you want to appear as a new line.

② Type additional **<BR>** tags wherever you want a line break.

**Note:** *You do not need a closing tag for the* <BR> *tag.*

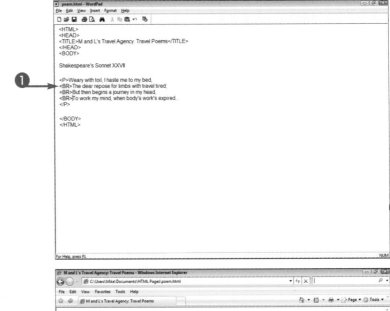

● When the page is displayed in a Web browser, each instance of the tag creates a new text line.

# Insert a Blank Space

You can insert blank spaces within a line of text to indent or add emphasis to your text. You can also use blank spaces to help position an element on a Web page, such as a graphic or photo.

## Insert a Blank Space

**1** Type ** ** in the line where you want to add a blank space.

To add multiple spaces, type the code multiple times.

The code stands for *nonbreaking space*. Web browsers will not create a line break where you insert these characters.

The browser displays blank spaces in the line.

● In this example, the blank spaces cause a paragraph to be indented.

The code   is a type of HTML entity. For more about entities, see the section "Insert Special Characters."

# Insert Preformatted Text

You can use the preformatted tags, `<PRE>` and `</PRE>`, to keep the line breaks and spaces you enter for a paragraph or block of text. Web browsers ignore hard returns, line breaks, and extra spaces between words unless you insert the preformatted tags. If you type a paragraph with spacing just the way you want it, you can assign the preformatted tags to keep the spacing in place.

**1** Type **<PRE>** above the text you want to keep intact.

**2** Type **</PRE>** below the text.

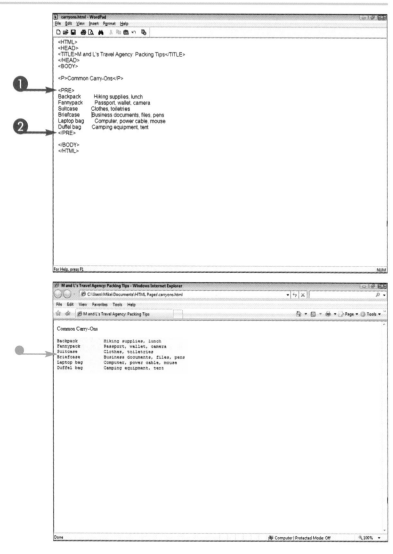

● When displayed in a Web browser, the text retains all your original line breaks and spacing.

Browsers display preformatted text in a monospace font by default. This can help you align elements within the text into columns.

# Insert a Heading

You can use headings to help clarify information on a page, organize text, and create visual structure. You can choose from six heading levels for a document, ranging from heading level 1 (<H1>), the largest, to heading level 6 (<H6>), the smallest. Headings appear as bold text on a Web page.

**You can use the ALIGN attribute to change the horizontal alignment of a heading, such as <H1 ALIGN="right">. See the section "Change Paragraph Alignment" to learn more about inserting alignment controls within your HTML tags.**

## Insert a Heading

① Type **<H?>** in front of the text you want to turn into a heading, replacing *?* with the heading level number you want to assign.

You can set a heading level from 1 to 6.

② Type **</H?>** at the end of the heading text, replacing *?* with the corresponding heading level.

③ Type additional heading tags for any other text that you want to emphasize on the page.

● The heading appears in bold text in the Web browser.

This figure shows an example of each heading size in descending order.

# Add Block Quotes

You can use block quotes to set off a paragraph from the rest of the document page. Block quotes are commonly used with quoted text or excerpts from other sources.

① Type **<BLOCKQUOTE>** in front of the text you want to turn into a block quote.

② Type **</BLOCKQUOTE>** at the end of the text.

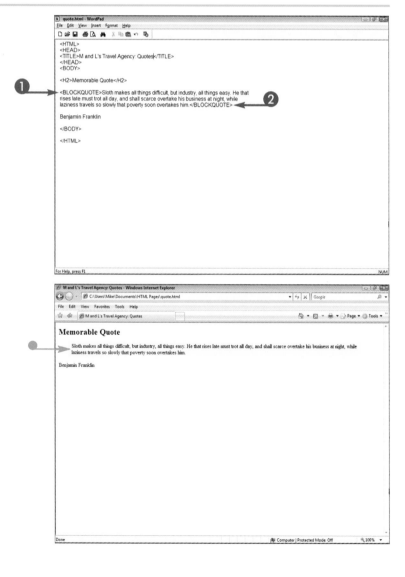

● The Web browser displays the block quote as inset text on the document page.

You can place text inside multiple <BLOCKQUOTE> tags to add more indenting.

# Insert a Comment

You can use comments to write notes to yourself within an HTML document. Comments do not appear when a browser displays a Web page. For example, you might leave a comment about a future editing task or leave a note to other Web developers viewing your HTML source code.

**You can also place comments around HTML code to turn that code off. HTML tags inside comments are not interpreted by the browser.**

## Insert a Comment

① Type **<!- -** where you want to place a comment.

② Type the comment text.

③ Type **- ->**.

The comment does not appear on the page when viewed in a Web browser.

You can use numbered lists on your Web page to display all kinds of ordered lists. For example, you can use numbered lists to show steps or prioritize items.

## Create a Numbered List

**PLACE TEXT IN A NUMBERED LIST**

1. Type **<OL>** above the text you want to turn into a numbered list.

2. Type **<LI>** in front of each item in the list.

3. Type **</LI>** after each list item.

4. Type **</OL>** after the list text.

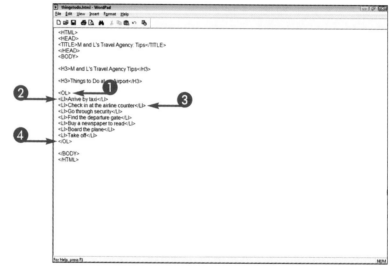

● The text appears as a numbered list on the Web page.

**SET A NUMBER STYLE**

1. Type **TYPE="?"** within the `<OL>` tag, replacing *?* with a number style code:

   **A:** A, B, C

   **a:** a, b, c

   **I:** I, II, III

   **i:** i, ii, iii

   **1:** 1, 2, 3

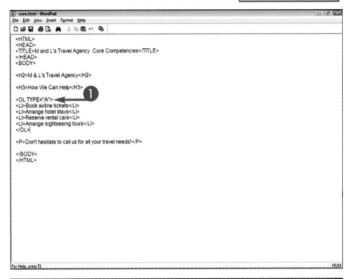

The numbered list is displayed in the style you selected.

● In this example, the list uses letters rather than numbers.

 **TIPS**

**How do I add another item to my numbered list?**
Simply insert the text where you want it to appear in the list and add the `<LI>` and `</LI>` tags before and after the text. The Web browser displays the updated list the next time you view the page.

**How do I start my numbered list with numbering that is different from the default?**
By default, a Web browser reads your numbered list coding and starts with the number 1. To start with a different number, you must add a START attribute to the `<OL>` tag. For example, if the numbering is to start at 5, the coding would read `<OL START="5" TYPE="1">`.

# Create a Bulleted List

You can add a bulleted list to your document to set a list of items apart from the rest of the page of text. You can use a bulleted list, also called an unordered list, when you do not need to show the items in a particular order.

**By default, bullets appear as solid circles. If you want to use another bullet style, you must add a TYPE attribute to the <UL> tag.**

## Create a Bulleted List

### PLACE TEXT IN A BULLETED LIST

1 Type **<UL>** above the text you want to turn into a bulleted list.

2 Type **<LI>** in front of each item in the list.

3 Type **</LI>** after each list item.

4 Type **</UL>** after the list text.

● The text appears as a bulleted list on the Web page.

**SET A BULLET STYLE**

1 Type **TYPE="?"** within the <UL> tag, replacing *?* with a bullet style code; for example, **circle**, **disc**, or **square**.

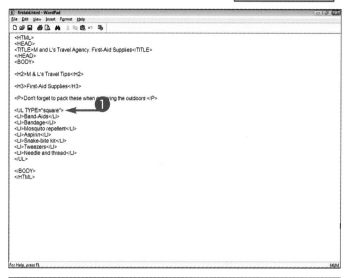

The bulleted list is displayed in the style you selected.

● In this example, the bulleted list uses square bullets.

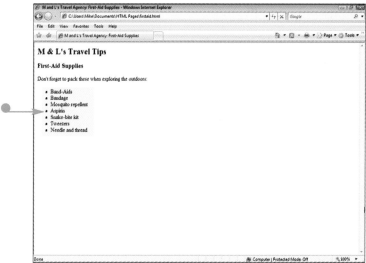

---

**TIPS**

**Can I stop a bulleted list for one line of text and continue it on the following line?**
Yes. If you leave off the <LI> and </LI> tags for a line of text within the list, a Web browser reads the line as regular text. However, you can insert a line break (<BR>) or use the paragraph or heading tags before the nonbulleted text line so that it appears as a separate line in the list. For example:

```
<UL>
<LI>Dogs</LI>
<LI>Cats</LI>
<BR>and the ever-popular
<LI>Potbellied pigs</LI>
</UL>
```

You can use a nested list to add a list within a list to your Web page. Nested lists allow you to display listed text at different levels within the list hierarchy. You can use both numbered and bulleted lists within an existing list.

## Create a Nested List

① Click where you want to insert a nested list, or add a new line within the existing list and type **<OL>** for a numbered list or **<UL>** for an unordered list.

**Note:** To create a numbered list, see the section "Create a Numbered List." To create a bulleted list, see the section "Create a Bulleted List."

② Type the new list text, including the **<LI>** and **</LI>** tags, using the same technique you used to create the original list.

③ Type **</OL>** or **</UL>** at the end of the nested list.

● The text appears as a nested list on the Web page.

Browsers usually set off nested lists with different bullet styles. In this example, a nested list gets an open circle.

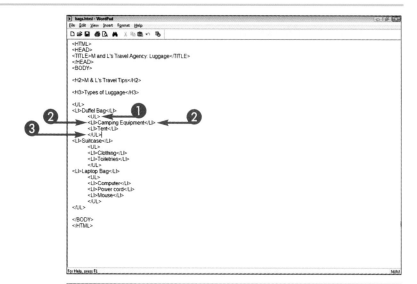

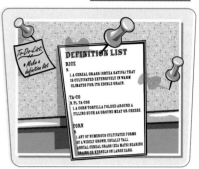

# Create a Definition List

You can use a definition list in your document to set text apart in the format of a glossary or dictionary.

## Create a Definition List

**1** Type **<DL>** above the text you want to set as a definition list.

**2** Type **<DT>** in front of each term and **</DT>** after each term.

**3** Type **<DD>** in front of each definition and **</DD>** after each definition.

**4** Type **</DL>** after the definition list text.

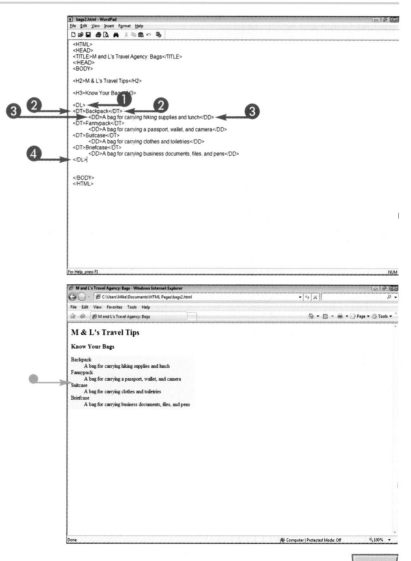

● The text appears as a definition list on the Web page.

# Insert Special Characters

You can use HTML code to insert special characters into your Web page text. Special characters are characters that do not usually appear on your keyboard.

**The codes used to insert special characters are called *entities*. Entities consist of number or name codes preceded by an ampersand and ending with a semicolon, such as &frac12; for the fraction 1⁄2 or &para; for a paragraph symbol.**

① Click where you want to insert a special character.

② Type the number or name code for the character, with an ampersand (&) before the code and a semicolon (;) following the code.

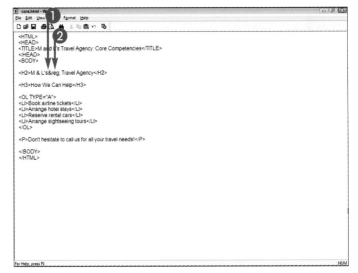

● The Web browser displays the designated character in the text.

# Special Characters

To properly insert many special characters into your Web page text, you need to know their entity codes. The following table lists the common special characters you can insert. For more on inserting these special characters, see the section "Insert Special Characters."

| Description | Special Character | Code | Description | Special Character | Code |
|---|---|---|---|---|---|
| copyright | © | `&copy;` | small o, slash | ø | `&oslash;` |
| registered trademark | ® | `&reg;` | em dash | — | `&mdash;` |
| trademark | ™ | `&trade;` | en dash | – | `&ndash;` |
| paragraph mark | ¶ | `&para;` | micro sign | µ | `&micro;` |
| nonbreaking space | | ` ` | macron | ¯ | `&macr;` |
| quotation mark | " | `&quot;` | superscript one | $^1$ | `&sup1;` |
| left angle quote | « | `&laquo;` | superscript two | $^2$ | `&sup2;` |
| right angle quote | » | `&raquo;` | superscript three | $^3$ | `&sup3;` |
| ampersand | & | `&amp;` | one-half fraction | ½ | `&frac12;` |
| inverted exclamation | ¡ | `&iexcl;` | one-fourth fraction | ¼ | `&frac14;` |
| inverted question mark | ¿ | `&iquest;` | three-fourths fraction | ¾ | `&frac34;` |
| broken vertical bar | ¦ | `&brvbar;` | degree sign | ° | `&deg;` |
| section sign | § | `&sect;` | multiply sign | x | `&times;` |
| not sign | ¬ | `&not;` | division sign | ÷ | `&divide;` |
| acute accent | ´ | `&acute;` | plus-or-minus sign | ± | `&plusmn;` |
| cedilla | ¸ | `&cedil;` | less-than sign | < | `&lt;` |
| bullet | • | `&bull;` | greater-than sign | > | `&gt;` |
| capital N, tilde | Ñ | `&NTilde;` | dagger | † | `&dagger;` |
| small n, tilde | ñ | `&ntilde;` | double dagger | ‡ | `&Dagger;` |
| capital A, tilde | Ã | `&Atilde;` | cent sign | ¢ | `&cent;` |
| small a, tilde | ã | `&atilde;` | pound sterling | £ | `&pound;` |
| capital A, grave accent | À | `&Agrave;` | euro | € | `&euro;` |
| small a, grave accent | à | `&agrave;` | yen sign | ¥ | `&yen;` |
| capital O, slash | Ø | `&Oslash;` | general currency | ¤ | `&curren;` |

# Formatting Text

You can apply formatting tags to control the appearance of text on your Web page. This chapter shows you how to add attributes and tags to make your text look its best.

# Make Text Bold

You can add bold formatting to your text to give it more emphasis or make your page more visually appealing. For example, you might make a company name bold in a paragraph or add bold to a list of items.

① Type **<B>** in front of the text you want to make bold.

② Type **</B>** at the end of the text.

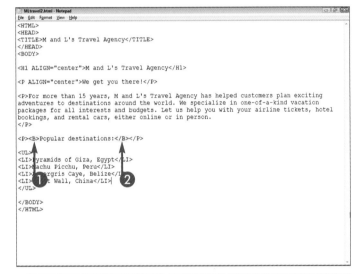

● When displayed in a Web browser, the text appears as bold.

**Note:** To create bold text using the font-weight property in CSS, see Chapter 11.

# Italicize Text

You can add italics to your text to give it more emphasis or make your page more visually appealing. For example, you might italicize a description under a heading to distinguish it from the rest of the page.

**Common uses for italicized text include emphasizing a new term or setting apart the title of a literary work.**

## Italicize Text

1 Type **<I>** in front of the text you want to italicize.

2 Type **</I>** at the end of the text.

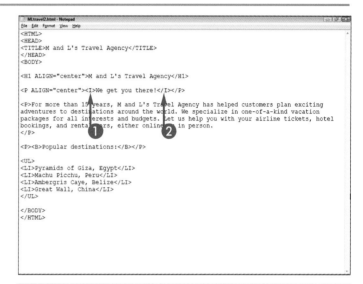

● When displayed in a Web browser, the text appears in italics.

***Note:*** *To italicize text using the font-style property in CSS, see Chapter 11.*

# Add Underlining to Text

You can add underlining to your text for added emphasis. For example, you might underline a term or an important name.

Use caution when applying underlining to Web pages because some users may mistake the underlined text for a hyperlink. See Chapter 6 to learn more about using links in Web pages.

① Type **<U>** in front of the text you want to underline.

② Type **</U>** at the end of the text.

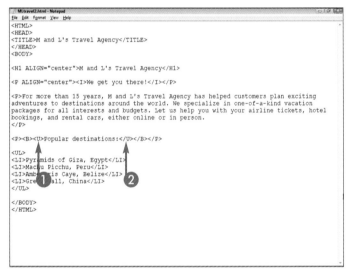

● The text appears underlined on the Web page.

*Note: To underline text using the text-decoration property in CSS, see Chapter 11.*

# Change Fonts

You can change the appearance of your text using the tags <FONT> and </FONT>, along with the FACE attribute. You can use the attribute to specify a font by name.

Not all Web browsers can display all fonts. It is best to assign common fonts typically found on most computers, such as Times New Roman and Arial. It is also a good idea to list more than one font name in the FACE attribute, in case the first font is not available on the viewer's computer.

## Change Fonts

① Type **<FONT FACE="?">** in front of the text you want to change. Replace *?* with one or more font names or families, separated by commas.

If the first font you list is not available on the user's computer, the second font will be used.

Commonly supported font families are *serif*, *sans serif*, and *monospace*.

② Type **</FONT>** at the end of the text.

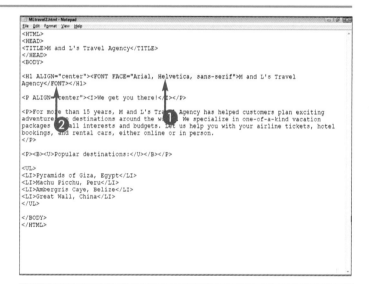

● The text appears in the new font on the Web page.

*Note: To change the font using the font-family property in CSS, see Chapter 11.*

You can change the font size of your Web page text using the SIZE attribute. You can specify seven font sizes in HTML. Font Size 1 creates the smallest text, while Font Size 7 creates the largest.

While the SIZE attribute lets you set the text size for a section of text, the **<BASEFONT>** tag lets you set the font size for the entire page.

## Change Font Size

**CHANGE A SECTION OF TEXT**

① Type **<FONT SIZE="?">** before the text you want to change, replacing ? with a number from 1 to 7.

② Type **</FONT>** at the end of the text.

③ Type additional **<FONT>** tags and **SIZE** attributes for any other text that you want to size.

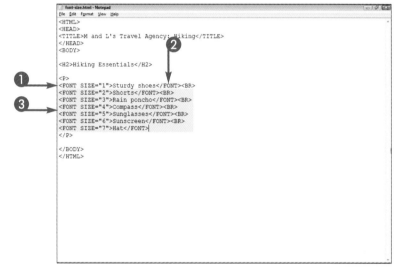

● The text appears at the designated font size on the Web page.

This figure shows samples of all seven font-size levels.

**Note:** *To change the font size using the font-size property in CSS, see Chapter 11.*

**CHANGE ALL THE TEXT**

① Type **<BASEFONT SIZE="?">** at the top of your Web page text, replacing *?* with a size you want from 1 to 7.

All the text appears at the new size in the Web browser.

***Note:*** *The <BASEFONT> tag does not affect the size of any headings (<H1>) within your Web page text.*

| Size<br>Attribute | Font<br>Size |
|---|---|
| 1 | 7 points |
| 2 | 10 points |
| 3 | 12 points |
| 4 | 14 points |
| 5 | 18 points |
| 6 | 24 points |
| 7 | 36 points |

**At what size will my text appear in my page if I size it using the SIZE attribute?**

The exact size of the text depends on which browser you use, although most modern browsers display at the same sizes. This table shows at what sizes Internet Explorer 6 and Firefox 2 display text.

**Can I set a size using something other than the seven size levels?**

Yes, using relative font sizing. If you type a plus (+) or minus (-) sign before a size number, the browser displays text at a size that is relative to the surrounding text. For example, if you type **<FONT SIZE="+2">**, the browser displays the text two sizes larger than the surrounding text. If you type **<FONT SIZE="-2">**, the browser displays the text two sizes smaller than the surrounding text.

# Change the Text Color

You can enhance your text by adding color. The COLOR attribute works with the <FONT> tag to change text on a page from the default black to a color. You can specify the color using a hexadecimal value or, for certain common colors, the color's name.

**Legibility is always a concern when it comes to applying color attributes to text. Be sure to choose a color that is easy to read on a Web page. Use caution when applying colored text to a colored background. Always test your page to make sure the colors do not clash and your text remains legible.**

## Change the Text Color

**CHANGE A SECTION OF TEXT**

1 Type **<FONT COLOR="?">** in front of the text you want to change, replacing *?* with the name or hexadecimal value of the desired color.

This example shows the color name for red.

2 Type **</FONT>** at the end of the text.

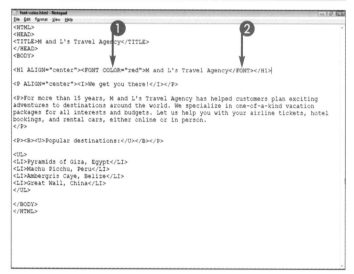

● The text appears in the designated color on the Web page.

**Note:** *To change the font color using the color property in CSS, see Chapter 11.*

**CHANGE ALL THE TEXT**

1 Within the <BODY> tag, type **TEXT="?"**, replacing *?* with the name or hexadecimal value of the desired color.

This example uses a hexadecimal value instead of a color name. Always precede a hexadecimal value with a # sign.

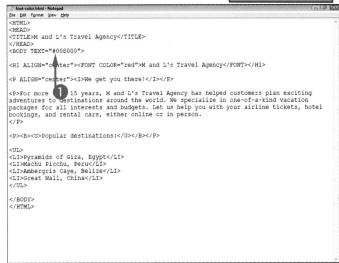

All the text appears in the new color in the Web browser.

● Text that you have colored using the FONT tag remains that color.

*Note: The TEXT attribute does not affect the color of links. To learn more about links, see Chapter 6.*

---

**TIP**

**What colors can I set for my Web page text?**

HTML coding sets colors using six-digit hexadecimal values preceded by a number sign (#), as shown in the table. Browsers can also understand the color names listed here.

| Color | Hexadecimal Value | Color | Hexadecimal Value |
|-------|-------------------|-------|-------------------|
| Aqua | #00FFFF | Navy | #000080 |
| Black | #000000 | Olive | #808000 |
| Blue | #0000FF | Purple | #800080 |
| Fuchsia | #FF00FF | Red | #FF0000 |
| Gray | #808080 | Silver | #C0C0C0 |
| Green | #008000 | Teal | #008080 |
| Lime | #00FF00 | White | #FFFFFF |
| Maroon | #800000 | Yellow | #FFFF00 |

# Adjust Margins

You can adjust the margins of your Web page to change the amount of space that appears at the top, bottom, left edge, or right edge. By default, the HTML margins are set at approximately 10 pixels. You can adjust the settings to suit your design needs.

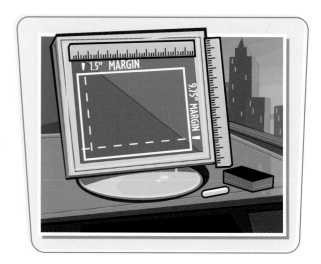

① Within the `<BODY>` tag, type **MARGIN="?"**.

Replace `MARGIN` with the margin attribute you want to change: **LEFTMARGIN**, **RIGHTMARGIN**, **TOPMARGIN**, **BOTTOMMARGIN**, **MARGINWIDTH**, or **MARGINHEIGHT**.

Replace *?* with the amount of indentation you want, measured in pixels.

You can set the margin for one side of the page or all four sides, all within the `<BODY>` tag.

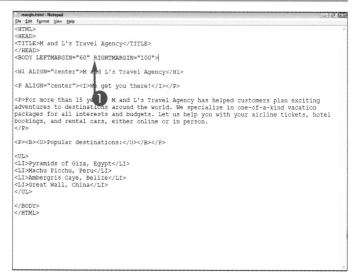

● The Web browser displays your page with the specified margins.

**Note:** *To learn how to change the alignment of text on a page, see Chapter 3.*

**Note:** *To adjust margins using style sheets, see Chapter 12.*

# Set a Background Page Color

You can add color to the background of the page using the BGCOLOR attribute. It is a good idea to choose a background color that does not obscure your text.

## Set a Background Page Color

① Within the <BODY> tag, type **BGCOLOR="?"**.

Replace *?* with a color name or hexadecimal value.

*Note: For a table of 16 color codes you can apply, see the section "Change the Text Color."*

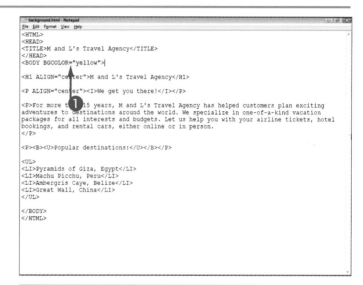

The page appears in the Web browser with a background color assigned.

*Note: To change the background using style sheets, see Chapter 11.*

# Add a Horizontal Line

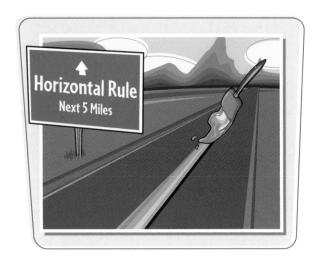

You can add a solid line, or *horizontal rule*, across your page to separate blocks of information. Horizontal rules must occupy a line by themselves and cannot appear within a paragraph.

**You can define the thickness and length of a horizontal line using the SIZE and WIDTH attributes.**

Add a Horizontal Line

### ADD A SIMPLE LINE

❶ Type **<HR>** where you want to insert a horizontal rule.

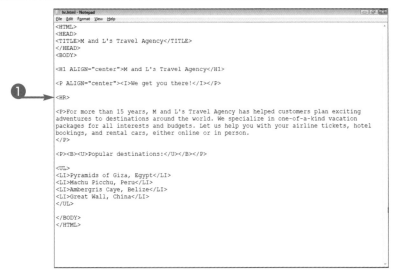

● The browser displays the line across the page.

## SET A LINE THICKNESS AND WIDTH

1 Within the `<HR>` tag, type **SIZE="?"**, replacing *?* with the thickness you want to assign, measured in pixels.

2 Within the `<HR>` tag, type **WIDTH="?%"**, replacing *?* with the percentage of the page you want the rule to extend across.

You can also set a numeric value to set the width of the rule in pixels.

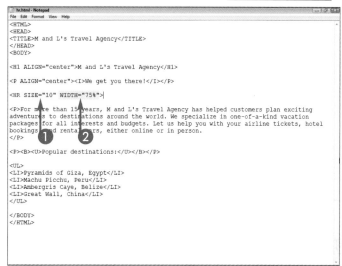

● The browser displays the line across the page.

**TIPS**

### How do I make my line appear more solid?

By default, the browser displays horizontal rules with shading, giving the lines a three-dimensional effect. To remove the shading, add the NOSHADE attribute to your `<HR>` tag so that it reads **<HR NOSHADE>**.

### Can I add color to a horizontal line?

Yes. You can insert the COLOR attribute and assign a color value to a line. For example, if you type **<HR COLOR="#0000FF">**, the browser displays the line as blue. See the section "Change the Text Color" for more about HTML colors.

# Adding Images

Are you ready to add images to your Web page? Images include photographs, logos, clip art, and any other visual object you can add to a Web page. This chapter shows you how to add and manipulate images, including photographs, graphic files, and background images.

# Understanding Web Page Images

You can use images in a variety of ways on your Web pages. Images include everything from graphics and clip art to photographs and other visual objects. Images can illustrate text, show a product, provide background decoration, or act as navigational buttons for a Web site. An important part of using images effectively on your own site is to understand how browsers display the images for others to view.

## Image File Formats

Although there are numerous file types used for images, JPEG and GIF are the two most popular types used on the Web. Both formats are cross-platform and offer file compression. PNG is a newer arrival in the image file format world and is gaining popularity among Web developers. The current versions of all of today's popular Web browsers can display JPEG, GIF, and PNG images.

## JPEG

JPEG, which stands for *Joint Photographic Experts Group*, supports 24-bit color, allowing for millions of colors. The JPEG format is commonly used with complex images, such as photos or graphics that use millions of colors and feature lots of detail. JPEG is not a good choice for solid-color artwork because it results in a larger overall file size, which translates to longer download times. JPEG images usually use a .jpg file name extension.

## GIF

GIF, which stands for *Graphics Interchange Format*, supports up to 256 colors. The GIF format is more commonly used for simple images, such as logos and graphics containing basic shapes and lines. If your image or graphic contains few colors and not a lot of detail, GIF is a good file format choice. A single GIF file can also store multiple images and display them as an animation. GIF images use a .gif file name extension.

## PNG

The PNG (*Portable Network Graphics*) format offers rich color support and advanced compression schemes, so it is a good choice for a variety of image types. Like JPEG, PNG supports 24-bit color, but it can also be saved with fewer colors, similar to GIF. Because PNG is a relatively new file format, use it if your intended audience most likely has up-to-date browsers. PNG images use a .png file name extension.

## Downloading Considerations

Browsers must download an image before users can view it on a Web page. Large images can take a long time to display, especially if Internet connection speeds are slow. For this reason, consider the overall file size of an image when deciding whether to add it to a Web page. If you fill your page with several large pictures, the download time for the page to fully display will be excessive.

## Optimize Images

Most image-editing programs allow you to adjust the quality of an image to control its file size. You can also control file size by shrinking or cropping an image. For best results, make sure your image file size does not exceed 60K. If you have larger image files, users may not be willing to wait for the pictures to download. With GIFs and some PNGs, you can decrease the number of colors in the image to reduce the file size.

# Prepare Your Images for the Web

You can use image-editing software to edit your images and make them Web-ready. Whether you plan to use photographs or graphics on an HTML page, you can save yourself some time and effort by preparing the images in an image-specific program first and then inserting them onto your pages using HTML.

**For more on images and the formats they use, see the section "Understanding Web Page Images."**

## Image-Editing Programs

A variety of programs are available for editing image files. Some programs, such as Adobe Photoshop Elements and Corel's Paint Shop Pro, are affordable and allow you to reduce the overall file size of an image as well as save it in a Web-friendly file format such as JPEG, GIF, or PNG. Paint, which comes free with Windows, also offers image-editing features that can help you optimize file size.

## Reduce the Image Width and Height

Image dimensions are important considerations when placing an image on a Web page. Images wider than the browser window will not be fully visible, requiring the user to scroll. You can use an image-editing program to resize an image. Cropping out areas of the image that you do not want to appear on the Web page can help reduce the overall image file size.

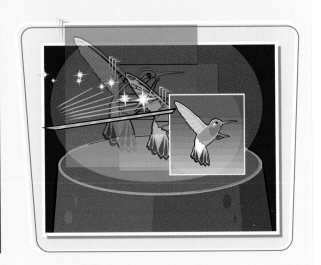

## Image Compression

Image-editing programs allow you to save your image as a specific file type and set a compression level. File compression used in JPEG images can sometimes reduce the file size by up to 90 percent. Many programs let you view the image both before and after compression to check for differences in quality.

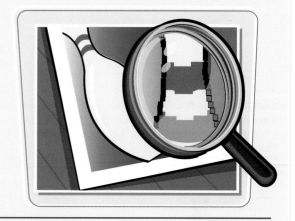

## Number of Colors

For GIF images and some PNG images, you can reduce the number of colors in the image to reduce the file size. For example, while GIF images can contain a maximum of 256 colors, an illustration with mostly solid-color regions may look just fine saved as a 16-color GIF. Most image editors allow you to compare an image at different color settings prior to saving.

## Alternative Text

Some Web users may turn off the browser's image-display setting to help speed up the downloading of Web pages. Also, some visually impaired users view the Web using screen readers that do not display images at all. To accommodate such users, be sure to include alternative text describing the images on your page. Alternative text can appear in place of the image and allows users to understand how the image relates to the rest of the page. For more information, see the section "Add Alternative Text."

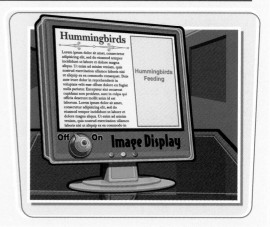

# Insert an Image

You can add images to your Web page to lend visual interest or illustrate a topic. For example, you can add a photograph of a product or a company logo to a business's Web page. HTML coding lets you display images as inline elements, which means they appear within the body of the page along with text.

**You can use image files from a digital camera or scanner, or you can create illustrations with a graphics program. If you are not the original author of the image, you need permission to use the image before placing it on a Web site.**

## Insert an Image

**INSERT A PHOTOGRAPH**

1 Type **<IMG SRC="?">** where you want to insert a photographic image, replacing *?* with the full path to the file you want to insert.

In this example, because the image was saved in the same folder as the HTML file, you reference it with just the file name.

● The Web browser displays the image on the page.

## INSERT A GRAPHIC FILE

1 Type **<IMG SRC="?">** where you want to insert a graphic, replacing *?* with the full path to the file you want to insert.

In this example, because the graphic was saved in an `images` subdirectory relative to the HTML file, you reference it with the subdirectory name followed by a slash (/) and then the file name.

● The Web browser displays the graphic on the page.

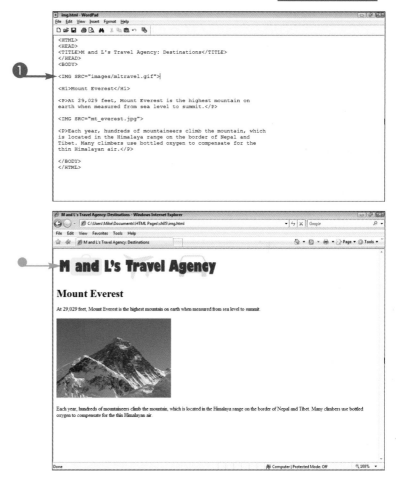

**TIPS**

### How can I download an image from a Web page?
Internet Explorer, Firefox, and most other Web browsers allow you to copy an image from a Web site by right-clicking the image and selecting a save command. If you save an image in the same folder as your HTML files, you can then use the image on your pages using the previous steps. Make sure you have permission from the image owner before using it on your Web site.

### Where can I find low-cost images to use on my Web site?
Many Web sites feature images that are in the public domain or are available for noncommercial use. Wikimedia Commons (http://commons. wikimedia.org) is one such site. If you have a little money to spend, you can license images from *microstock* Web sites, which are known for low-cost, downloadable images. iStockPhoto (www.istockphoto.com) is a popular microstock site.

# Specify an Image Size

If your image appears too big or too small on a Web page, you can use image attributes in your HTML coding to change the size. You can set the width and height of an image in pixels or as a percentage of the overall window size.

① Click inside the `<IMG>` tag and type **WIDTH="?"**, replacing *?* with the width measurement you want to set.

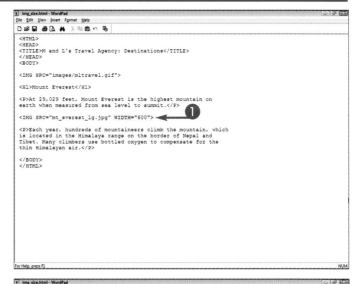

② Type a space.

③ Type **HEIGHT="?"**, replacing *?* with the height measurement you want to set.

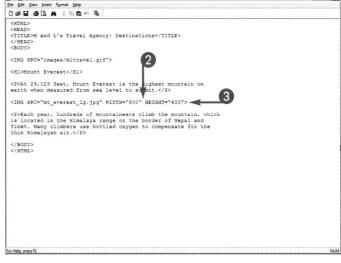

● You can also set the attribute value as a percentage. This tells the browser to display the image at a percentage of the browser window size.

When giving a percentage value, be sure to follow it with a percent sign (%).

● The Web browser displays the image at the specified size on the page.

*Note: If you specify only one dimension, whether the width or the height, for your image, the browser sizes the other dimension proportionally based on the original size.*

---

**TIPS**

**What size should I set for a Web page image?**
The best size for an image depends on how you want to use it on the Web page. The vast majority of Web users access pages with their monitors set at least 800 pixels in width and 600 pixels in height. At these settings, browsers can usually display images that are 750 pixels in width and 400 pixels in height without requiring the user to scroll. Making your images smaller decreases download time and can allow users to see more than one image at a time, depending on the layout.

**Is it better to resize an image in an editing program or using HTML coding?**
Resizing images using HTML can reduce the quality of your images, especially if you use HTML to enlarge them. Also, shrinking an image using HTML won't actually reduce its file size, which means it won't download any faster. For these reasons, it is better to resize images using an image editor. This allows you to maintain an image's quality and optimize its file size.

# Add Alternative Text

For users who have images turned off in their browsers, you can add alternative text that identifies the images on your page. Alternative text, sometimes called *placeholder text*, can describe what appears in an image and is an important addition to your Web page code.

## Add Alternative Text

**1** Click inside the `<IMG>` tag and type **ALT="?"**, replacing *?* with alternative text describing the image.

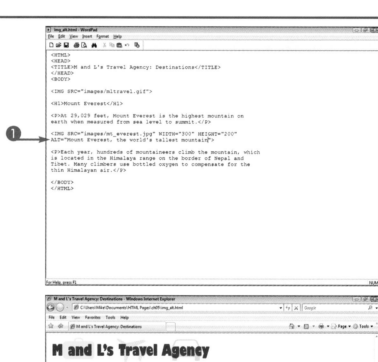

● If the user's browser has images turned off, or if the image can't be found on the Web server, the browser displays the alternative text in lieu of the image.

**Note:** *Alternative text can also help search engines determine the type of image content that is on your page.*

# Create an Image Label

You can add a label that appears whenever the user moves the mouse pointer over a particular image on a Web page. You can use labels to offer detailed information about the image.

Labels work differently from alternative text. Alternative text appears on the page itself when images are turned off. A label appears in a pop-up box when the user moves the mouse over the image.

## Create an Image Label

① Within the <IMG> tag, type **TITLE="?"**, replacing *?* with the image label you want to appear.

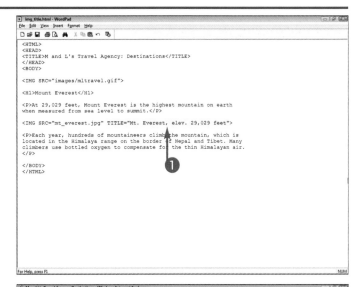

```
<HTML>
<HEAD>
<TITLE>M and L's Travel Agency: Destinations</TITLE>
</HEAD>
<BODY>

<IMG SRC="images/mltravel.gif">

<H1>Mount Everest</H1>

<P>At 29,029 feet, Mount Everest is the highest mountain on earth
when measured from sea level to summit.</P>

<IMG SRC="mt_everest.jpg" TITLE="Mt. Everest, elev. 29,029 feet">

<P>Each year, hundreds of mountaineers climb the mountain, which is
located in the Himalaya range on the border of Nepal and Tibet. Many
climbers use bottled oxygen to compensate for the thin Himalayan air.
</P>

</BODY>
</HTML>
```

● The label appears when you move the mouse pointer over the image in the browser window.

**Note:** *Label text can also help search engines determine the type of image content that is on your page.*

# Add Copyright Text to Images

You can add copyright information below or next to an image to give yourself credit as the author. If you are using an image from another source, be sure to get permission first. You can add copyright text to credit the source of the image.

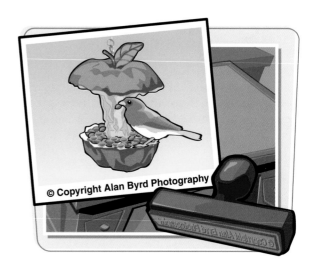

© Copyright Alan Byrd Photography

① Type **&copy;** to create the copyright symbol.

**Note:** *For more about adding special characters to a page, see Chapter 3.*

② Type a space, and then type the copyright text you want to add.

**Note:** *To control the font and font size using tags, see Chapter 4.*

● In this example, a line break tag (<BR>) puts the copyright text on a new line.

● The copyright text appears in the browser window.

# Align an Image Horizontally

You can use the `left` and `right` alignment attributes to control the horizontal positioning of an image on a page. The alignment attributes also control how text wraps around the image.

You can also align an image vertically on a page. See the section "Align an Image Vertically" to learn more.

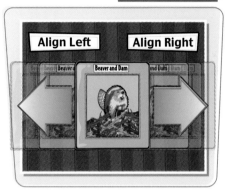

## Align an Image Horizontally

① Click inside the `<IMG>` image tag and type **ALIGN="?"**, replacing *?* with the alignment you want to apply, either **left** or **right**.

The Web browser aligns the image as specified.

● In this example, the image is aligned to the right.

**Note:** To center-align an image, see the section "Center an Image."

**Note:** For greater control over image alignment, consider placing your images in tables. Learn more about using tables in Chapter 7.

# Align an Image Vertically

You can use the alignment attributes to control the vertical positioning of an image on a page relative to text that follows it. The alignment attributes are `top`, `middle`, and `bottom`.

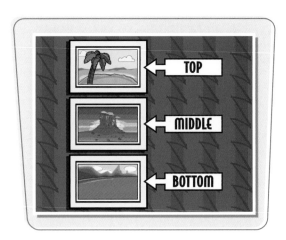

**1** Click inside the `<IMG>` tag and type **ALIGN="?"**, replacing ? with the alignment you want to apply, either **middle**, **top**, or **bottom** (**bottom** is the default).

If the image shares the same line as text, the alignment attribute controls the position of the image relative to the text.

The Web browser aligns the image as specified.

● In this example, the image is middle-aligned with existing text.

**Note:** *For greater control over image alignment, consider placing your images in tables. Learn more about using tables in Chapter 7.*

# Center
# an Image

You can center your image on the page using a `<DIV>` tag and the `align` attribute. Centering an image can give it more emphasis and help it stand out from the text or other page elements.

## Center an Image

1 Click before the `<IMG>` tag and type **`<DIV>`**.

2 Click inside the `<DIV>` tag and type **`ALIGN="center"`**.

3 Click after the closing bracket of the `<IMG>` tag and type **`</DIV>`**.

● The image appears centered on the Web page.

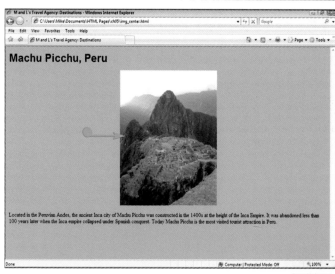

# Wrap Text Between Images

You can place two images side by side and wrap text between the two. To create this effect, you align one image to the left and the other to the right.

## Wrap Text between Images

① Use <IMG> tags to insert the two images above the text you want to wrap.

② Click inside the first <IMG> tag and type **ALIGN="left"**.

③ Click inside the second <IMG> tag and type **ALIGN="right"**.

● The text wraps between the two images on the Web page.

**Note:** *To learn how to add space between an image and surrounding text, see the section "Add Space around an Image."*

You can stop text wrapping around your images using the line break tag along with the `clear` attribute.

## Stop Text Wrap

① Click where you want to end the text wrap and type **<BR CLEAR="?">**, replacing *?* with the margin you want to clear, either **left**, **right**, or **all**.

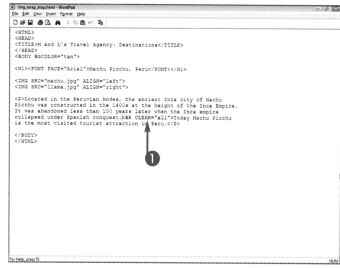

The text wrapping ends at the selected point on the page.

● In this example, the next paragraph starts on a different line from the images.

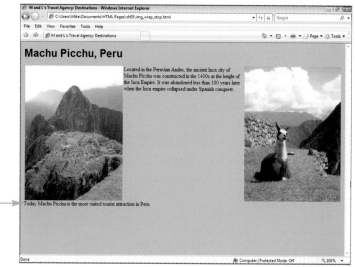

# Set an Image Border

You can add a border to an image to give it added emphasis or make it look more attractive on the page. You can define the thickness of the border in pixels.

## Set an Image Border

**1** Click inside the `<IMG>` tag and type **BORDER="?"**, replacing *?* with the thickness value you want to apply.

To remove a border you no longer want, replace *?* with **0**.

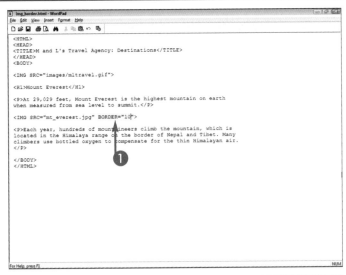

● The Web browser displays a black border around the image.

**Note:** You can use style sheets to put a border with a custom color around the image. See Chapter 11 for details.

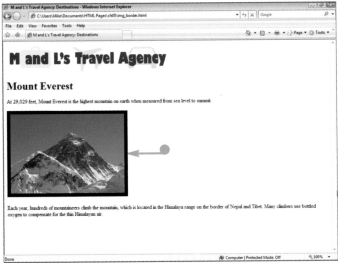

# Add Space Around an Image

Most Web browsers display only a small amount of space between images and text. You can increase the amount of space, also called *padding*, to make the page more visually appealing and easier to read. You can control padding on the left and right sides of an image with the HSPACE attribute. You can control the padding above and below an image with the VSPACE attribute.

**The values used with the horizontal and vertical attributes specify the padding in pixels.**

## Add Space around an Image

① Click inside the <IMG> tag and type **HSPACE="?"** or **VSPACE="?"**, replacing *?* with the amount of space you want to insert.

You can add one or both attributes to an image.

If you add both attributes, separate them with a space in the HTML coding.

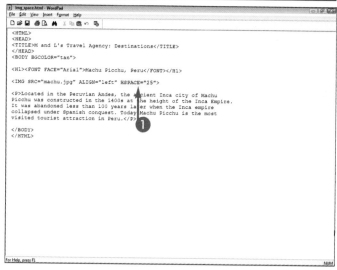

● The Web browser displays the image with the specified amount of space around it.

The HSPACE and VSPACE attributes add space to two sides at a time. To add space to just one side, for example the bottom of an image, use style sheets. See Chapter 12 for details.

# Add a Background Image

You can turn an image into a background for your Web page by setting an attribute in the <BODY> tag. When selecting an image for a background, try to factor in how your text will appear against the image. You may need to change the color of the text to make it legible.

**If you use a large image file, it fills the entire background. If you use a smaller image, the browser tiles the image across and down the page to fill the background with a repeating pattern.**

## Add a Background Image

1. Click inside the <BODY> tag and type **BACKGROUND="?"**, replacing *?* with the path to the image file you want to use.

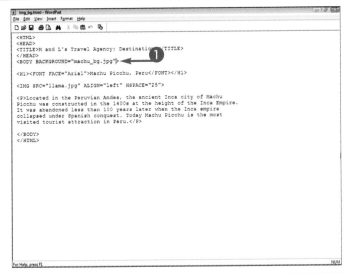

● The Web browser displays the image as the page background.

*Note: To learn how to change the text color, see Chapter 4.*

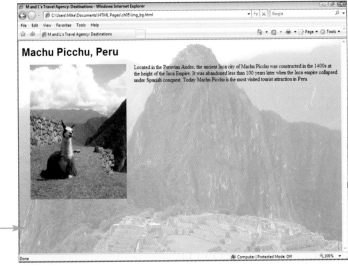

# Create an
# Image Banner

You can use banners at the top of your Web pages to advertise a product or service, or to give your Web site a consistent look and feel. You can use a GIF, JPEG, or PNG image as a banner.

**Full banners are typically 468 pixels wide and 60 pixels tall, but yours can be whatever size suits your page. You can assign the banner size while creating the banner in a graphics-editing program, or you can set the image size using HTML coding. To learn how to set image height and width, see the section "Specify an Image Size" earlier in this chapter.**

### Create an Image Banner

① At the top of the page, before any body text, type **<IMG SRC="?">**, replacing ? with the path to the banner file you want to use.

② Type **WIDTH="?"** within the <IMG> tag, replacing ? with a value in pixels.

③ Type **HEIGHT="?"** within the <IMG> tag, replacing ? with a value in pixels.

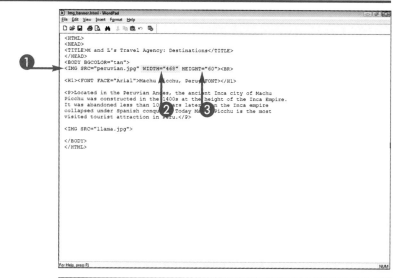

● The Web browser displays the image as a banner at the top of the page.

*Note: To learn how to create an image map at the top of your Web pages, see Chapter 14.*

# Adding Links

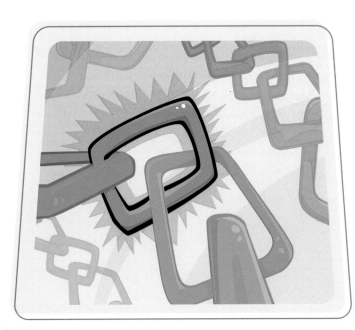

Are you ready to start adding links to your Web pages? This chapter shows you how to create links in your HTML documents to allow users to jump to other Web sites or to other pages within your own site. You also learn how to add e-mail links and control the appearance of links.

# Understanding Links

Hyperlinks, or *links* for short, are what make Web pages different from other computer documents. Any publicly accessible Web page can be connected to another by creating a link. Links enable users to navigate from one topic to the next on a Web site and from one Web site to another. The user clicks the link and the browser opens the destination page.

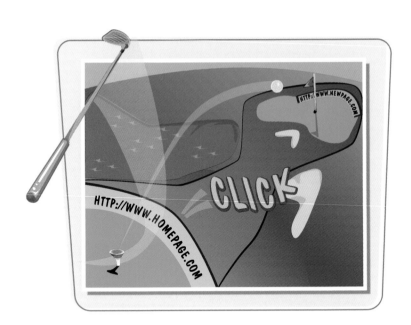

## Types of Links

Links can be text or images. Text links typically appear as underlined, differently colored words on a page. Any image on a Web page can also be turned into a link. For example, graphical site maps and navigation bars that appear at the top or side of a page make it easy for users to access other pages on the same Web site. When a user holds the mouse pointer over a link, the pointer takes the shape of a pointing hand, indicating the presence of an active, clickable link.

## Link to External Web Pages

You can use links on your Web page to direct users to other pages on the Internet. For example, you might include a link on your company Web page to a local city directory detailing activities and hotels in the area. Or you might add a link on a product page to the manufacturer's Web site.

## Link to Other Pages on Your Site

If your Web site consists of more than one page, you can include links to other pages on the site. For example, your main page may provide links to pages about your business, products, and ordering information as well as to a map of your location. If you maintain a blog, the home page will usually link to postings that you have created in the past.

## Link to Other Areas on the Same Page

If your Web page is particularly long, you can provide links to different areas on the page. For example, at the top of a page, you might include links to each section heading or photo that appears below. This allows users to jump right to the information they want to view without having to scroll.

## Absolute and Relative Links

You can use two types of links in your HTML documents: absolute and relative. *Absolute links* use a complete URL to point to a specific page on a specific Web server. *Relative links* use shorthand to reference a page and don't specify the server. You generally use relative links to reference documents on the same Web site.

## Anchor Tags

The HTML code you use to create a link is called an *anchor tag*, consisting of the beginning `<A>` and the ending `</A>`. The `HREF` attribute works within the opening anchor tag to define the URL, or Web address, to which you want to link. You can learn more about using URLs in the next section, "Understanding URLs."

# Understanding URLs

Every page on the Web has a unique address called a *URL*. Short for *Uniform Resource Locator*, a URL identifies the domain name of the Web server and the directory path to the file on that server. Absolute links specify a complete Web page URL, whereas relative links use shorthand to specify pages relative to the page containing the link.

## HTTP Prefix

All URLs for Web pages include the standard HTTP (HyperText Transfer Protocol) prefix, as in http://www.example.com. While most browsers automatically insert the http:// prefix for you when you type an address such as www.example.com, you must include the prefix when referencing URLs in your HTML.

## FTP or MAILTO Prefix

There may be times when you use a prefix other than HTTP in your URLs. If you are linking to a document that resides on a file transfer site, you use the FTP prefix (ftp://). If you want to create a link that opens an e-mail program, allowing a user to send an e-mail message, you use the MAILTO prefix (mailto:).

## Domain Name

Following the prefix in a URL is the domain name of the Web server where the page is stored. Typically, domain names correspond to the company or organization hosting your Web page files. Hosts can include commercial companies, educational institutions, and government agencies. In the URL http://www.example.com, "example.com" is the name of the domain, with "www." specifying a Web server at that domain. Occasionally you may use a numeric IP (Internet Protocol) address such as 208.215.179.146 in your URL instead of a domain name.

## Directory Path and File Name

Following the domain name in a URL is information about the file name of the HTML page and the directories in which the page is stored. For example, the page located at the URL http://www.example.com/pages/home.html has the file name "home.html" and is stored inside a directory named "pages" on the Web server. You use slashes (/) to separate the domain name, directories, and file name. When you reference a Web site's home page, you will often leave off the path and file name from a URL, as in http://www.example.com. In such cases, the server returns a default page for the site, usually titled index.html, located in the Web server's root folder.

## URL Errors

One of the easiest mistakes you can make when creating a link is to type the wrong URL. This causes users to get an error message when they click the link. One misplaced letter or missing slash in a URL can result in a broken link. Renaming or rearranging the file structure on your Web server may also break links, requiring you to rewrite the URLs in your HTML.

# Link to Another Page

You can create a link in your HTML document that, when clicked, takes the visitor to another page on the Web. You can link to a page on your own Web site or to a page elsewhere on the Web.

**To create a link, you must first know the URL of the page to which you want to link, such as http://www.wiley.com.**

**INSERT A TEXT LINK**

1 Type the text you want to use as a link.

2 Type **<A HREF="?">** in front of the text, replacing *?* with the URL of the page to which you want to link.

3 Type **</A>** at the end of the link text.

● The Web browser displays the text as an underlined link.

● Anytime the user moves the mouse pointer (👆) over the link, it takes the shape of a hand pointer (👆).

● The URL for the link appears in the status bar.

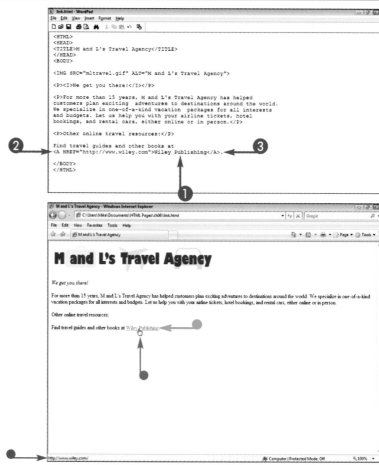

**INSERT AN IMAGE LINK**

1 Add the image you want to use as a link using the <IMG> tag.

*Note: To learn how to add images to a page, see Chapter 5.*

2 Type **<A HREF="?">** in front of the image code, replacing *?* with the URL of the page to which you want to link.

3 Type **</A>** after the image code.

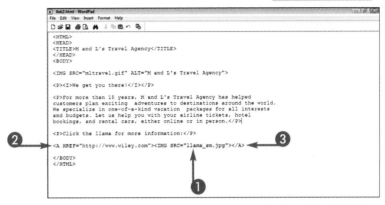

● The Web browser displays the image as a link.

● Anytime the user moves the mouse pointer (⊕) over the link, it takes the shape of a hand pointer (🖑).

● The URL for the link appears in the status bar.

---

**TIPS**

**How do I link to another page on my Web site?**
You can link to another page on your site using a relative link. In a relative link, you can specify the location of the destination page relative to the page that contains the link without specifying the domain name of the server. If the destination page is located in the same directory as the containing page, you can simply specify the filename, as in <A HREF="photos.html">. If the destination page is in a subdirectory relative to the containing page, you need to specify that subdirectory as well, as in <A HREF="media/photos.html">.

**My link image includes a border. How do I remove the border?**
When you turn an image into a link, a browser automatically places a border around the image. To remove the border, type **BORDER="0"** in the <IMG> tag, as in <A HREF=http:// www.example.com><IMG SRC= "vacation.jpg" BORDER="0"></A>.

# Open a Linked Page in a New Window

You can add instructions to an HTML link that tell the browser to open the link page in a new browser window. You may add this instruction if you want to keep a window to your own site open so the user can easily return to your page.

**You use a target attribute within the link anchor element (<A>) to open links in new windows. To make all the links on your page open in new windows, you can use the** `BASE` **element. To learn more about how links and URLs work, see the sections at the beginning of this chapter.**

Open a Linked Page in a New Window

### LINK TO A NEW WINDOW

1 Click within the <A> tag for the link you want to edit and type **TARGET="?"**, replacing *?* with a name for the new window.

Other links on your Web page can reference the same target name to open pages in the same new window.

If you want the link to open in a new, unnamed window, type **"_blank"**.

● When the link is clicked, the linked page opens in the targeted window.

## MAKE ALL LINKS OPEN NEW WINDOWS

1 Click between the `<HEAD>` and `</HEAD>` tags and type **`<BASE TARGET="?">`**, replacing *?* with a name for the new window, such as main.

If you want the link to open in a new, unnamed window, type **"_blank"**.

● When the user clicks any of the links on the page, the linked page opens in the targeted window.

**TIPS**

### Do I need to specify a name for the new window?

No. Rather than worry about what to name a new window, you can simply leave the window unnamed. You do this by using the `TARGET="_blank"` attribute. A new, unnamed window opens.

### Should I open a new window for every link?

Probably not. If a new window opens every time a link is clicked on your pages, users may quickly become overwhelmed by the number of open windows. You may want to open new windows only when links lead to a page outside the current Web site. This way, the current Web site remains open on the user's computer.

# Link to an Area on the Same Page

You can add links to your page that take the user to another place on the same page. This is particularly useful for longer documents. For example, you can add links that take the user to different headings in your document.

**To link to places on the same page, you must assign names to the areas to which you want to link. You can do this with the anchor tag (\<A\>) and the NAME attribute. Such assigned names are sometimes called *named anchors*.**

### NAME AN AREA

**1** Click in front of the section of text to which you want to create a link and type **\<A NAME="?"\>**, replacing *?* with a unique name for the area.

It is best to keep your names short and simple, using only letters and numbers.

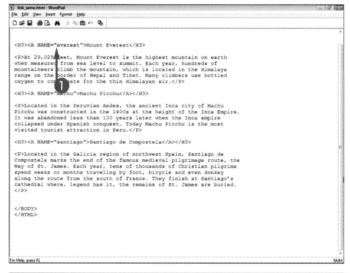

**2** Type **\</A\>** at the end of the section.

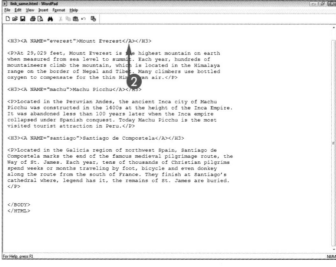

## CREATE A LINK TO THE AREA

**1** In front of the text or image you want to turn into a link, type **<A HREF="#?">**, replacing *?* with the name of the section to which you want to link.

*Note: Be careful not to leave out the pound sign (#) when linking to other areas of a page.*

**2** Type **</A>** after the link text.

*Note: To use an image as a link, see the section "Insert a Link to another Page."*

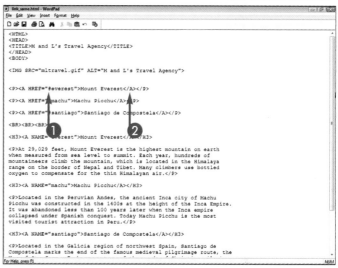

● When a user clicks the link, the browser scrolls to the designated section of the page.

---

**TIPS**

**Can I place a link at the bottom of my page that returns the user to the top of the page?**

Yes. It is a good idea to add a link to the bottom of a long page to help the user navigate to the top again without having to scroll. To create such a link, create a named anchor at the top of the page following the steps shown in this section. Then insert a link that references that named anchor. Good text to use for such a link is "Return to Top" or "Back to Top."

**How do I link to a specific location on another page on my Web site?**

You can use the same technique shown in this section to link to a section on another page. First, name the area on the other page using the `<A NAME="?">` tag and attribute. Then create a link to the page, adding a # and then the name of the relative link, such as `<A HREF="page.html#section1">`.

# Link to Another File Type

You can add links to non-HTML resources, such as Word document files, spreadsheet files, image files, compressed files, and more. To make such files Web-accessible, you must store them in the same locations on the Web server as your HTML files.

**Thanks to special plug-ins, some Web browsers can open certain non-HTML files. For a file that it can't open, a browser may prompt users to save the file on their computers.**

## Link to another File Type

**1** Type the text for the link.

It is good form to include a description on the page that identifies what type of file the link opens.

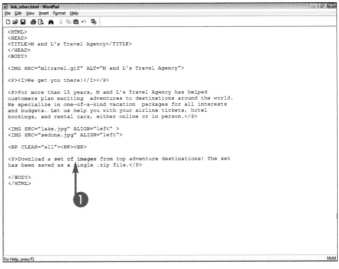

**2** Type **<A HREF="?">**, replacing *?* with the full path and name of the file.

**3** Type **</A>** at the end of the link text.

● The link appears on the Web page.

When the link is clicked, the browser may display the file in the browser window.

**Note:** *To open the file in a new window, see the section "Open a Linked Page in a New Window."*

If the browser cannot open the file, a File Download dialog box may appear that allows the user to download the file to his or her computer.

**TIPS**

### Can I include links to plain-text files?

Yes, and most browsers will be able to open and display such files. Because plain-text files do not include HTML formatting, browsers display the text unformatted and without inline images or other features.

### What happens if the user cannot download or open the file?

If the user encounters problems accessing a non-HTML file, his or her browser or computer may display an error message. To help with any problems that might occur, be sure to include information about the file format and size on the Web page; also include links to any useful tools that can help the user work with the file. For example, if the link is to a PDF file, include a link to the Adobe Web site where the user can download the Adobe Acrobat Reader program, which can read PDFs.

# Link to an E-mail Address

You can create a link in your Web page that allows users to send an e-mail message. Adding e-mail links is a good way to solicit feedback and questions from your Web site visitors.

**1** Type the text you want to use as an e-mail link.

It is standard practice to use the e-mail address as the text link.

**2** In front of the link text, type **<A HREF="mailto:?">**, replacing *?* with the e-mail address you want to use.

**3** Type **</A>** at the end of the link text.

100

● The link appears in the Web browser.

● When the link is clicked, the user's e-mail editor opens with the To field prefilled with the e-mail address.

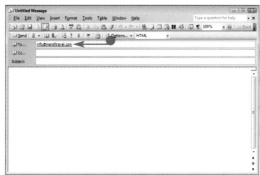

**TIPS**

**Can I specify a subject for an e-mail message?**

Yes. You can use the ?subject parameter within the link tag to include a subject line with the e-mail message. When the user clicks the link and the e-mail client opens, the subject area is prefilled. You can use this technique to help recognize e-mail generated from your Web site. For example:

```
<A HREF="MAILTO:webmaster@
example.com?subject=comments">
E-mail a comment</>
```

**Is it safe to use my e-mail address in a link?**

You should use caution when placing a personal e-mail address on a Web page. E-mail addresses on Web pages are notorious magnets for unsolicited e-mail, because such addresses can be harvested automatically by spamming tools that crawl the Web. For this reason, you may want to create a separate e-mail account just for your Web-generated e-mail messages. See your Internet service provider for more information.

## Change Link Colors

You can control the color of links on a page. Links can appear as different colors depending on whether or not they have been clicked before. You can also define the color that a link turns when a user clicks it.

You assign link colors in the <BODY> tag. Use the LINK attribute to assign a color to unclicked links. Use the ALINK attribute, which stands for *active link*, to specify the color that appears when a link is being clicked. Use the VLINK attribute, which stands for *visited link*, to change the color of previously clicked links.

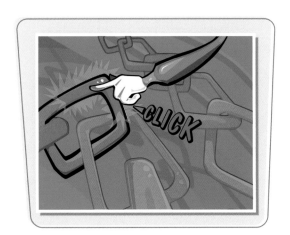

### Change Link Colors

① Click within the <BODY> tag and type **LINK="?"**, replacing ? with the color value you want to apply to the unselected links on your page.

*Note: To learn more about HTML color, see Chapter 4.*

② Type a space.

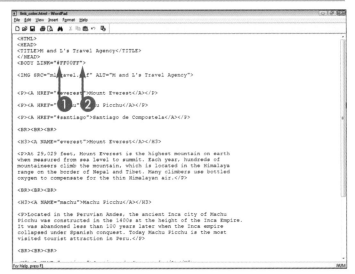

③ Type **ALINK="?"**, replacing ? with the color value you want to apply to active links on your page.

④ Type a space.

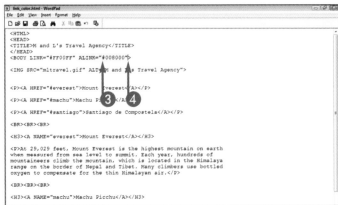

⑤ Type **VLINK="?"**, replacing *?*
with the color value you want to
apply to the previously selected
links on your page.

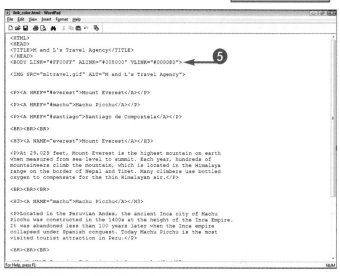

● The browser displays the links in
the colors you chose.

**Note:** To learn how to change link colors using
CSS, see Chapter 11.

**TIPS**

**Can I type color names rather than hexadecimal values?**
Yes. You can use any of the 16 Web-safe colors by name rather
than by hexadecimal value to change link colors. For example, you
can type:

**<BODY LINK="teal" VLINK="gray" ALINK="red">**

and achieve the same effect as typing:

**<BODY LINK="#008080" VLINK="#808080"
ALINK="#FF0000">**

For a list of color names and their hexadecimal
values, see Chapter 4.

**How do I remove underlines
from my text links?**

You can remove the underlining
that browsers apply to links using
Cascading Style Sheets, or
CSS. CSS gives you
greater formatting
control over your
Web page text. To
learn more about
CSS, see Chapter 11.

# CHAPTER

# 7

# Working with Tables

Are you looking for a way to organize data on your Web page into rows and columns? Or to divide your page into sections for placing headers, footers, and navigation links? This chapter shows you how to use HTML tables to do all of this.

# Understanding Table Structure

HTML tables enable you to effectively present large amounts of data in rows and columns. You can also use tables to organize the overall structure of a Web page. For example, you can create a two-column table that organizes a list of navigational links in one column and the main text and image content in another.

## Table Structure

Every table is basically a rectangle containing rows and columns. The places where the columns and rows intersect are called *cells*. Each cell can hold Web page content. Using HTML attributes, you can set the size of an entire table as well as the size of particular cells. You can also turn borders of a table and its cells on or off, depending on whether or not you want to draw attention to the table's structure.

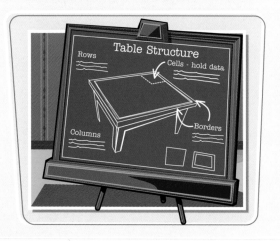

## Cell Spanning

Cells can span two or more columns or rows to form bigger containers for data. For example, a table may include a title cell at the top that spans multiple columns across the table, or one that extends downward across several rows. When you span cells in a table, interior cell walls disappear to create larger cells.

## Traditional Tables

You can use traditional tables on a Web page to present data in a tabular format. For example, you might insert a table to hold a list of products and prices or to display a class roster. You can set a fixed width and height for the table to make it fit in with the rest of the page content.

## Presentation Tables

You can use a presentation-style table to display the content on the page in interesting ways. Instead of defining an exact size, you can specify a table size using percentages. Whenever the user resizes his or her browser window, the table resizes as well. This allows for a more "liquid" layout. This type of table is good for page layouts as well as data tables.

## Table Elements

The building blocks of HTML tables are the <TABLE>, <TR>, and <TD> tags. The <TABLE> element defines the table itself. The <TR> tag defines a table row. The <TD> tag defines the table data, or cell content. In addition to these codes, you can assign table headers, captions, and column groups. You can also create tables within tables, called *nested tables*.

## Preparing to Create a Table

Before you start the task of creating any kind of table, whether it is strictly for data or to control the page layout, stop and sketch out what you want the table to look like and what type of data you want each cell to hold. A little planning beforehand can help you build your table faster and more accurately.

# Add a Table

You can insert a table onto your page to organize data or control the page layout. HTML tables are made up of cells arranged into rows and columns. You can assign different page elements to different cells to control the positioning of those elements on the page. Cells can hold text, images, and other Web page content.

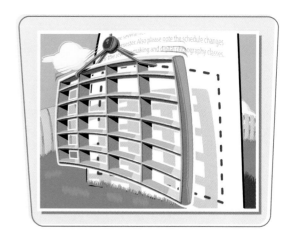

Add a Table

① Type **<TABLE>** where you want to insert a table.

② Type **<TR>** to start the first row in the table.

   To make it easier to distinguish between rows, type each row tag on a new line.

③ Type **<TD>** for the first cell you want to create.

④ Type the cell data.

***Note:*** *If you want your first row to include bold column labels, you can use the <TH> tag instead of <TD>. See the section "Add Column Labels" to learn more.*

⑤ Type **</TD>** to complete the cell.

⑥ Repeat steps **3** to **5** to add cells.

   To make it easier to distinguish between cells, you can place each cell on a new line in your HTML document.

⑦ Type **</TR>** at the end of the first row.

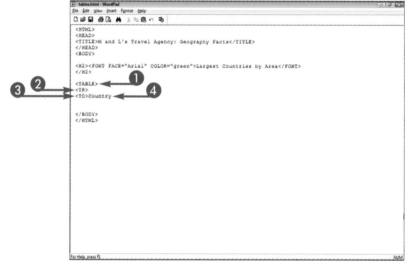

8 Continue adding rows and cell data as needed.

9 Type **</TABLE>** at the end of the table data.

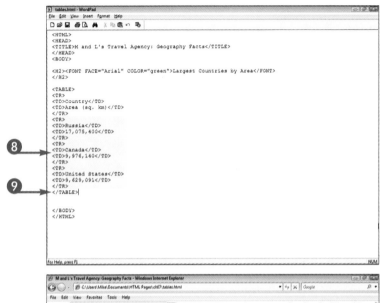

The Web browser displays the data in a tabular format.

● In this example, the table cells need some padding and spacing or borders.

*Note:* See the sections "Assign a Table Border" and "Adjust Cell Padding and Spacing" to learn more.

**TIPS**

### How do I set a size for a table?
You can set the dimensions of a table as exact pixel values or as percentages of the browser window using the <TABLE> tag's WIDTH and HEIGHT attributes. If you want to set a fixed size and have the entire table width visible in browsers, set the width at 750 pixels or less, because most users surf the Web with their monitors set to at least 800 pixels wide. For more information, see the section "Adjust the Table Size."

### What is the best way to build a table?
Before you start coding your table, draw it out on paper to organize the cell contents, designate column headers and rows, and determine its general layout and size. When you are ready to begin coding, start by typing the tags to define the table structure, putting numbers in the cells as placeholders. You can check the structure in a Web browser to see how it looks, then return to your editor and start filling in the real cell data.

# Assign a Table Border

Table borders make your cells easier to distinguish and give the table a visible structure on a page. A border is simply a line that appears around the table as well as around each cell within the table. By default, a table does not have a border unless you specify one. You can use the BORDER attribute to turn table borders on or off.

**When you set a border thickness, it applies only to the outer edge of the table, not to the cells within the table. Border thickness is measured in pixels. Borders appear gray unless you specify a color. See the section "Adjust Cell Padding and Spacing" to learn how to control interior borders.**

## Assign a Table Border

① In the <TABLE> tag, type **BORDER="?"**, replacing *?* with the value for the border thickness you want to set.

*Note: See the section "Add a Table" to learn how to create a basic table.*

② To set a border color, type **BORDERCOLOR="?"** in the <TABLE> tag, replacing *?* with the color value you want to apply.

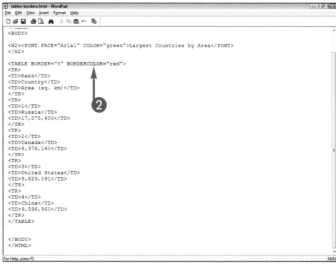

● In this example, the browser displays a table with a default gray border.

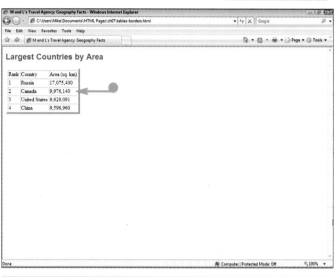

● In this example, the browser displays the same table with a colored border.

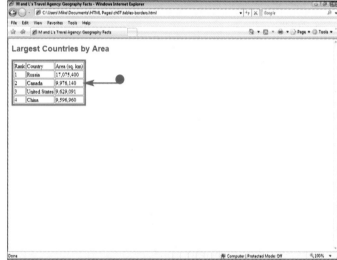

**TIPS**

**Can I specify a border with a style sheet?**

Yes. In your style sheet, type **TABLE** or **TD**. Then type **{BORDER: *VALUES*}**, replacing *VALUES* with a border size (in pixels), border style, and border color, separating the values with spaces. For example, to create a 1-pixel, solid-red border, type **{BORDER: 1px solid red}**. See Chapter 11 to learn more about applying borders with style sheets.

**Style Sheet**

**Do I need to add borders if I am using a table as a layout for my Web page?**

No. It is usually not a good idea to use the BORDER attribute for table layouts. With a layout, you want the table structure to define different sections of the page invisibly. If you assign a border, the browser adds a border to every section, which can distract from your page content.

# Adjust Cell Padding and Spacing

You can use padding to add space between the border and the contents of a cell. You can use spacing to increase the border size or distance between cells. Padding and spacing size is measured in pixels.

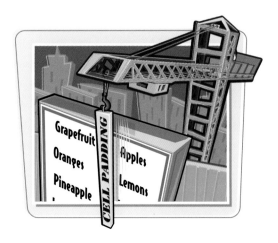

**SET CELL PADDING**

1. In the <TABLE> tag, type **CELLPADDING="?"**, replacing *?* with the pixel value you want to assign.

● In this example, a table border is turned on to show the padding more clearly.

● The Web browser displays the designated amount of space between the cell contents and the cell borders.

**SET CELL SPACING**

1 In the `<TABLE>` tag, type **CELLSPACING="?"**, replacing *?* with the pixel value you want to assign.

● In this example, a table border is turned on to clearly show the padding.

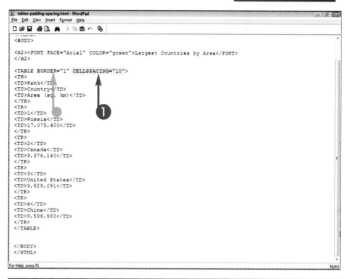

● The Web browser displays the designated amount of space for the cell borders.

---

**TIPS**

**What happens if I set the spacing and padding values to 0?**

If you set the CELLSPACING and CELLPADDING values to 0, the browser removes any spacing or padding between the cells. You may use this technique to make images in adjacent cells appear as a single image. You can set the BORDER attribute to 0 as well to remove the border between cells.

**How do I control the padding on just one side of a cell?**

The CELLPADDING attribute applies padding to all sides of cells equally. To control padding on just one side of a cell, you can apply a style rule to a `<TD>` tag using style sheets. For example, you can apply 10 pixels of padding to the top of a table cell using the padding-top property. See Chapter 12 for information on controlling padding with style sheets.

# Adjust Cell Width and Height

You can control a cell's width using the WIDTH attribute and its height using the HEIGHT attribute. This enables you to allocate more space to columns or rows that have more content. If you do not set a specific width or height, the content of the cell determines the cell's size.

**You can specify dimensions using a pixel value or using a percentage relative to the width or height of the overall table.**

---

## Adjust Cell Width and Height

### SET CELL WIDTH

**1** In the <TD> tag, type **WIDTH="?"**, replacing *?* with the value or percentage you want to set for the cell.

*Note: See the section "Adjust the Table Size" to set the width of the entire table.*

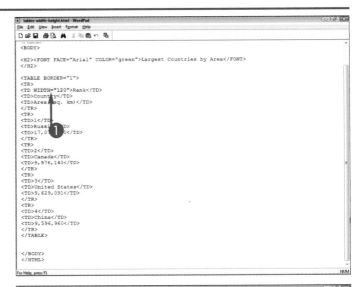

● The Web browser displays a set width for the cell, as well as all the other cells in the same column.

## SET CELL HEIGHT

**1** In the `<TD>` tag, type
**HEIGHT="?"**, replacing *?* with
the pixel value or percentage you
want to set for the cell.

**Note:** *See the section "Adjust the Table Size" to
set the height of the entire table.*

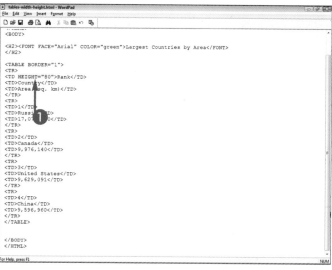

● The Web browser displays a set
height for the cell, as well as all
the other cells in the same row.

Largest Countries by Area

| Rank | Country | Area (sq. km) |
|------|---------------|---------------|
| 1 | Russia | 17,075,400 |
| 2 | Canada | 9,976,140 |
| 3 | United States | 9,629,091 |
| 4 | China | 9,596,960 |

**TIPS**

**If I want to precisely control the dimensions in my table, do I need to set a width and height for all the cells?**

If you have a table with more than one cell, no. When you set a width for one cell, this also sets the width for the cells above or below. When you set a height for a cell, this also sets the height for all the cells to the left or right of it. Because of this, you need to set the width or height only once for each row or column.

**Can I set the width for a single cell and not have it affect the other cells?**

When you change the width of a cell, all the other cells in that column adjust to the same width. If you want one cell to span one or more columns, you can use another set of codes to control the individual cell width. See the section "Extend Cells across Columns and Rows" to learn more.

# Add Column Labels

If you are building a table to populate with data, you can add labels, also called *headers,* to the top of each column using the <TH> tag. For example, if your table lists products and prices, your column headers might include labels such as Product Number, Product Name, and Price. Column headers appear in bold type and are centered within each cell.

## Add Column Labels

**1** Type **<TH>** after the <TR> tag for the row you want to use as your column labels.

**Note:** *See the section "Add a Table" to learn how to create a basic table.*

**2** Type label text for the first column.

**3** Type **</TH>** at the end of the label.

**4** Repeat steps **1** to **3** to add as many column labels as you need, ending the row with the </TR> tag.

● The Web browser displays the labels as column headers in the table.

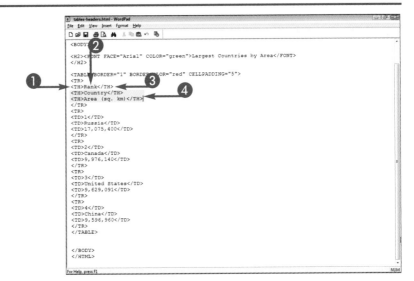

# Create Newspaper-Style Columns

You can use the table format to present columns of text on your Web page, much like a newspaper. For example, you may want to organize your text into two or three columns. Paragraphs of text are contained within each column.

**You can use the vertical alignment attribute to make each column align at the top of the table.**

### Create Newspaper-Style Columns

① Within the `<TR>` and `</TR>` tags, type **`<TD VALIGN="top">`** to start the first column of text.

*Note: See the section "Add a Table" to learn how to create a basic table.*

● You can optionally specify a `WIDTH` attribute to constrain a column's width.

② Type your column text.

③ Type **`</TD>`** at the end of the text.

④ Repeat steps **2** and **3** to add more columns and text.

The Web browser displays the text as columns on the page.

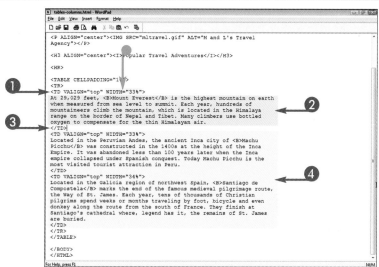

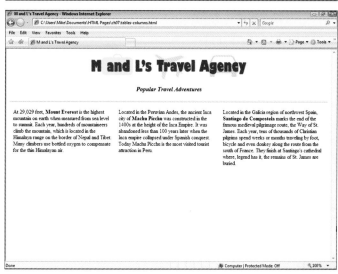

# Create Side Navigation

You can use a table to create a two-column layout for your page. You can use a narrow column on the left to hold navigation links and a larger column on the right to hold the main content.

**1** Start your table by typing **<TABLE>** and **<TR>** tags.

**2** Type **<TD VALIGN="top" WIDTH="?">**, replacing *?* with the pixel value or percentage value you want to assign for the navigation column.

**3** Type your navigation links. You can use the <BR> tag to put links on different lines.

**Note:** *For more information about links, see Chapter 6.*

**4** Type **</TD>** at the end of the link text.

**5** Type **<TD VALIGN="top" WIDTH="?">**, replacing *?* with the pixel value or percentage value you want to assign for the main content column.

**6** Type your main content.

**7** Type **</TD>**, **</TR>**, and then **</TABLE>** to close the table.

When the table displays in a browser, the links appear to the left of the main content.

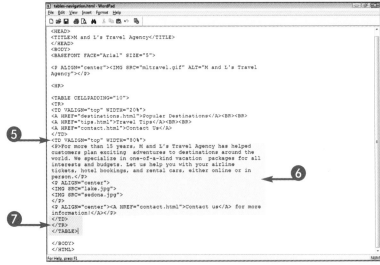

# Add a Table Caption

You can add a caption to your table to help users identify the information contained within the table. Table captions can appear at the top or bottom of the table. By default, captions appear above the table unless you specify another alignment attribute. Captions always appear on a separate line of text from the table.

**You can format your caption text using the HTML formatting tags. See Chapter 4 to learn more.**

Daily Sports

Matt Zigaitis in Victory Lane after 3rd consecutive HTML 800 win

## Add a Table Caption

**1** Add a new line directly below the `<TABLE>` tag.

*Note: See the section "Add a Table" to learn how to create a basic table.*

**2** Type **<CAPTION>**.

To place the caption below the table, type **ALIGN="bottom"** within the `<CAPTION>` tag.

**3** Type the caption text.

**4** Type **</CAPTION>** at the end of the caption text.

● The Web browser displays the caption above or below the table.

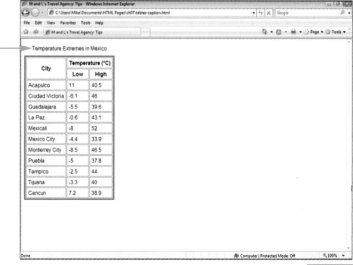

# Control which Borders to Display

Ordinarily, when you assign a border to a table, it surrounds both the table and the individual cells. You can control which external and internal borders appear in your table using the FRAME and RULES attributes. For example, you can turn off the top and bottom borders of a cell or display the entire right side of the table without a border. By controlling which borders appear, you can create a custom table.

**This section includes a list of all external and internal border values for quick reference.**

Control Which Borders to Display

## CONTROL EXTERNAL BORDERS

1 In the BORDER attribute for the table, type **FRAME="?"**, replacing *?* with the value for the border display you want to set.

You can use void, above, below, rhs, lhs, hsides, vsides, or border.

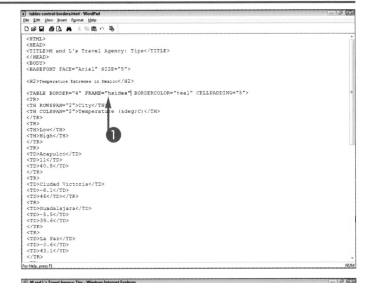

The Web browser displays the table with the external borders you specified.

● In this example, the sides of the table are hidden.

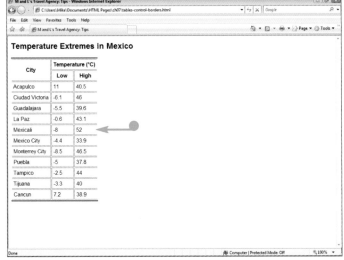

## CONTROL INTERNAL BORDERS

① In the BORDER attribute for the table, type **RULES="?"**, replacing *?* with the value for the border display you want to set.

You can use none, cols, rows, groups, or all.

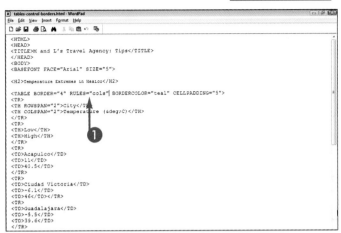

The Web browser displays the table with the internal borders you specified.

● In this example, the inside row borders are hidden.

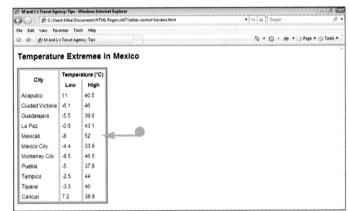

**TIP**

### What values do I use to define external or internal borders?

| External Borders | |
| --- | --- |
| **Value** | **Display** |
| VOID | No external borders |
| ABOVE | A border above the table |
| BELOW | A border below the table |
| RHS | A border on the right side of the table |
| LHS | A border on the left side of the table |
| HSIDES | Borders on the top and bottom of the table |
| VSIDES | Borders on the left and right sides of the table |
| BORDER | Borders on every side of the table (default) |

| Internal Borders | |
| --- | --- |
| **Value** | **Display** |
| NONE | No internal borders |
| COLS | Borders between columns |
| ROWS | Borders between rows |
| GROUPS | Borders between column and row groups |
| ALL | Borders throughout the table cells (default) |

# Adjust the Table Size

You can control the exact size of a table using the `WIDTH` and `HEIGHT` attributes in the `<TABLE>` tag. You can specify a table size in pixels or set the size as a percentage of the browser window.

When setting a width in pixels, limit the value to 750 pixels to ensure the table fits on the screen. If you prefer a more flexible table, set the size as a percentage. This allows the table to be resized if the browser window is resized.

## Adjust the Table Size

### SET A TABLE SIZE IN PIXELS

1 In the `<TABLE>` tag, type **WIDTH="?"**, replacing *?* with the pixel value you want to assign.

2 Type a space.

3 Type **HEIGHT="?"**, replacing *?* with the pixel value you want to assign.

**Note:** *The* `HEIGHT` *attribute is not as well supported as the* `WIDTH` *attribute and may not display properly in all browsers.*

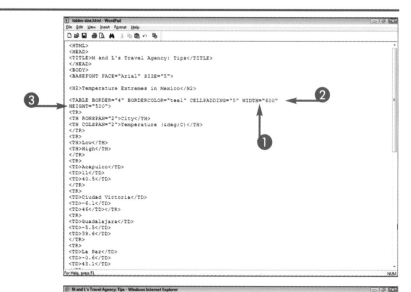

● The Web browser displays the table at the specified size.

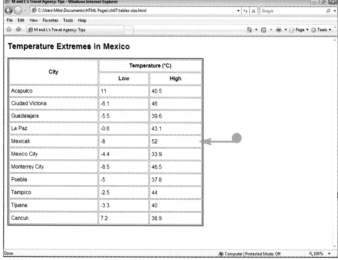

Temperature Extremes in Mexico

| City | Temperature (°C) | |
|---|---|---|
| | Low | High |
| Acapulco | 11 | 40.5 |
| Ciudad Victoria | -6.1 | 46 |
| Guadalajara | -5.5 | 39.6 |
| La Paz | -0.6 | 43.1 |
| Mexicali | -8 | 52 |
| Mexico City | -4.4 | 33.9 |
| Monterrey City | -8.5 | 46.5 |
| Puebla | -5 | 37.8 |
| Tampico | -2.5 | 44 |
| Tijuana | -3.3 | 40 |
| Cancun | 7.2 | 38.9 |

### SET A TABLE SIZE AS A PERCENTAGE

① In the `<TABLE>` tag, type **WIDTH="?"**, replacing *?* with the percentage value you want to assign.

You can add a height setting if your table needs one by typing **HEIGHT="?"** in the `<TABLE>` tag.

**Note:** *The* `HEIGHT` *attribute is not as well supported as the* `WIDTH` *attribute and may not display properly in all browsers.*

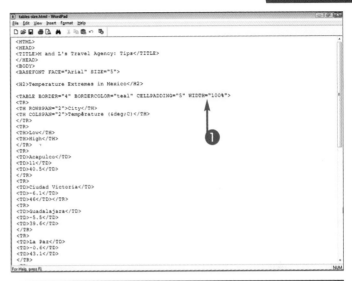

● The Web browser displays the table at the specified size.

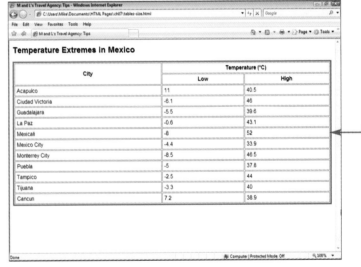

**TIPS**

| **Is it possible to set a table too small for its contents?** | **To what size does a browser set my table if I do not specify an exact width?** |
|---|---|
| No. If you accidentally make a table too small for the contents, the browser ignores the measurements and tries to make the table fit as best it can. On the other hand, if you set a table too wide, users are forced to scroll to see parts of the table. For best results, do not make your table wider than 750 pixels. | If you do not set a width using the `WIDTH` attribute, the browser sizes the table based on the cell contents. When text is in the table, the browser expands the table enough to fit its largest contents but not past the right edge of the browser window. If a table contains large images, it may extend beyond the browser window. |

# Change Cell Alignment

You can control the alignment of data within your table cells using the ALIGN and VALIGN attributes. The ALIGN attribute controls horizontal alignment: left, center, and right. By default, all table data you enter into cells is left-aligned. The VALIGN attribute controls vertical alignment: top, middle, and bottom. By default, the table data is vertically aligned to appear in the middle of each cell.

You can add alignment attributes to a single cell, a row, or all the data in the table. To learn how to position a table on the page, see the section "Change Table Alignment."

**SET HORIZONTAL ALIGNMENT**

1. Click inside the tag for the cell, row, or table you want to align.

*Note: You can also align column or row groups. See the section "Create Column and Row Groups" to learn more.*

2. Type **ALIGN="?"**, replacing ? with a horizontal alignment attribute: left, center, or right.

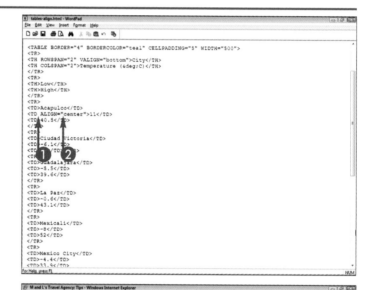

The Web browser displays the table with the specified alignment.

- In this example, the contents of a single cell are centered.

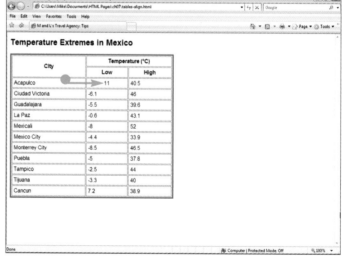

## SET VERTICAL ALIGNMENT

1. Click inside the tag for the cell, row, or table you want to align.

*Note: You can also align column or row groups. See the section "Create Column and Row Groups" to learn more.*

2. Type **VALIGN="?"**, replacing *?* with a horizontal alignment attribute: `top`, `middle`, or `bottom`.

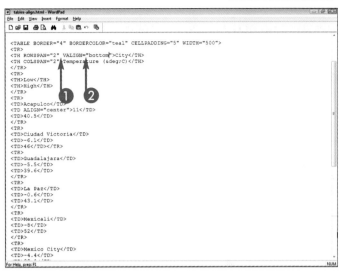

The Web browser displays the table with the specified alignment.

● In this example, a single column heading is bottom-aligned.

**Temperature Extremes in Mexico**

| City | Temperature (°C) | |
| --- | --- | --- |
| | Low | High |
| Acapulco | 11 | 40.5 |
| Ciudad Victoria | -6.1 | 46 |
| Guadalajara | -5.5 | 39.6 |
| La Paz | -0.6 | 43.1 |
| Mexicali | -8 | 52 |
| Mexico City | -4.4 | 33.9 |
| Monterrey City | -8.5 | 46.5 |
| Puebla | -5 | 37.8 |
| Tampico | -2.5 | 44 |
| Tijuana | -3.3 | 40 |
| Cancun | 7.2 | 38.9 |

**TIPS**

**Can I override the alignment of a column or row group for a single cell?**

Yes. You can set the alignment for a column or row and then override the alignment for an individual cell within the group. Simply add the alignment attribute to the cell. See the section "Create Column and Row Groups" to learn more.

**How do I justify data in a table cell?**

Justification sets both left and right alignment and stretches the text to span the area between the cell borders. Although there is an HTML attribute for justification, `justify`, not all Web browsers currently support the setting.

J-U-S-T-I-F-Y

# Extend Cells across Columns and Rows

You can create a larger cell in your table by extending the cell across two or more columns or rows. The ability to span cells, also called *merging cells*, allows you to create unique cell structures within your table. For example, you might include a large cell across the top of a table to hold a heading or an image.

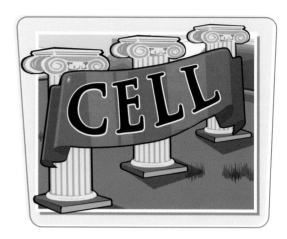

**EXTEND CELLS ACROSS COLUMNS**

1 Click inside the tag for the cell you want to extend across columns.

2 Type **COLSPAN="?"**, replacing ? with the number of columns you want to span.

The Web browser displays the cell spanning the designated number of columns.

● In this example, a heading column spans the top of the table.

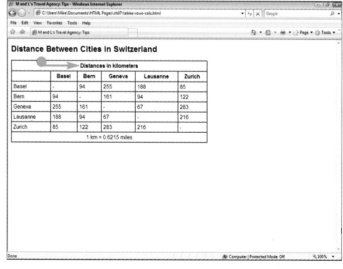

**EXTEND CELLS ACROSS ROWS**

1 Click inside the tag for the cell you want to extend across rows.

2 Type **ROWSPAN="?"**, replacing *?* with the number of rows you want to span.

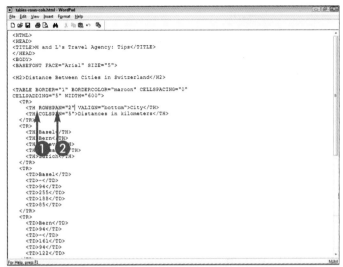

The Web browser displays the cell spanning the designated number of rows.

● In this example, a heading spans two rows at the top of the table.

● In this example, a heading also spans five columns. You can combine column and row spanning to create complex table designs.

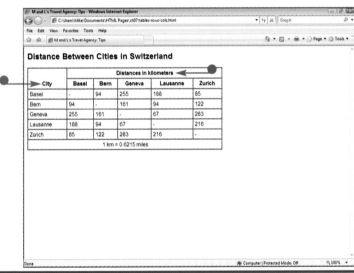

Distance Between Cities in Switzerland

| City | Distances in kilometers | | | | |
| --- | --- | --- | --- | --- | --- |
| | Basel | Bern | Geneva | Lausanne | Zurich |
| Basel | - | 94 | 255 | 188 | 85 |
| Bern | 94 | - | 161 | 94 | 122 |
| Geneva | 255 | 161 | - | 67 | 283 |
| Lausanne | 188 | 94 | 67 | - | 216 |
| Zurich | 85 | 122 | 283 | 216 | - |
| 1 km = 0.6215 miles | | | | | |

 **TIPS**

**Can I extend a cell across columns and rows at the same time?**

Yes. If you add the COLSPAN and ROWSPAN attributes to the same row or header tag, you can make a cell span horizontally and vertically in the table. Just remember to remove cells in the columns and rows you want the current cell to span.

**How can I set off a row that spans the top of my table?**

You can create a title cell for a table by adding a top cell that spans all the cells beneath it. To set that cell off from the others, you can add a background color. See the section "Add a Background Color to Cells" for more information. You can also make that cell a header cell by using the <TH> tag. See the section "Add Column Labels" for details.

# Create Column and Row Groups

You can define a group of columns in your table and set attributes across that group using the <COLGROUP> tag. This saves you from having to apply attributes separately to all the cells in the columns. You can use the <COL> tag to add special formatting to columns that differ from other columns in a group.

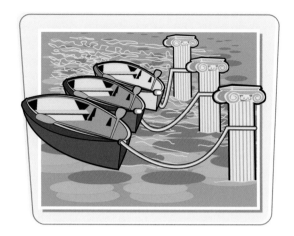

## CREATE A COLUMN GROUP

① Add a line where you want to insert a new column group and type **<COLGROUP SPAN="?"**, replacing *?* with the number of columns you want to include in the group.

● You can type any formatting attributes you want to assign the group within the <COLGROUP> tag.

② Type **</COLGROUP>** to end the group.

③ Repeat steps **1** and **2** for each column group you want to create.

Any formatting you assign to the group is applied to every cell in the group.

● In this example, one group has a gray background color, while the other has a purple background color.

**Note:** See the section "Add a Background Color to Cells" to learn more.

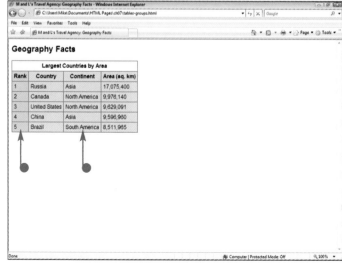

**CREATE A NONSTRUCTURAL COLUMN GROUP**

1. After a `<COLGROUP>` tag, add a line where you want to create a new column definition and type **`<COL SPAN="?"`**, replacing *?* with the number of columns you want to format.

2. Type any formatting attributes you want to assign the columns within the `<COL>` tag.

   You do not need a closing tag for the `<COL>` tag.

3. Repeat steps **1** and **2** for each column you want to create in the column group.

   Any formatting is applied to the columns in the group.

● In this example, two purple columns have a narrower width and a third purple column has a wider width.

*Note: See the section "Adjust Cell Width and Height" to learn more about changing cell dimensions.*

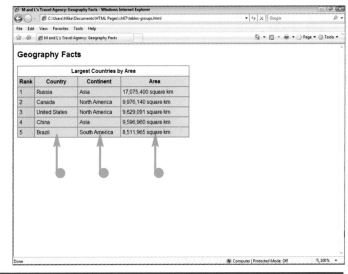

 **TIPS**

**Can my table include both grouped and ungrouped columns?**

Yes. For example, your table might include a group of columns set aside for certain data, while the remaining cells remain ungrouped.

**If my column group includes a column header and I assign an alignment to the group, does the header alignment change, too?**

No. Header cells are not affected by alignment you assign to the column group. Browsers read the `<TH>` tag and automatically set center alignment and bold text. You can, however, align the cell separately using the alignment attributes. See the section "Change Cell Alignment" to learn how to add alignment coding to a table cell.

continued

# Create Column and Row Groups *(continued)*

You can use row groups to divide a table into horizontal sections. You create row groups using the <THEAD> and <TBODY> tags. The <THEAD> tag creates a header for the row group. You use the <TBODY> tag to define the actual row groups. If the row group requires a footer, you can add one with the <TFOOT> tag.

**CREATE A ROW GROUP**

① Before the first header row you want to group, type **<THEAD>**.

● You can add any formatting you want to apply to the group within the <THEAD> tag.

*Note: See the section "Add a Background Color to Cells" to learn more about adding color to tables.*

② Type **</THEAD>** after the last row you want to include in the header group.

③ Type **<TBODY>** above the first row you want to include in the group.

● You can type any formatting attributes you want to assign the group within the <TBODY> tag.

④ Type **</TBODY>** after the last row you want to include in the group.

To create multiple row groups, repeat steps **3** and **4** for the other rows you want to group together in the table.

⑤ Type **<TFOOT>** above the first row you want to include in the footer group.

● You can type any formatting attributes you want to assign the group within the <TFOOT> tag.

⑥ Type **</TFOOT>** after the last row you want to include in the footer group.

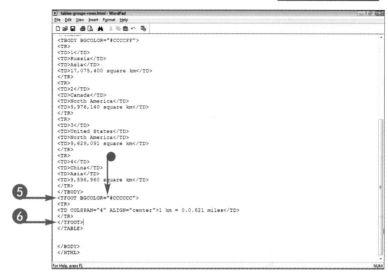

The Web browser displays the row groups in the table.

In this example, row groups are assigned different background colors to help distinguish each group.

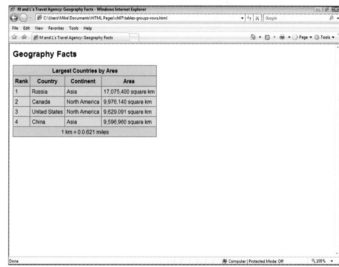

**TIPS**

**After I assign a column or row group, how do I align every cell in the group?**

You can add the ALIGN attribute to the <THEAD>, <TFOOT>, or <TBODY> tag to assign alignment to the entire group. For example, if you type **<TBODY ALIGN="right">**, all the cell content in the group aligns to the right of the cells.

**How do I add borders between my groups?**

You can specify exactly which cell and table borders appear in your table using the FRAME attribute. For example, you might set a thick, colored border at the top and bottom of a row group to make the group stand out from the rest of the table. See the section "Control Which Borders to Display" earlier in this chapter to learn more.

# Add a Background Color to Cells

You can add color to individual cells in your table or to certain rows and columns. You can use background color to draw attention to the cell contents.

**When applying a background color, be careful not to choose a color that makes the table data difficult to read. See Chapter 4 to learn more about setting color values in HTML.**

## Add a Background Color to Cells

① Click the tag for the cell or row to which you want to add a background color.

② Type **BGCOLOR="?"**, replacing *?* with the color value you want to assign.

*Note: See Chapter 4 to learn more about assigning color values.*

To add color to a particular column, you can add the color attribute to each cell in the column or to a column group tag.

*Note: See the section "Create Column and Row Groups" to learn more.*

To add color to a row, you can add the color attribute to the `<TR>` tag.

The Web browser displays the background color in the cell, row, or column.

● In this example, a color is added to a single cell.

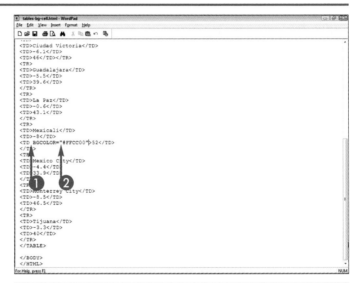

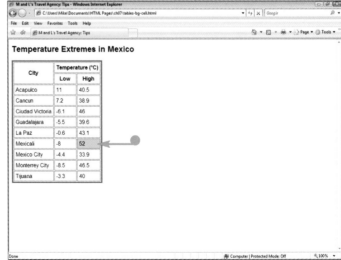

# Add a Background Color to a Table

You can add a background color that appears behind the entire table of data. You can use a background color to make the table stand out from the rest of the Web page.

**When applying a background color, be careful not to choose a color that makes the table data difficult to read. See Chapter 4 to learn more about setting color values in HTML.**

## Add a Background Color to a Table

1 Within the <TABLE> tag, type **BGCOLOR="?"**, replacing *?* with the color value you want to assign.

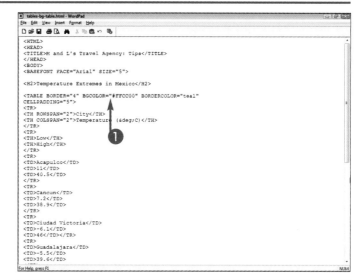

```
<HTML>
<HEAD>
<TITLE>M and L's Travel Agency: Tips</TITLE>
</HEAD>
<BODY>
<BASEFONT FACE="Arial" SIZE="5">

<H2>Temperature Extremes in Mexico</H2>

<TABLE BORDER="4" BGCOLOR="#FFCC00" BORDERCOLOR="teal"
CELLPADDING="5">
<TR>
<TH ROWSPAN="2">City</TH>
<TH COLSPAN="2">Temperature (&deg;C)</TH>
</TR>
<TR>
<TH>Low</TH>
<TH>High</TH>
</TR>
<TR>
<TD>Acapulco</TD>
<TD>11</TD>
<TD>40.5</TD>
</TR>
<TR>
<TD>Cancun</TD>
<TD>7.2</TD>
<TD>38.9</TD>
</TR>
<TR>
<TD>Ciudad Victoria</TD>
<TD>-6.1</TD>
<TD>46</TD></TR>
<TR>
<TD>Guadalajara</TD>
<TD>-5.5</TD>
<TD>39.6</TD>
```

● The Web browser displays the table with the specified background color.

**Note:** *To add color to a specific cell, see the section "Add a Background Color to Cells."*

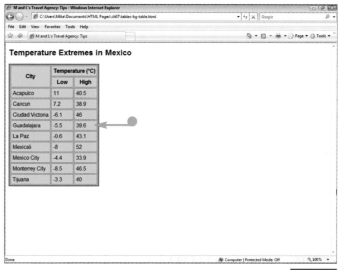

### Temperature Extremes in Mexico

| City | Temperature (°C) | |
|---|---|---|
| | Low | High |
| Acapulco | 11 | 40.5 |
| Cancun | 7.2 | 38.9 |
| Ciudad Victoria | -6.1 | 46 |
| Guadalajara | -5.5 | 39.6 |
| La Paz | -0.6 | 43.1 |
| Mexicali | -8 | 52 |
| Mexico City | -4.4 | 33.9 |
| Monterrey City | -8.5 | 46.5 |
| Tijuana | -3.3 | 40 |

# Insert an Image in a Cell

You can add an image to any cell in your table. If you are using a table as a page layout structure, for example, you might place images in different cells to illustrate your page. If you are using a table strictly to hold data, you might insert a photo of your content, such as a product picture.

**You can also use the** BACKGROUND **attribute to add an image to the entire table. See the section "Insert a Background Image" to learn more.**

① Click in the cell in which you want to add an image, right after the opening <TD> tag, and type **<IMG SRC="?">**, replacing *?* with the name and path of the image file you want to use.

*Note: See Chapter 5 to learn how to add and work with images.*

● The Web browser displays the cell with the specified image.

# Insert a Background Image

You can add a background image to appear behind your entire table. Background images can give your table a more interesting design.

When using an image as a background, be careful the design and colors do not clash with the table data or make it illegible. You may need to change the text color to make it stand out from the underlying background image. See Chapter 4 to learn how to assign color to text.

## Insert a Background Image

**1** Click in the `<TABLE>` tag and type **BACKGROUND="?"**, replacing *?* with the name and path of the image file you want to use.

**Note:** See Chapter 5 to learn how to add and work with images.

● The Web browser displays the table with the specified background image.

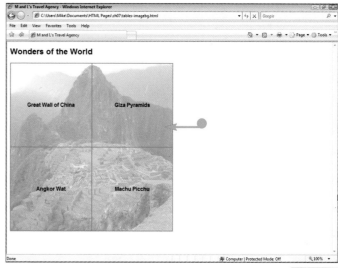

# Change Table Alignment

You can control the positioning of a table on your Web page using the ALIGN attribute. You can use this attribute to center a table or align it on the left or right side of the page. The ALIGN attribute also determines the way in which text wraps around your table element. For example, if you align the table to the right, text wraps around the left side of the table.

① Click in the `<TABLE>` tag and type **ALIGN="?"**, replacing *?* with the alignment you want to apply: `left`, `right`, or `center`.

**Note:** *Text will not wrap around a centered table, but it will wrap around those that are left- or right-aligned.*

To stop text from wrapping, type **<BR CLEAR="?">** before the text, replacing *?* with the alignment value you want to clear.

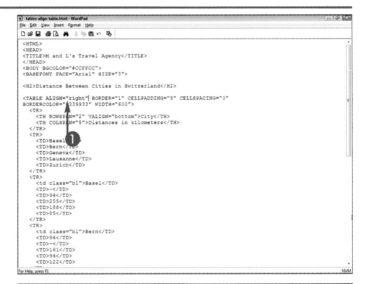

The Web browser displays the table with wrapping text.

● In this example, the table is right-aligned, with text wrapping around the left side.

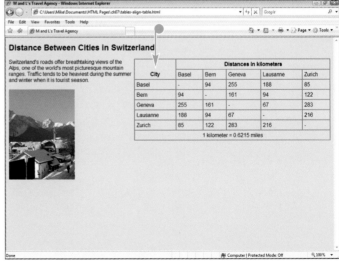

● In this example, the table is left-aligned, with text wrapping around the right side.

*Note: Tables are automatically left-aligned unless you specify an alignment value.*

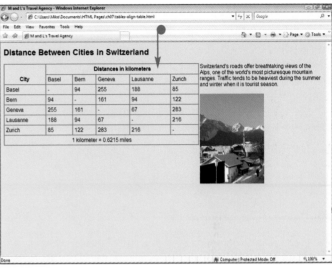

● In this example, the table is center-aligned, and no text wrapping occurs.

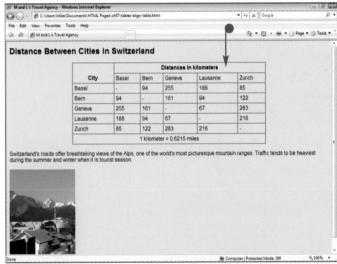

**TIPS**

**How do I control line breaks in a cell?**
To create a line break in a cell, you can use the `<BR>` tag or the `<P>` tag. These are the same text formatting tags used for regular page text. See Chapters 3 and 4 to learn more about line breaks and other text formatting. See the next section, "Control Text Wrapping in Cells," to learn how to control the way in which text wraps within a table cell.

**Can I center a table using a style sheet?**
Yes. You can type **MARGIN-RIGHT: AUTO** or **MARGIN-LEFT: AUTO** in the table's style sheet to center a table. However, you need to specify the table width first. See Chapters 10, 11, and 12 to learn more about style sheets. See the section "Adjust the Table Size" to learn how to set a table width.

# Control Text Wrapping in Cells

Depending on the size of the table, Web browsers automatically wrap text in cells when needed. You can control the wrapping by using line breaks within the cell, or you can turn off text wrapping completely.

**1** Click inside the cell tag for the text you want to control and type **NOWRAP**.

To specify where a line breaks, type **<BR>**.

You can also use the <P> tag to control line breaks in a cell.

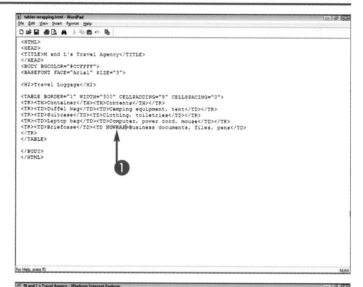

● The Web browser displays the text without breaking the line.

138

# Nest a Table within a Table

You can create a table within a table, or a *nested table*. Nested tables allow you to create a more complex table layout.

## Nest a Table within a Table

① Within the main table, add a line in the cell in which you want to add another table.

② Create the nested table just like a regular table.

**Note:** See the section "Add a Table" to learn how to create a basic HTML table.

To help distinguish the nested table from the main table, consider using indents or new lines when entering the nested table data.

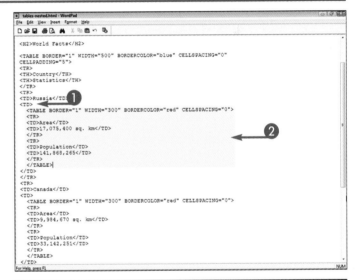

● The Web browser displays the table within the main table.

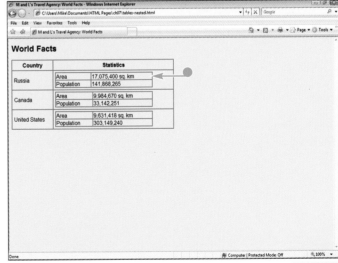

# Working with Frames

Are you looking for a way to enhance your Web site layout? Frames can help you present multiple pages to your Web site visitors all on one screen. This chapter shows you how to create framesets and add frames to your Web site.

# Understanding Frames

You can use frames to divide your Web page into sections and allow users to access different pages in your Web site from one screen. Although frames are not as widely used as they once were, they can still serve as a valuable tool to help you create a dynamic structure for your Web site.

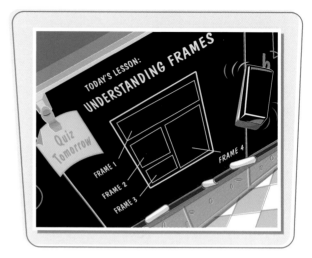

## Frame Basics

Browser windows are typically made up of a single frame displaying a single HTML document. If a page's content exceeds the size of the frame, scroll bars appear allowing the user to view different parts of the page. With multiple frames, the browser window displays several HTML documents at one time, each frame acting as a separate screen. Each frame can display its own scroll bars to allow users to view different portions of the Web page appearing within the frame.

## Ways to Use Frames

You can find numerous uses for frames with a multipage Web site. You can use frames to display a fixed page at the top of the screen and a scrollable page in the remainder of the screen. For example, you might use a navigation page at the top with links to pages on your site. When a user clicks a link in the top frame, the frame below displays the content. Or you might use side-by-side frames to display a picture in one frame and text in another.

## Frame Advantages

When deciding whether to use frames in your Web site, take time to examine the pros and cons of frames. On the pro side, frames are helpful with larger Web sites, especially when you want to keep certain information in view at all times. Frames offer a great way to display a navigation bar in one location without needing to include navigational links on every page in your site. Frames can make it easier for users to navigate a large Web site.

## Frame Disadvantages

On the con side, users might not see your frame content as you envision; monitor resolution settings vary, and what you think is the perfect size for a frame may not be so on another user's screen. Depending on the Web page, not all page content looks good in smaller frames. Although newer browsers support the use of frames, some older versions do not. You may need to design a nonframe version of your site to accommodate users without frame support. Frames can also complicate your HTML page coding, and when they are not working properly they can cause user frustration. For example, if users are unable to view all of the links in a navigation-oriented frame, they may not be able to reach certain pages in your Web site.

## Framesets and Frames

You use several HTML documents to create frames in a Web site. A frameset document defines the overall frame architecture, including the number, size, and organization of the frames. You also need a separate HTML page for each frame. You can save the frameset document as a separate file and link the pages to the frame structure. See the section "Create Frames" to learn how to make a frameset document.

## Nested and Inline Frames

If your Web site requires a more complex frame structure, you can nest a frameset within the original frameset. This gives you the flexibility of dividing a frame into more frames. See the section "Create a Nested Frameset" to learn how to do this. You can also insert a single frame within any Web page on your site without needing to define a frameset document. See the section "Create an Inline Frame" to learn more.

# Create Frames

You can use frames to divide the Web browser window into panes. This allows you to display different pages in the browser window at the same time. For example, you might use one frame to display a navigational page that lists links to different pages on your Web site and show the result of a clicked link in another frame.

**You can use the <FRAMESET> and <FRAME> tags to define the frame structure. The <FRAMESET> tag creates a frameset, dividing the window into sections, while the <FRAME> tag specifies which page goes into which frame.**

## Create Frames

① Create and save a new HTML document, including only the basic <HTML>, <HEAD>, and <TITLE> tags.

***Note:*** *To learn how to create HTML documents, see Chapter 2.*

② Below the </HEAD> tag, type **<FRAMESET** and a space.

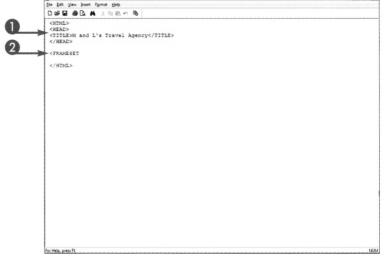

③ Define the frameset to include two or more rows or columns and specify a size in pixels for the rows or columns.

To create frames in rows, type **ROWS="?,?">**, replacing ? with the height of each row in your frameset.

To create frames in columns, type **COLS="?,?">**, replacing ? with the width of each column in your frameset.

You can also set a row or column size as a percentage by typing the value followed by a percentage sign, such as **30%**.

④ Type **<FRAME NAME="?"**, replacing *?* with a name for the frame.

⑤ Type a space and **SRC="?">**, replacing *?* with the name and location of the Web page you want to appear in the frame.

⑥ Repeat steps **4** and **5** for each frame you specified in step **3**.

⑦ Type **</FRAMESET>**.

The Web browser displays the frames.

● In this example, two row frames appear in the browser window.

You can use a nested frameset to combine rows and columns in a frameset.

***Note:*** *To create a frameset with both rows and columns, see the section "Create a Nested Frameset."*

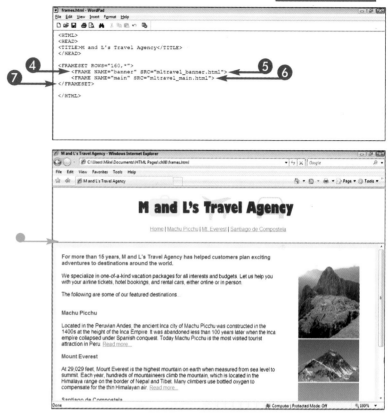

### Do I need to declare a frameset document for my framed pages?

It is good practice to include a document declaration in your pages. You can specify that your frameset page is of type Frameset at the top of your HTML code. The declaration might look like this:

```
<!DOCTYPE HTML PUBLIC "-//W3C/DTD HTML
4.01 Frameset//EN" "http://www.w3.org/
TR/REC-html40/frameset.dtd">
```

See Chapter 2 to learn more about document declarations.

### Do I have to specify a row height or column width for each frame?

Yes, but the height or width can be a wildcard character. After you define the first frame size, you can use an asterisk (*) to assign the remaining window space to other frames. For example:

```
<FRAMESET ROWS="65,*,60">
```

In this frameset, the middle frame is sized to take up whatever space remains after the other two frames are sized.

# Customize Frame Borders

You can change the thickness of your frame borders using the BORDER attribute. By default, Web browsers display the borders around your frames at a thickness of 6 pixels. You can set your frame borders to another size as well as control the color of the borders.

**CHANGE THE FRAME BORDERS**

1 Within the <FRAMESET> tag, type **BORDER="?"**, replacing *?* with a thickness value in pixels.

● The Web browser displays the frames with the designated border thickness.

## CHANGE THE BORDER COLOR

**1** Within the `<FRAMESET>` tag, type **BORDERCOLOR="?"**, replacing *?* with a color value.

**Note:** *You can learn more about HTML colors in Chapter 4.*

● The Web browser displays the frames with the designated color.

**TIPS**

### How do I hide my frame borders completely?

To hide all the frame borders, type **FRAMEBORDER="0"** in the `<FRAMESET>` tag. This coding makes the content of each frame blend together, creating what appears to be one large Web page. In some browsers, you may still see a small space between the panes. To remove this space, type **BORDER="0"** in the `<FRAMESET>` tag.

### Is there another way I can control frame border thickness?

You can use the FRAMESPACING attribute to control the thickness of frame borders. However, only Internet Explorer supports this attribute; it is not part of the formal HTML standard. To set a border thickness, type **FRAMESPACING="?"** in the `<FRAMESET>` tag, replacing *?* with the thickness value you want to set. Border thickness is measured in pixels.

# Control Frame Margins

You can control the amount of space that appears between a frame border and the contents of the frame. Using the MARGINWIDTH and MARGINHEIGHT attributes, you can set margins for the top, bottom, left, and right sides of your frames. Margin space is measured in pixels.

① Within the <FRAME> tag, type **MARGINWIDTH="?"**, replacing *?* with the amount of space you want to set for the left and right margins.

② Type a space and **MARGINHEIGHT="?"**, replacing *?* with the amount of space you want to set for the top and bottom margins.

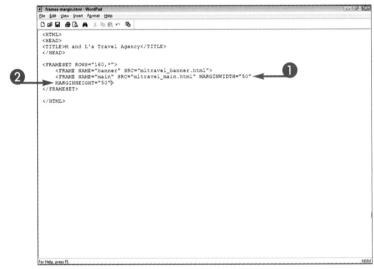

The Web browser displays the frames with the designated margins.

● In this example, the bottom frame now has increased margins all around the inside of the frame.

In the example, the bottom frame features content in a white table on a teal background.

# Add Alternative Text

You can use the `<NOFRAMES>` tag to insert alternative text for users whose browsers do not support frames. In some cases, the user may have decided to turn off frame display. Alternative text can alert them to the content they are missing.

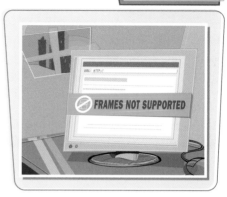

## Add Alternative Text

**1** Directly above the `</FRAMESET>` tag, add a line and type **<NOFRAMES>**.

**2** Type any alternative text you want to appear.

**3** Type **</NOFRAMES>**.

If the user's browser does not support frames, or the frame display is turned off, a page appears with the alternative text.

# Prevent Frame Resizing

By default, users can resize the frames in your Web page, allowing them to view more information in a frame. You can control your page layout by restricting frame resizing. This can be useful if you need the frame dimensions to remain fixed so that the content is viewed correctly.

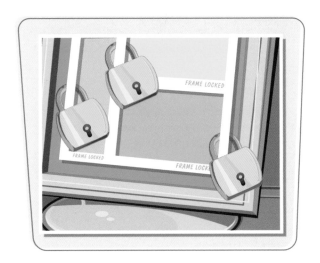

① Type **NORESIZE** inside the `<FRAME>` tag of the frame you want to control. You do not assign a value to the NORESIZE attribute.

You can repeat step **1** for any other frames for which you want to prevent resizing.

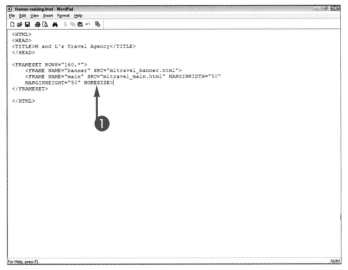

The user is not able to resize the frame in the browser window.

● In this example, resizing is turned off in the top frame.

# Hide or Display Frame Scroll Bars

Web browsers automatically display scroll bars if a frame's content exceeds the size of the frame. You can use the SCROLLING attribute to control when scroll bars appear. A yes value displays scroll bars, while a no value hides the scroll bars.

## Hide or Display Frame Scroll Bars

① Click inside the <FRAME> tag of the frame you want to control.

② Type **SCROLLING="?"**, replacing *?* with **yes** to display scroll bars or **no** to hide scroll bars.

You can repeat steps **1** and **2** to control the scroll bars in other frames.

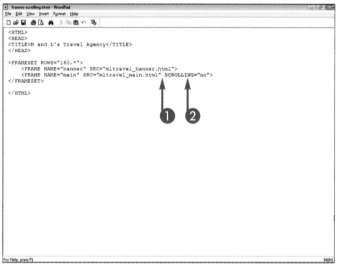

The browser displays or hides scroll bars as instructed.

● In this example, the scroll bars are hidden for the bottom frame.

You can make links on your pages open content in specific frames. To target links to particular frames, you must identify each frame with a unique name and then reference that name with the <A> tag's TARGET attribute. You can also open a page into the entire browser window by using a TARGET value of "_top". This breaks the user out of the current frameset.

**To learn how to assign names to frames, see the section "Create Frames."**

**OPEN IN A FRAME**

① Open the HTML file where the link should appear.

② Type **<A HREF="?"**, replacing *?* with the target page.

③ Type a space and **TARGET="?">**, replacing *?* with the frame name.

*Note: To name frames, see the section "Create Frames."*

④ Type the link text.

⑤ Type **</A>**.

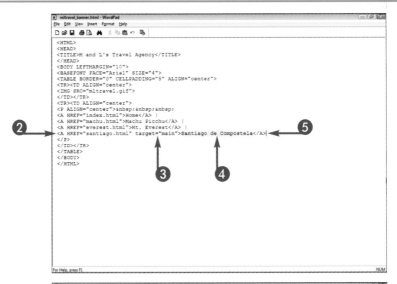

● The browser displays the link.

● When the user clicks the link, the page opens in the frame you specified.

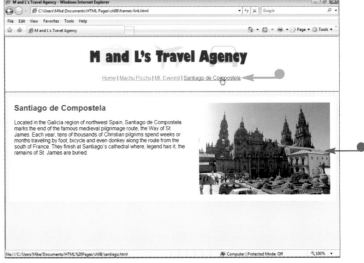

**OPEN ON TOP OF A FRAMESET**

1 Open the HTML file where the link should appear.

2 Type **<A HREF="?"**, replacing *?* with the target page.

3 Type a space and **TARGET="_top">**.

*Note: To name frames, see the section "Create Frames."*

4 Type the link text.

5 Type **</A>**.

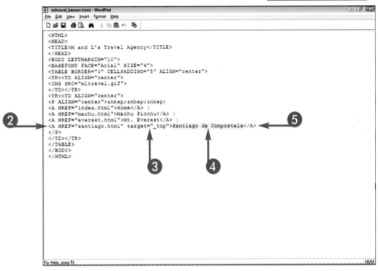

● When the user clicks the link, the page opens on top of the existing frameset.

In step **3**, you can type **TARGET="_parent">** to open the page in the parent frameset of a nested frameset.

## TIPS

**How do I make all the links open in the same frame?**

To make all page links open in the same frame, you can add the target frame information to the <HEAD> tag. Inside the <HEAD> tag, type **<BASE TARGET="?">**, replacing *?* with the name of the target frame. You must name the target frame in the frameset document in order to reference the name with the TARGET attribute.

**Can I make the target link open in a new window?**

Yes. You can use the TARGET attribute to instruct the browser to open the target link in a new window. To open the linked page in a new, unnamed window, use the _blank value. For example:

```
<A HREF="mypage.html" TARGET="_blank">
Click here to view the page</A>
```

In this code, when the user clicks the link, the document mypage.html opens in a new browser window.

# Create a Nested Frameset

You can nest a frameset within another frameset, creating a combined frameset. For example, you might place a two-frame frameset within the largest frame of your main frameset.

**You create a nested frameset the same way you created the initial frameset. See the section "Create Frames" to learn more about creating a frameset document and defining frames.**

## Create a Nested Frameset

1 In the frameset document, add a line where you want to insert a nested frameset.

2 Type **<FRAMESET ROWS="?,?">** to insert rows, or type **<FRAMESET COLS="?,?">** to insert columns, replacing ? with the row or column values for your frames.

3 Add the frame tags to define the frame names and source pages.

4 Type **</FRAMESET>** to complete the nested frameset.

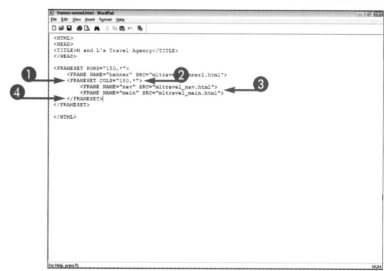

The Web browser displays the frameset within the original frameset.

● In this example, the nested frameset consists of two columns that appear below a row frame.

# Create an Inline Frame

You can create a floating frame, also called an *inline frame,* that appears within the content of a Web page. Inline frames do not require a frameset.

## Create an Inline Frame

1 Type **<IFRAME SRC="?"** where you want to insert an inline frame, replacing *?* with the name and location of the page you want to appear within the inline frame.

2 Type a space and **NAME="?"**, replacing *?* with the name of the inline frame.

3 Type a space and **WIDTH="?" HEIGHT="?">**, replacing *?* with width and height values.

4 Type **</IFRAME>**.

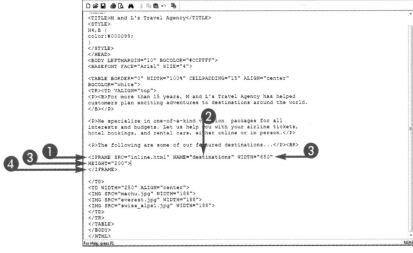

● The Web browser displays the inline frame.

Inline frames can be useful for inserting long passages of legal text, such as terms and conditions.

# CHAPTER 9

# Creating Forms

Looking for a way to allow your Web site visitors to communicate with you? This chapter shows you how to build forms that gather information from users and teaches you about the various ways to process the information.

# Understanding Forms

You can use forms to collect information from the people who visit your Web site. For example, you might enable visitors to send you feedback, post comments on articles, or purchase goods or services from your business. Before you jump into building your own forms, take a moment to study how forms work and the various ways you can use them on your own Web site.

## How Forms Work

Forms use input elements to collect data from a user, such as text fields and check boxes. After a user fills in the data, he or she can click a button to submit the form, and the browser sends the data back to the Web server. As the Web developer, you decide how to handle the data. For example, you can write a script to parse the data and send back a custom Web page in response, have a program store the data in a database, or receive the data via e-mail. Most form data is processed by CGI scripts on the Web server. You can learn more about various ways to process your data in the section "Gather Form Data" later in this chapter.

## HTML for Forms

Web page forms have three important parts: a <FORM> tag, form input elements, and a Submit button. When designing and building a form, you write HTML to define the different objects that allow users to type or select information. These objects can include text fields, radio buttons, check boxes, and more. All forms should include a Submit button for sending the data to a Web server for processing.

## Form Design

Before coding the HTML for a form, spend time thinking about how you want the user to interact with the form, what sort of data you want to collect, and how you want the form to look. Be sure to add label text to your form elements that explains what type of information you want from the user, and give users enough space to type their input. You should also explain how the information is to be used, especially if the user is submitting personal data.

## Types of Forms

You can create different types of forms. For example, you can create a search form that allows users to search your Web site for information by submitting keywords. You can add data-collection forms to gather information from users, such as names, addresses, and e-mail addresses. Your form may be as simple as a guest book or as complex as a detailed survey. You can also use forms to help customers add items to an online shopping cart and make a purchase on your site.

## Controlling Data Entry

You can control how a user enters data into your form. For example, you can guide the user from one input field to the next by controlling the tab order. See the section "Change the Tab Order" to learn more. You can also control the type of data entered into a field. For example, you can limit the phone number text field so that it accepts only numbers, not characters. You can use JavaScript programs to help alert users to invalid form data. See Chapter 13 to learn more about JavaScript.

## Confirmation

After the form data is processed, a script typically displays a message in the browser window noting whether or not the form data was sent successfully. You might also code your script so that it sends a confirmation message by e-mail. It is always good practice when collecting form data to provide visitors with a confirmation or assurance that some sort of action will be taken based on their submission. This confirmation is usually a page that you code using HTML.

# Types of Form Elements

Forms are made up of a variety of input elements. Some elements, such as text boxes, give users a way to add information in a free-form manner. Others, such as radio buttons, constrain what the user can submit. You can mix different types of input elements in a single form.

## Text Boxes

Text boxes are input fields designed specifically for users to type data into, such as typing a name or comment. A text box can be a single line to collect a limited number of characters, such as a phone number or postal code. Text boxes can also be large, multiline fields that allow for submitting paragraphs of input. In single-line text boxes, you can control the maximum number of characters a user can type.

## Check Boxes

Check boxes enable a user to select one or more options from a list. For example, if you want to collect information about a user's familiarity with computers, you can place a set of check boxes next to a list of computer applications. When designing a form, you have the option of presenting check boxes as already checked.

### Radio Buttons

Radio buttons are the small, circular buttons found on forms, named for their resemblance to the buttons found on older automobile radios. Like check boxes, radio buttons are used to present several choices to the user. Unlike with check boxes, however, users may select only one radio button in a set. For example, if you include a feedback form on your page that rates your Web site, you might include radio buttons for the values Excellent, Good, Average, and Poor. The user can select only one of the four options.

### Menus and Lists

Menu and list input elements enable you to present a large set of choices in a form. In a drop-down menu, a user clicks a box to open a list of options from which he or she can select only one. For example, users will often choose from a drop-down menu when selecting their state or country in an address form. You can also present data as a scrollable list and allow users to select one option or multiple options.

### Submit and Reset Buttons

Users need a way to send their data to the Web server. They can do this using a Submit button, which usually appears at the end of the form input elements. Data is collected only after the user clicks this button. You might also add a Reset button to your HTML form that allows the user to reset all the input fields and start over.

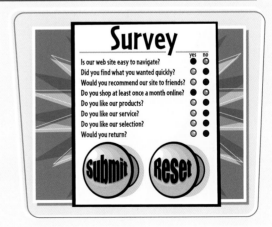

# Gather Form Data

After a user submits data from a form to a Web server, you must do something with the information. Before you begin creating your form, you need to know how the collected data will be processed. Your Web host can usually help you set up programs known as *scripts* to process the form information.

## CGI Scripts

The form data you collect will most likely be processed by CGI (Common Gateway Interface) scripts. These scripts are often written in Perl, PHP, or Java and run on the same Web server that serves your HTML pages. Scripts take form data and do something useful with it, such as putting it into a database, writing it to a file, creating a customized HTML response page, or sending the information to an e-mail address.

## Finding CGI Scripts

You can write your own CGI scripts if you know a programming language such as Perl, PHP, or Java, or you can adapt one of the many free CGI scripts available on the Web. Sites like the CGI Resource Index (http://cgi.resourceindex.com), Matt's Script Archive (www.scriptarchive.com), and HotScripts.com (www.hotscripts.com) are good places to start. You should also check with your Web host to see what it provides.

## CGI Scripts and Web Servers

Many Web hosts offer CGI scripts for processing form data. If your Web host does, you need to find out the location of the server's CGI-bin directory. A CGI-bin directory is a place on Web servers where CGI scripts are stored (the directory may be called something else, depending on the server). If your Web host does not allow CGI scripts, you might consider using a form hosting service to process your form results. Sites such as Creative Digital Resources (www.creative-dr.com) and Response-O-Matic (www.response-o-matic.com) offer free form processing.

## Preparing a Script

To adapt a CGI script to your own form, you need to adjust the script variables and path names to suit your Web server. You must also transfer the CGI script to your server using FTP (File Transfer Protocol). Be sure to check with the Web host regarding where to store the CGI file. Some prefer to store scripts in a central CGI-bin directory, while others let you store them in your own folders as long as the scripts have a particular file extension.

## Sending Data to Databases

Another use for CGI scripts is to send form data to a database. Database programs are designed to store and manage large amounts of data. CGI scripts translate requests from the Web server into a format readable by a database. If you plan to use your form data in conjunction with a database, you need to learn more about how databases work with the Web.

## Sending Data to an E-mail Address

If you do not want to use a CGI script, you can use a command directly in your <FORM> tag to send form data to an e-mail address. This action returns a list of field names and the values entered in each. This option is useful only if the form is simple; more complex forms require scripts or databases to process and make sense of the information. To learn more about sending form data via e-mail, see the section "Send Form Data to an E-mail Address."

# Create a Form

You can use a form to gather information from the people who visit your Web site. To create a form, you use the <FORM> tag to point to the CGI script that will process the form, define the form elements, and display a Submit button to send the data to the script.

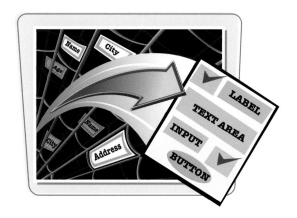

① Click where you want to insert a form and type **<FORM METHOD="?"**, replacing *?* with **post** or **get**.

The type of method to use can depend on the information you are collecting or the script that processes the form data.

If you are including a file upload element in your form, use the `post` method.

② Type a space and **ACTION="?">**, replacing *?* with the name and location of the CGI script you want to use to process the form data.

**Note:** *You may need to contact your Web host to determine the name and path of the CGI script.*

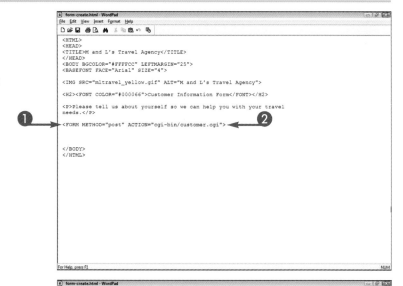

③ Type **</FORM>**.

You can now add input elements to your form between the <FORM> and </FORM> tags.

**Note:** *See the remaining sections in this chapter to learn more about adding input elements.*

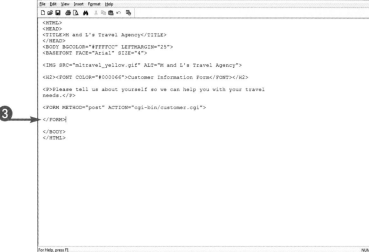

# Send Form Data to an E-mail Address

You can instruct the browser to send form data to an e-mail address. You might pursue this route if you are creating a simple form or if your Web server does not support CGI scripts.

## Send Form Data to an E-mail Address

① Click where you want to insert a form and type **<FORM METHOD="post"**.

② Type a space and **ENCTYPE="text/plain"**.

③ Type a space and **ACTION="mailto:?">**, replacing ? with the e-mail address to which you want to send the form data.

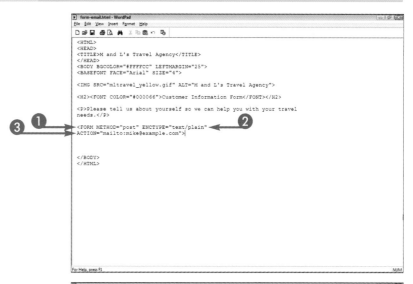

④ Type **</FORM>**.

You can now add input elements to your form between the <FORM> and </FORM> tags.

**Note:** See the remaining sections in this chapter to learn more about adding input elements.

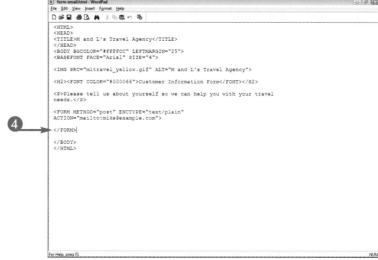

# Add a Text Box

You can add a text box to your form to allow users to type a single-line reply or response. When creating a text box, you must identify the input field with a unique name. You can also control the text box size and the maximum number of characters a user can type in the field.

**By default, browsers display the text box field at a width of 20 characters. You can make the text box wider using the SIZE attribute. You can control the number of characters allowed in a text box by specifying a value with the MAXLENGTH attribute.**

## Add a Text Box

① Between the `<FORM>` and `</FORM>` tags, add a new line for the text box.

② Type **`<INPUT TYPE="text"`**.

③ Type a space and **`NAME="?"`**, replacing ? with a unique identifier for the text box.

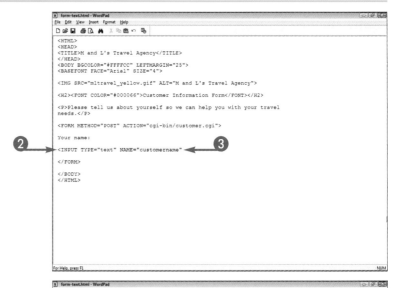

④ Type a space and **`SIZE="?"`**, replacing ? with a width in characters.

⑤ To define a maximum number of characters for the field, type **MAXLENGTH="?">**, replacing *?* with the maximum number of characters allowed.

**Note:** *Do not forget to type a closing bracket (>) at the end of your input element tag.*

● The Web browser displays the text box in the form.

The user can click inside the text box and type the required information.

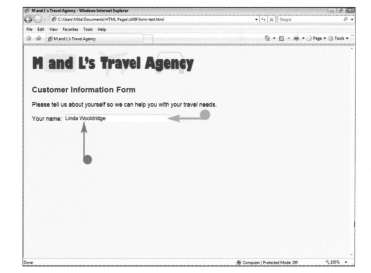

**TIPS**

### Can I add a default value to a text box?

Yes. A default value is text that appears in the text box when the user views the form. You can use default values to display instructions about the type of data required, give users an example of the data you are looking for, or show a popular choice or response. To specify a default, you can add the VALUE attribute to the <INPUT> tag. For example:

```
<INPUT TYPE="text" NAME="email"
VALUE="Enter your e-mail address">
```

### How do I create a password text box?

Browsers handle password text boxes a bit differently from regular text boxes. Instead of displaying the characters that are typed, the input field displays the data as asterisks (*). This prevents others from seeing the password text. To create a text box for password entry, you specify the password type in the <INPUT> tag. Your code might look like this:

```
<INPUT TYPE="password"
NAME="password" SIZE="45">
```

# Add a Large Text Area

If your form requires a larger text-entry box, you can create a large text area that holds multiple lines of text. For example, if you create a feedback form, you can use a large text area to allow users to type paragraphs of text.

**When defining a text area, you can control the size of the text box and how text wraps within the field. Text area size is measured in rows and columns, based on character height.**

## Add a Large Text Area

① Between the <FORM> and </FORM> tags, add a new line for the large text box.

② Type **<TEXTAREA**.

③ Type a space and **NAME="?"**, replacing ? with a unique name for the text area.

*Note: You can use the <BR> or <P> tag to separate input elements onto different lines in your form.*

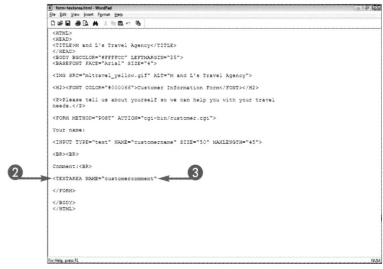

④ Type a space and **ROWS="?"**, replacing ? with the number of rows you want to specify to determine the height of the text area.

⑤ Type a space and **COLS="?"**, replacing ? with a number of character columns to determine the width of the text area.

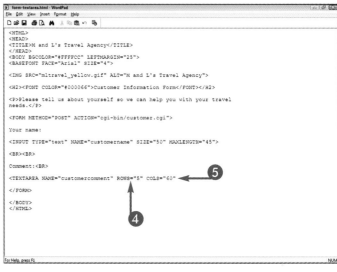

⑥ Type a space and **WRAP="?">**, replacing *?* with a text wrap control.

**soft** wraps text within the text area but not in the form results.

**hard** wraps text within both the text area and the form results.

**off** turns off text wrapping, forcing users to add line breaks manually as they type.

⑦ Type **</TEXTAREA>**.

● You can add a default message between the <TEXTAREA> and </TEXTAREA> tags.

● The Web browser displays the text box in the form.

● The user can click inside the text box and type information.

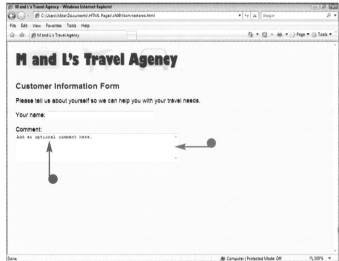

**TIPS**

**What happens if the user types more than can be viewed in the text area?**

If the user types more text than is visible in the text area, scroll bars become active at the side of the text box. Scroll bars allow the user to scroll and view the text. The text area automatically holds as much text as the user needs to type, up to 32,700 characters.

**Is there a way to keep users from typing text into a large text area?**

Yes. You can use the READONLY attribute if you want to display default text in a text area and do not want users to move or edit the text. For example, you might use a large text area to explain something about your form or offer detailed instructions. You place the READONLY attribute, without assigning it a value, within the <TEXTAREA> tag.

# Add Check Boxes

You can add check boxes to your form to allow users to select from one or more options. You can group the check boxes under a single NAME attribute.

① Between the `<FORM>` and `</FORM>` tags, type **`<INPUT TYPE="checkbox"`**.

② Type a space and **`NAME="?"`**, replacing ? with a unique name for the check box.

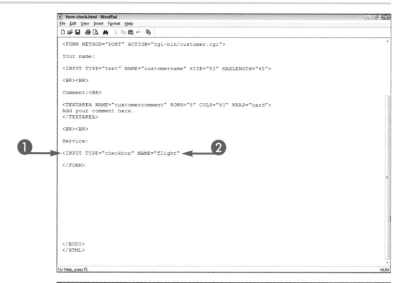

③ Type a space and **`VALUE="?">`**, replacing ? with a value to be assigned if the check box is checked.

**Note:** *The check box value does not appear on the form.*

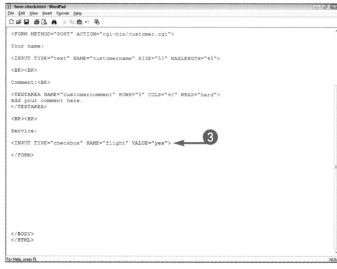

④ Type the text you want to appear beside the check box.

⑤ Repeat steps **1** to **4** to create more check boxes for a group of check box options.

**Note:** You can optionally use <BR> or <P> tags to separate input elements onto different lines in your form.

● The Web browser displays the check box in the form.

● The user can click the box to insert a check mark.

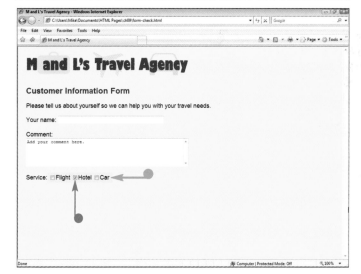

### How do I automatically show the check box as selected?

You can use the CHECKED attribute to show a check box as selected by default when the user views that page. You add the CHECKED attribute to the <INPUT> tag:

```
<INPUT TYPE="checkbox"
NAME="favoritecolors"
VALUE="Blue" CHECKED>
```

### How do I separate my check boxes onto separate lines?

You can use the <P> or <BR> tag. Your code might look like this:

```
<P>What type of movie do you like the best?</P>

<INPUT TYPE="checkbox" NAME="genre"
VALUE="Drama">

<BR><INPUT TYPE="checkbox" NAME="genre"
VALUE="Comedy">

<BR><INPUT TYPE="checkbox" NAME="genre"
VALUE="Action">
```

# Add Radio Buttons

You can use radio buttons if you want to allow users to choose only one item from a group. The user clicks a button to activate the selection.

① Between the `<FORM>` and `</FORM>` tags, type **<INPUT TYPE="radio"**.

② Type a space and **NAME="?"**, replacing ? with a unique name for the radio button group.

③ Type a space and **VALUE="?">**, replacing ? with a value describing the radio button.

**Note:** The radio button value does not appear on the form.

④ Type the text you want to appear beside the radio button.

⑤ Repeat steps **1** to **4** to add more radio buttons to the group, using the same name for all the buttons in a set.

**Note:** *You can optionally use <BR> or <P> tags to separate input elements onto different lines in your form.*

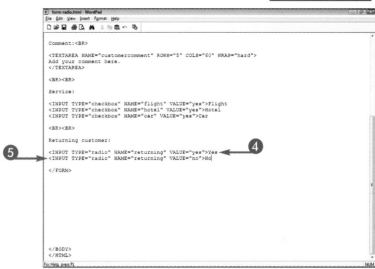

- The Web browser displays the radio buttons on the form.

- The user can click the radio button to select that option.

### What happens if I give radio buttons in a set different names?

When radio buttons have different NAME attributes, the browser treats them as parts of different radio button sets. This means the user is able to turn more than one of them on at a time by clicking. Make sure all the radio buttons in a set have the same NAME attribute to avoid this.

### Can I show a particular radio button as selected by default?

Yes. You can use the CHECKED attribute to show one radio button in the group as selected by default. The CHECKED attribute is inserted after the VALUE attribute in your HTML code. Your code might look like this:

```
<INPUT TYPE="radio" NAME="agerange"
VALUE="40-50" CHECKED>
```

# Add a Menu List

You can add a menu to a form to give users a list of choices. Menus allow you to display choices as a drop-down list that appears when the user clicks the list. By storing a long list of choices as a drop-down list, you can free up space for other input items in the form.

① Between the <FORM> and </FORM> tags, type **<SELECT NAME="?"**, replacing ? with a unique name for the menu.

② Type a space and **SIZE="?">**, replacing ? with the height, measured in character lines, for the menu input.

If you want to display a drop-down menu, set the height to 1.

③ Start a new line and type **<OPTION VALUE="?">**, replacing ? with a descriptive word for the menu item.

④ Type the text you want to appear in the menu list.

⑤ Repeat steps **3** and **4** to add more menu items to the list.

⑥ To make one menu item appear as selected in the list, type **SELECTED** after the VALUE attribute.

⑦ Type **</SELECT>**.

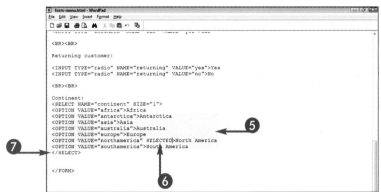

The Web browser displays the menu on the form.

● The user can click here to display the drop-down list.

● The user can click a list item to make a selection.

---

**TIPS**

**How do I display the entire menu on my form?**

Type the number of menu entries as the SIZE attribute value. This makes the menu appear as a rectangular box that displays all the items in the list. If the menu list is long, it may take up more room on the form than you want, making users scroll to view the selections. If you prefer to save room on your form, keep the menu size at 1. This creates a drop-down menu list.

**How can I create a submenu?**

Use the <OPTGROUP> tag and the LABEL attribute:

```
<SELECT NAME="favoriteflower">
<OPTGROUP LABEL="Perennial">
<OPTION VALUE="Daisy">Daisy<OPTION
VALUE="Lily">Lily</OPTGROUP><OPTGROUP
LABEL="Annual"><OPTION VALUE="Petunia">
Petunia<OPTION VALUE="Impatiens">Impatiens
</OPTGROUP></SELECT>
```

Not all browsers support the <OPTGROUP> tag.

# Add a Submit Button

You can add a Submit button to your form so users can send you the data they enter. Most Web page developers add the Submit button to the bottom of the form. You can choose any label you want for the button, as long as it is easy for users to understand that they need to click it to submit their data.

① Between the <FORM> and </FORM> tags, type **<INPUT TYPE="submit"**.

② Type a space and type **VALUE="?">**, replacing *?* with the text you want to appear on the button.

● The browser displays the button on the form.

When the user clicks the button, the form data is processed and sent to the destination specified in the <FORM> tag.

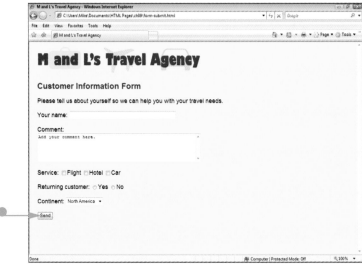

# Add a Reset Button

You can add a Reset button to your form to allow users to clear the data they have entered. For example, the user may want to type different information, or change his or her mind about submitting the information. A Reset button lets users erase all the information they typed into the various input fields.

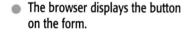

**Add a Reset Button**

1 Between the <FORM> and </FORM> tags, type **<INPUT TYPE="reset"**.

2 Type a space and **VALUE="?">**, replacing ? with the text you want to appear on the button.

● The browser displays the button on the form.

When the user clicks the button, the form is reset to its original settings.

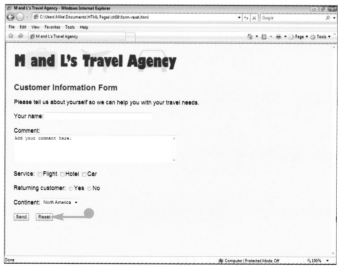

# Add Active Labels

To make your form easier to use, you can identify the text beside an input element as a label. The browser treats the text as an active form element, which means if the user clicks it, the input element changes to reflect the selection. For example, if you make the text next to a check box a label, the user can click the text as well as the check box to select the option.

① Click inside the tag for the form element you want to label and type **ID="?"**, replacing ? with a descriptive word for the element.

② Before the text, type **<LABEL FOR="?">**, replacing ? with the word you assigned in step **1**.

③ Type the label text and then **</LABEL>**.

You can repeat steps **1** to **3** to add more labels.

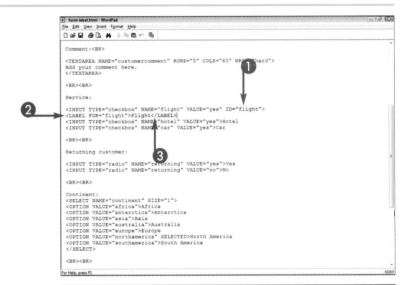

● The user can move the mouse pointer over the label to make the input element active as well as click to activate the input element.

Visitors filling out your form can navigate from one input element to the next by clicking the element or pressing the Tab key. By default, the Tab key follows the order in which you entered the input elements in your HTML document. You can change the tab order to move the user around the form in a different order.

## Change the Tab Order

1 Click inside the first form element tag and type **TABINDEX="?"**, replacing *?* with a number representing the element's position in the tab order.

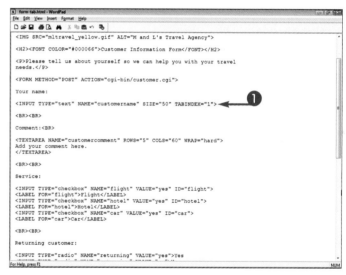

2 Repeat step **1** for the remaining elements.

***Note:*** *You can type a negative number to exclude an input element from the tab order.*

Users can move through your form using Tab in the order you specified.

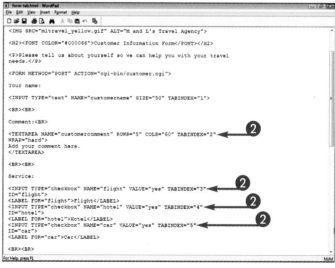

# Add a File Upload Element

If you want users to send you files, such as resumes or photos, you can add a file upload element to your form. When you add the upload element, a Browse button appears with the field, allowing users to locate the file they want to send.

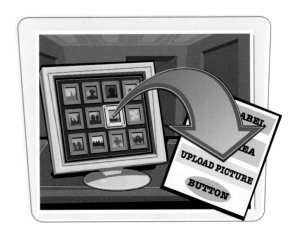

**The upload element works only if your <FORM> tag's METHOD attribute is set to post. See the section "Create a Form" to learn more about specifying a method.**

## Add a File Upload Element

① Make sure the <FORM> tag method is set to post.

② Within the <FORM> tag, type **ENCTYPE="multipart/form-data"**.

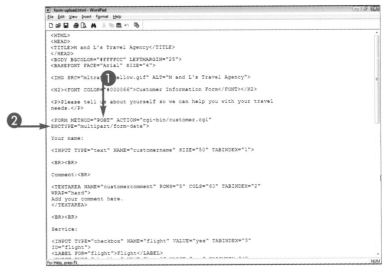

③ Type the text you want to appear next to the upload element.

④ Type **<INPUT TYPE="file"**.

⑤ Type a space and then
**NAME="?"**, replacing *?* with a
name for the input field.

⑥ Type a space and **SIZE="?">**,
replacing *?* with the character
length for the size of the input
field.

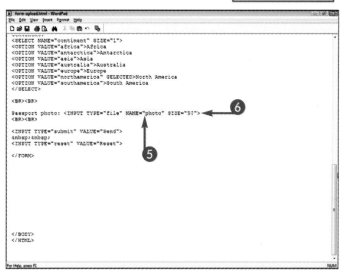

● The Web browser displays the
upload element on the form.

Users can type the path to the file
they want to upload, or click
**Browse** to locate the file.

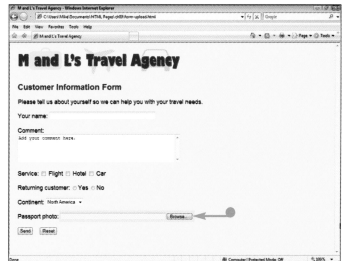

### What happens to the uploaded file after it is submitted?

You need a CGI script to process the uploaded
file on your server. Unless your Web host offers an
uploading script, you may need to adapt a script
from the Internet. You can find numerous free
CGI scripts on the Internet. Visit www.
cgi-resources.com or www.hotscripts.com
to search for an upload script.

### What if my Web server is limited to certain file types for uploads?

You can use the ACCEPT attribute to list
the files your server can process. You list
the files by their MIME (Multi-purpose
Internet Mail Extensions) types. Your HTML
code may look like this:

```
<INPUT TYPE="file" NAME="userfiles"
ACCEPT="image/gif, image/jpeg, image/
png">
```

# Group Form Elements

If your form is particularly long, you can organize the different parts into groups. For example, you might group personal information separately from questionnaire data. Groups appear set off from the rest of the page with a border. You can assign a title to the group to distinguish the form elements from other input fields on the form. Not all browsers support form groups.

## Group Form Elements

① Type **<FIELDSET>** above the first input element you want to place in a group.

② Type **</FIELDSET>** after the last input element you want to place in the group.

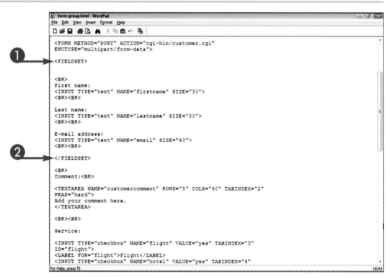

③ Below the <FIELDSET> tag, type **<LEGEND**.

④ Type a space and **ALIGN="?">**, replacing ? with an alignment for the group title (left, right, top, or bottom).

⑤ Type a title for the group.

⑥ Type **</LEGEND>**.

You can repeat steps **1** to **6** to define other groups of input elements on your form.

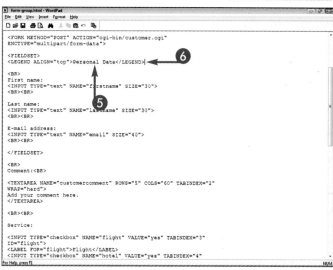

● The Web browser displays the grouped elements together.

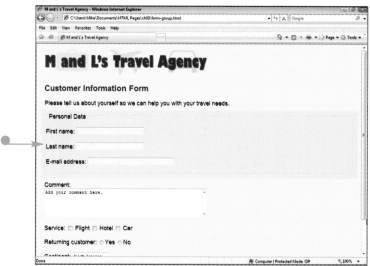

**TIPS**

**Is there another way to organize my form elements besides the <FIELDSET> tag?**

You can also arrange your form elements into tables on your Web page. For example, a table row makes a nice receptacle for a related group of input fields. You can size a table cell to fit as many form fields as you require. To learn more about creating HTML tables, see Chapter 7.

**Can I disable a form element?**

Yes. You can add the DISABLED attribute to an input element's tag to display the field. For example:

```
<INPUT TYPE="file" NAME="userfiles"
ACCEPT="image/gif, image/jpeg, image/png"
DISABLED="disabled">
```

You may want to disable a field until the user fills out certain other required data. You can then use JavaScript on your page to enable the field. See Chapter 13 to learn more about JavaScript.

# 10

# Creating Style Sheets

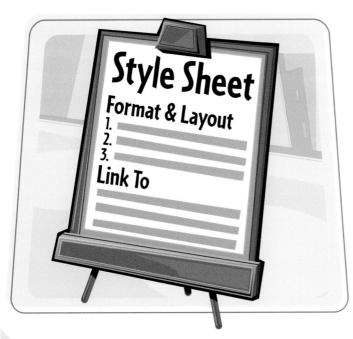

Looking for an easy way to apply complex styles to your Web page content? This chapter shows you how to use Cascading Style Sheets, or CSS, to assign formatting to your HTML documents and across your Web site.

# Understanding Style Sheets

You can use Cascading Style Sheets, or CSS, to exercise precise control over the appearance of your HTML documents. Style sheets can help you maintain a consistent look and feel throughout your Web site. By relegating formatting controls to a separate CSS document, you can free your HTML documents of repetitive coding and concentrate on the content that makes up your pages. Like HTML documents, CSS documents are simple text files.

### Defining Style Sheets

A style sheet is usually a text file that is separate from your HTML document. Style sheets can also be internal, residing within your HTML code. A style sheet holds formatting codes that control your Web page's appearance. You can use style sheets to change the look of any Web page element, such as paragraphs, lists, backgrounds, and more. Anytime you want to apply the formatting from an external style sheet to an HTML document, you attach the style sheet to the page using a LINK tag. Style sheet files have a .css file extension.

### Controlling Multiple Pages

You can link every page in your Web site to a single style sheet. Any changes you make to the style sheet formatting are reflected in every HTML document linking to the sheet. By storing all the formatting information in one place, you can easily update the appearance of your site's pages in one fell swoop. This can be a real timesaver if your site consists of lots of pages.

### Style Sheet Syntax

Style sheets are made up of rules, and each rule has two distinct parts: a selector and a declaration. The selector specifies the element to which you want to apply a style rule, and the declaration specifies the formatting for the selector. For example, in the style rule H2 {color: silver}, the selector is H2 and {color: silver} is the declaration. When applied to a page, this rule will make all level 2 headings appear in silver.

## Style Sheet Declarations

A declaration consists of one or more property and value pairs such as `font-size: 12px` or `position: absolute`. The property and value are separated by a colon; multiple property-value pairs in a declaration are separated by semicolons. It is good form to put each property-value pair on a separate line when writing your rules. Similar to HTML, you can add extra spaces and line breaks to your style sheet code to make it more readable. Learn more about writing style rules in Chapter 11.

## Style Classes

If you want to apply formatting only to a particular instance of a tag, you can use a class attribute inside that tag. You can assign a distinct name to a class and add a style rule that applies only to that class. For example, perhaps you want to add special formatting to one paragraph but not others. You define the style rule on your style sheet, and then refer to the class name in that paragraph tag.

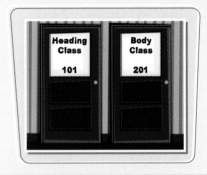

## Inheritance

Tags you add inside other tags inherit the outer tag's formatting, unless you specify otherwise. For example, if you define a `<BODY>` style, any tags you nest within the `<BODY>` tags inherit that formatting. HTML inheritance makes it easy to keep the formatting consistent as you add new items within an element. The inheritance relationships between different styles in a document is known as the *cascade*.

## External and Internal Style Sheets

You can connect an HTML document to an external or internal style sheet. Internal style sheets exist within an HTML page, between the `<HEAD>` and `</HEAD>` tags, while external style sheets are separate files. External style sheets are useful because you can link them to more than one HTML document. You might use an internal style sheet if your site consists of a single page.

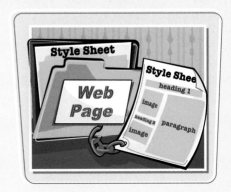

# Create an External Style Sheet

You can use an external style sheet to define formatting and layout instructions and then apply those instructions to your HTML documents. You can save the style sheet as a text file and assign the .css file extension to identify the file as a Cascading Style Sheet.

**For more on style sheets and how they work, see the section "Understanding Style Sheets."**

① Create a new document in your text editor.

**Note:** *To create and save HTML documents, see Chapter 2.*

② To create a style rule, type the element tag for which you want to define formatting properties.

This example shows how to create a style rule for level 2 headings.

③ Type a space.

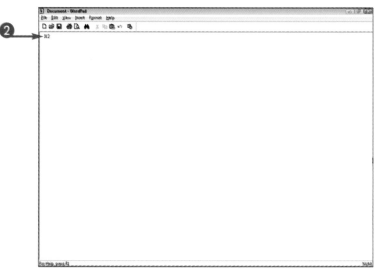

④ Type **{**.

⑤ Type one or more declarations.

Each declaration includes a property and a value separated by a **:**.

Separate multiple declarations with semicolons.

In this example, the rule includes setting a font and a font style.

**Note:** *To learn more about writing specific style rules, see Chapter 11.*

⑥ Type **}** to end the rule.

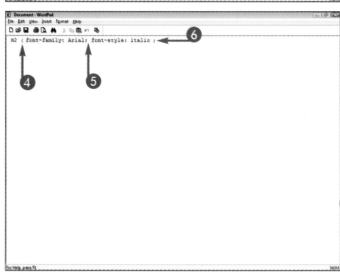

⑦ Repeat steps **2** to **6** to continue adding rules to your style sheet.

⑧ Click **File**.

⑨ Click **Save**.

The Save As dialog box appears.

⑩ Navigate to the folder that contains your HTML pages.

⑪ Type a unique filename for your style sheet and a .css extension.

⑫ Click **Save**.

Your text editor saves the new style sheet.

*Note: To learn how to apply a style sheet to an HTML document, see the section "Link to a Style Sheet."*

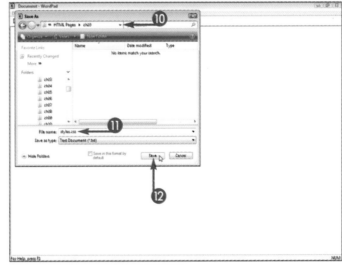

**Do style declarations need to be on a single line?**

No. Similar to HTML, you can add line breaks and spaces within your CSS without changing the effects of your rules. It can be a good idea to put each CSS declaration on a separate line to make it easier to view and edit your rules. You can also use tabs to make CSS properties and values line up with one another.

Font: Arial
Style: Italic
Color: Red

**Can I override the normal styles of an HTML tag with CSS?**

Yes. You may use CSS to change how HTML tags normally appear, even making some tags behave like others. For example, you can change the style of a heading tag so that it looks just like regular paragraph text, or vice versa. See Chapter 11 for some of the many types of styles you can apply to tags with CSS.

# Link to a Style Sheet

You can link to a style sheet to assign a set of formatting rules to your HTML document. You can link multiple documents to the same style sheet to give all the pages in your site a consistent look and feel.

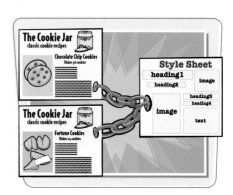

## Link to a Style Sheet

① Open the HTML document you want to link to a style sheet.

**Note:** To learn how to create a style sheet, see the section "Create an External Style Sheet."

② Click within the <HEAD> and </HEAD> tags and add a new line.

③ Type **<LINK REL="stylesheet" TYPE="text/css"**.

④ Type a blank space and **HREF="?">**, replacing ? with the name of the style sheet. If the style sheet is located in a subfolder, also specify the path.

The style sheet is now linked with the page.

You can test your page in a browser to see the style sheet results.

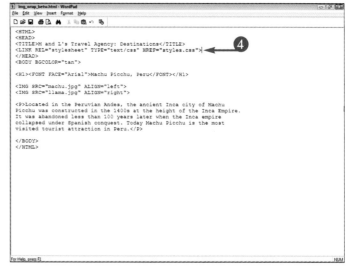

# Add Comments to a Style Sheet

You can add comments to your style sheet to describe and identify your style rules. For example, you might add a comment describing the effect of the rule when it is applied to text. Web browsers do not interpret comment information in style sheets.

## Add Comments to a Style Sheet

① In your style sheet document, type **/\*** to begin your comment.

**Note:** *To learn how to create a style sheet, see the section "Create an External Style Sheet."*

② Type your comment text.

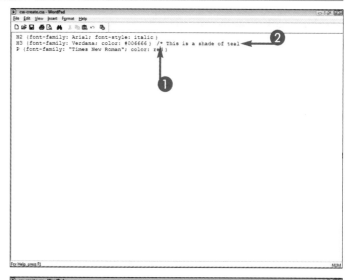

③ Type **\*/** to end the comment.

When the page is displayed in a Web browser, the comments are ignored.

# Create an Internal Style Sheet

You can create an internal style sheet that resides within the <HEAD> tag of your HTML document. Internal style sheets are handy if your Web site consists of a single page because you can change both style rules and HTML in the same file.

① Within the <HEAD> and </HEAD> tags, add a new line and type **<STYLE>**.

② Add a new line and type the element tag for which you want to create a style rule.

In this example, a new style rule is created for the H2 element.

③ Type **{**.

④ Type the properties and values for the rule.

If you intend to add more than one declaration to the rule, be sure to separate declarations with a semicolon.

⑤ Type **}** to end the rule.

**Note:** To learn more about writing style rules, see Chapter 11.

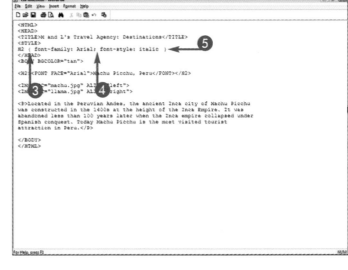

**6** Repeat steps **2** to **5** to continue adding style rules to your internal style sheet.

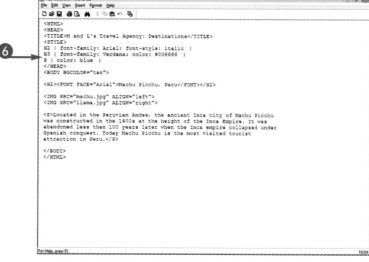

**7** Add a new line and type **</STYLE>**.

You can save your page and test it in a browser to see the results.

***Note:*** *To learn more about viewing HTML documents in a browser, see Chapter 2.*

### Do all browsers recognize style sheets?

Some older browsers do not support style sheets, so they ignore the <STYLE> tags. However, the content inside the <STYLE> tags is not ignored in these browsers, so any coding you type between the <STYLE> tags appears on the page. You can prevent an older browser from displaying style tag coding by typing **<!--** and **-->** before and after the style rules.

### Can I link another Web page to my internal style sheet?

No. A page cannot access another page's internal style sheet. If you want multiple Web pages to take advantage of a set of style rules, you must define those rules in an external style sheet and link the pages to the sheet. An internal style sheet is useful only if you want to apply those styles to a single HTML document. See the section "Create an External Style Sheet" to learn more.

# Create a Class

You can create a CSS class to apply a style rule to specific HTML tags. For example, if you want the introductory paragraphs formatted differently from all the other paragraphs, you can create a class specifically for the introductory paragraphs. After you create the class, the browser applies it to all the paragraphs to which the class is assigned.

**You can set up a class in your external or internal style sheet, and then use the CLASS attribute to assign rules to an HTML tag. To learn more about creating style sheets, see the sections "Create an External Style Sheet" and "Create an Internal Style Sheet."**

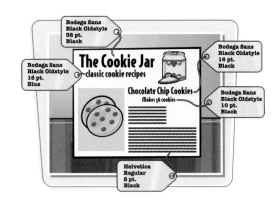

## Create a Class

**DEFINE A CLASS**

① In your external or internal style sheet, type the tag for which you want to create a class.

② Type a period.

③ Type a name for the class.

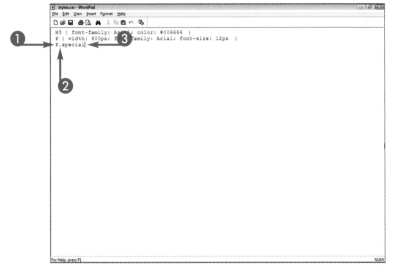

④ Type {.

⑤ Type one or more declarations for the class.

Separate multiple declarations with semicolons.

**Note:** To learn more about writing style rules, see Chapter 11.

⑥ Type } to end the style rule.

Your class is now defined.

If you are editing an external style sheet, save the sheet.

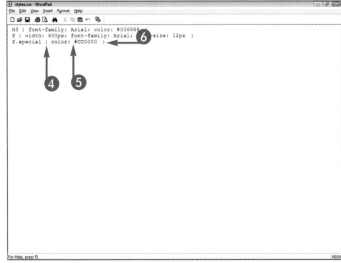

## ASSIGN A CLASS

**1** Open the HTML document and click in the tag to which you want to assign a class.

**2** Type **CLASS="?"**, replacing *?* with the class name.

You can assign multiple classes by separating class names with a space.

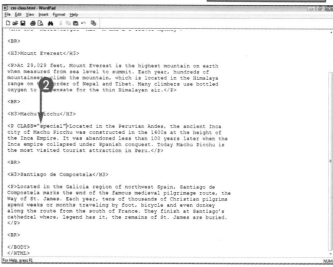

**3** Open the HTML document in a Web browser.

*Note: To learn about viewing an HTML document in a Web browser, see Chapter 2.*

● The Web browser applies the styles associated with the class to the tag content.

---

**TIPS**

### What is a generic class?
You can use a generic class to format more than one type of tag. For example, you might use a generic class to format both paragraphs and level 3 headings in a document. When defining a generic class, simply type a period followed by the class name, such as .myclass. When applying the class, use the class name, such as `<P CLASS="myclass">` or `<H3 CLASS="myclass">`.

### How do class styles affect styles that have already been applied to a tag?
When you apply a class to a tag, the class-based rules override any conflicting rules already assigned to the tag. For example, if you turn the paragraph text for a page red with the style `P {color:red;}` and then apply the class `P.bluetext {color:blue;}` to a paragraph, the text in that paragraph appears blue instead of red.

# Apply a Style with the DIV Tag

You can apply styles to different sections of your Web page using the `<DIV>` tag. You can define style classes for the `<DIV>` tag in your external or internal style sheet, and then apply those classes in your HTML document.

You can associate a class with `<DIV>` content using the `CLASS` attribute. For more information about creating classes, see the section "Create a Class."

Apply a Style with the DIV Tag

### SET UP A DIV CLASS

1. In your external or internal style sheet, type **DIV.?**, replacing *?* with the class name you want to assign for the `DIV` style.

2. Type **{**.

3. Type the declarations for the `DIV` style.

    Separate multiple declarations with semicolons.

*Note: To learn more about writing style rules, see Chapter 6.*

4. Type **}**.

    The style rule is complete.

    If you are editing an external style sheet, save the sheet.

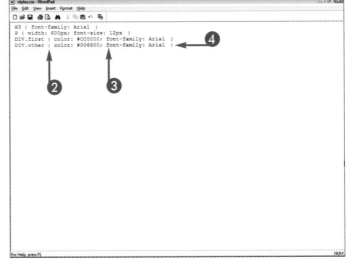

**APPLY THE DIV TAG**

① In the HTML document, click in front of the section to which you want to assign a DIV tag and add a line.

② Type **<DIV CLASS="?">**, replacing *?* with the DIV class name.

③ Type **</DIV>** at the end of the section.

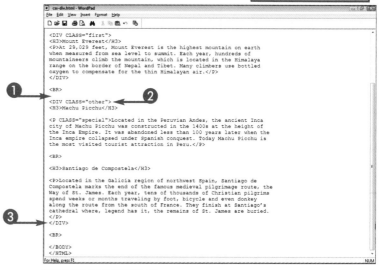

④ Open the HTML document in a Web browser.

*Note: To learn about viewing an HTML document in a Web browser, see Chapter 2.*

● The Web browser applies the style to the HTML section.

**TIPS**

**How do I format specific text within a paragraph or other section?**

You can use the <SPAN> tag to apply formatting to a portion of text in an HTML document. Unlike the <DIV> tag, the <SPAN> tag is an inline tag; it does not add blank lines before and after the text.

① Define a class for the <SPAN> tag.

② Before the text you want to format, type **<SPAN CLASS="?">**, replacing *?* with the SPAN class name.

③ After the text you want to format, type **</SPAN>**.

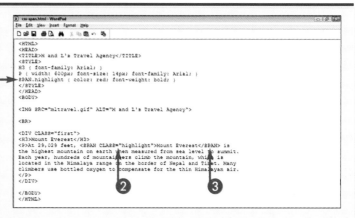

# Apply a Style Locally

You can apply a style to a single instance of a tag in your document using an HTML attribute. The STYLE attribute allows you to apply a style rule to a tag without having to define the rule separately in an internal or external style sheet.

**When you apply a style locally, it overrides any styles found in external or internal style sheets for the same tag. Applying styles locally works best for one-time changes. You should use internal or external style sheets for styles you plan to apply more than once.**

## Apply a Style Locally

① Click in the tag for the element you want to change and type **STYLE="?"**, replacing *?* with the style declarations you want to assign.

Separate multiple declarations with semicolons.

***Note:*** *To learn more about writing style rules, see Chapter 11.*

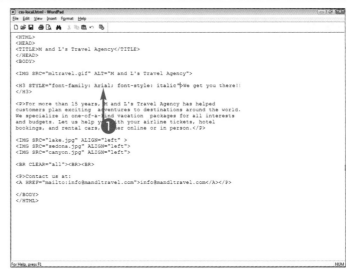

② Open the HTML document in a Web browser.

***Note:*** *To learn about viewing an HTML document in a Web browser, see Chapter 2.*

● The Web browser applies the style to the tag content.

# Apply a Style Using the ID Attribute

You can use the ID attribute to assign a style rule to an individual Web page element. IDs are like classes except that classes can be associated with multiple elements on the page.

**If you want to assign a style rule to more than one element of the same tag, create a class instead. See the section "Create a Class" to learn more.**

## Apply a Style Using the ID Attribute

**1** Open your external style sheet or scroll to your internal style sheet.

**2** Type the tag to which you want to assign an ID.

**3** Type **#?**, replacing ? with the ID name.

**4** Type a space and define the style rule.

**5** In the tag element for which you want to create a style rule, type **ID="?"**, replacing ? with the ID name.

The style is applied.

# Formatting Text with Style Sheets

Ready to start formatting your Web page with Cascading Style Sheets, or CSS? This chapter shows you how to apply formatting to your HTML elements using style sheet properties.

You can make Web page text bold using the `font-weight` property in a style rule. The property allows you to control the amount of boldness. Setting text to bold can help emphasize it on a page. The font-weight values are `lighter`, `normal`, `bold`, and `bolder`. You can also use a numeric value

① Click inside the tag declaration and type **font-weight:**.

**Note:** *To learn more about writing style sheets and rules, see Chapter 10.*

② Type a space.

③ Type a weight value (**bold** or **bolder**).

You can use the `normal` value to remove boldness that may be inherited from previous style rules.

You can use the `lighter` value to decrease the weight of text.

You can also specify a number value using a multiple of 100 from 100 to 900 to control the boldness level. Not all browsers support this feature.

The Web browser bolds all the text to which the tag is applied.

In this example, all the paragraphs are now bold.

**Note:** *To learn how to link a style sheet to all the pages on your Web site, see Chapter 10.*

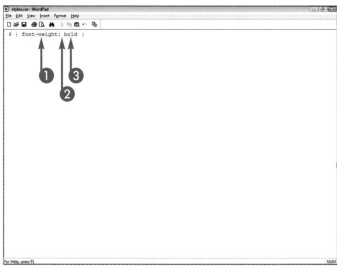

# Italicize Text

You can use the `font-style` property to italicize Web page text. Applying italics is an easy way to add emphasis to text. The `font-style` values are `italic`, `oblique`, and `normal`.

## Italicize Text

① Click inside the tag declaration and type **font-style:**.

*Note: To learn more about writing style sheets and rules, see Chapter 10.*

② Type a space.

③ Type an italics value (**italic** or **oblique**).

You can use the `normal` value to remove italics that may be inherited from previous style rules.

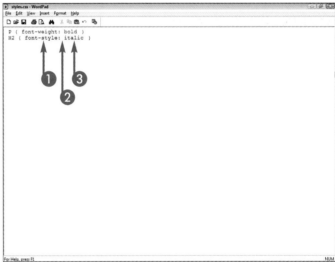

The Web browser italicizes all the text to which the tag is applied.

● In this example, the slogan text is italicized.

# Indent Text

You can indent the first line in a paragraph using the `text-indent` property in a style rule. You can set the indentation as a specific measurement value or as a percentage of the overall text block width.

You can indent the first line of a paragraph

## Indent Text

① Click inside the tag declaration and type **text-indent: ?**, replacing *?* with the amount of space you want to indent.

You can set the size measurement in pixels (**px**), millimeters (**mm**), centimeters (**cm**), inches (**in**), points (**pt**), picas (**pc**), x-height (**ex**), or **em**.

You can also set an indent size as a percentage of the text block width, such as 20%.

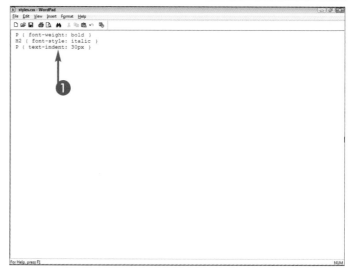

The Web browser indents the first line of all the text to which the tag is applied.

● In this example, all the <P> tags are indented.

***Note:*** *To indent text with margins, see Chapter 12.*

# Change the Font Size

You can use the `font-size` property to change the font size for a document's text. Rather than going through your document and changing each instance of a tag, you can use a style sheet rule to change the font size for all instances of the tag in your document.

## Change the Font Size

① Click inside the tag declaration and type **font-size:** and a space.

② Type a font size in points (**pt**), pixels (**px**), millimeters (**mm**), centimeters (**cm**), inches (**in**), picas (**pc**), x-height (**ex**), or **em**.

You can also type a descriptive (**xx-small**, **x-small**, **small**, **medium**, **large**, **x-large**, or **xx-large**) font size.

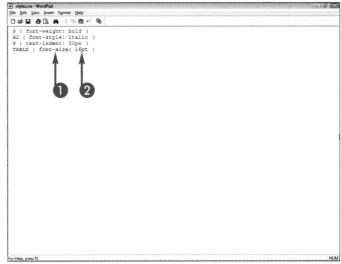

The Web browser assigns the font size for any text to which the tag is applied.

● In this example, the style is assigned to the links inside a table.

***Note:*** *Learn how to create tables in Chapter 7.*

# Change the Font

To change the font of your Web page text, you can use the font-family property. You can specify a font by name. Because not all fonts are available on all computers, you should designate a second and even third font choice. This way, if the computer does not have the first choice installed, the browser tries to display the next choice instead.

**To ensure most browsers can display your font, assign a common font, such as Arial, Verdana, Courier, or Times New Roman.**

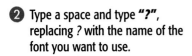

① Click inside the tag declaration and type **font-family:**.

**Note:** To learn more about writing style sheets and rules, see Chapter 10.

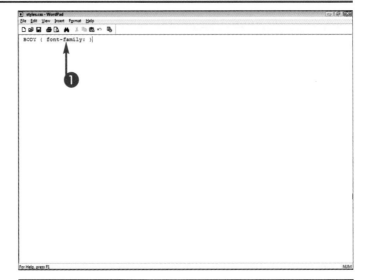

② Type a space and type **"?"**, replacing ? with the name of the font you want to use.

Be sure to enclose font names in double quotes.

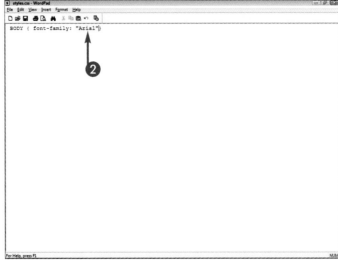

③ To designate a second, alternative font choice, type a comma, a space, and the second font name.

You can repeat step **3** to assign additional fonts.

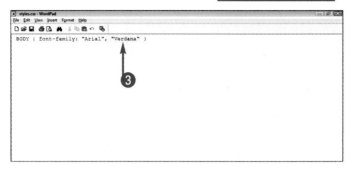

The Web browser uses the assigned font for any text to which the tag is applied.

In this example, the style rule is applied to the <BODY> tag, so all the body text is affected.

**TIPS**

**Can I change multiple font settings at the same time?**

Yes. You can write a style rule that combines several font settings in one fell swoop using the font property. For example, you can designate the font style, font size, and font for a particular tag rather than writing three different rules for the tag. Your combined rule might look like this:

P {font: italic 18pt "Times New Roman", "Arial"}

Some browsers may require you to type the properties in a particular order, such as font style before font size.

**Is there a way to include a font with my page so users can see it even if they do not have the font installed?**

If the users are viewing the page with Internet Explorer, yes. You can embed the font in your Web page. If you embed the font, you must store it on the Web server, and it must use the Embedded Open Type, or EOT, format. You can use a special program, called WEFT, to convert an installed font into the EOT format. Visit www.microsoft.com/typography/web/embedding/weft/ to learn more. Replace *?* with the name of the embedded font.

You can use the `text-transform` property to change the text case for a tag. For example, you may want all `<H2>` text to appear in all capital letters. The property controls how the browser displays the text regardless of how it was typed.

**You can choose from four case values:** `capitalize`, `uppercase`, `lowercase`, **and** `none`. **Use the** `capitalize` **value if you want the first character of each word to appear capitalized. Use the** `none` **value to leave text as is. The** `none` **value cancels any case values the text may have inherited.**

## Change the Text Case

① Click inside the tag declaration and type **text-transform:** and a space.

② Type a text case value (**capitalize**, **uppercase**, **lowercase**, or **none**).

*Note: To learn more about writing style sheets and rules, see Chapter 10.*

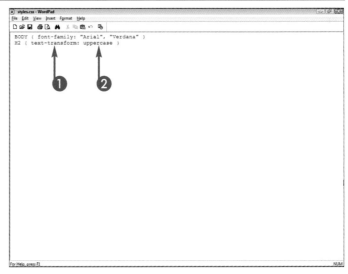

The Web browser assigns the text case to the content.

● In this example, text within the `<H2>` tags is displayed in uppercase letters.

You can control the horizontal positioning of block-level text in your page using the `text-align` property. Block-level text includes paragraphs, tables, and other elements that are preceded and followed by a blank line. You can align text to the left or right, center the text, or create justified text. By default, most browsers align text to the left unless instructed otherwise.

## Change Text Alignment

1 Click inside the tag declaration and type **text-align:** and a space.

2 Type an alignment (**left**, **center**, **right**, or **justify**).

This example shows multiple declarations in a single rule. Separate multiple declarations with semicolons.

**Note:** To learn more about writing style sheets and rules, see Chapter 10.

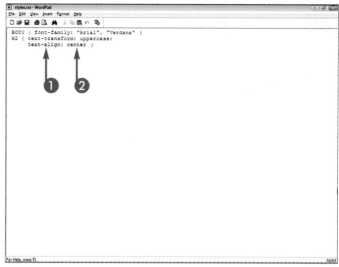

The Web browser assigns the alignment to the content.

● In this example, text within the `<H2>` tags is centered.

# Control Line Spacing

You can use the `line-height` property to adjust the spacing, or *leading*, between lines of text. Adjusting line spacing can make your Web page text easier to read. The line spacing value is specified as a multiple of the height of the element's font.

## Control Line Spacing

**1** Click inside the tag declaration and type **line-height:** and a space.

**2** Type a value for the spacing.

This example uses a value of 2.0 to make the spacing two times the current font height.

You can also set a percentage or an absolute value for the spacing.

**Note:** *To learn more about writing style sheets and rules, see Chapter 10.*

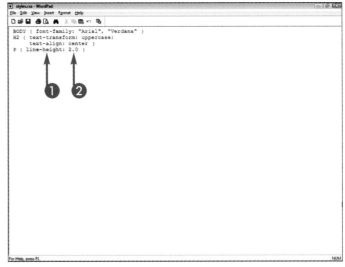

The Web browser assigns the line spacing to the content.

● In this example, text within the `<P>` tags displays extra line spacing.

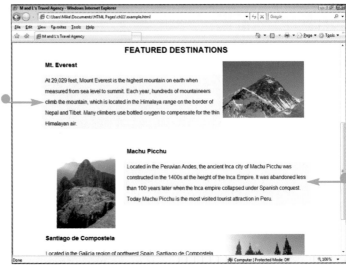

# Control Letter Spacing

You can control the spacing between characters, or *kerning*, using the `letter-spacing` property. Letter spacing changes the appearance of your text by increasing or condensing the space between letters.

**You can specify letter spacing in points (pt), pixels (px), millimeters (mm), centimeters (cm), inches (in), picas (pc), x-height (ex), or em.**

## Control Letter Spacing

① Click inside the tag declaration and type **letter-spacing:** and a space.

② Type a value for the spacing.

**Note:** *To learn more about writing style sheets and rules, see Chapter 10.*

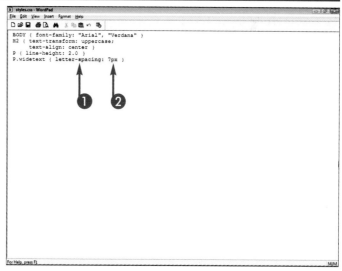

The Web browser assigns the letter spacing to the content.

● In this example, letter spacing is applied to the slogan using a style-sheet class.

**Note:** *See Chapter 10 to learn more about creating classes in your style sheets.*

# Add Color to Text

You can use the `color` property to change the color of text in your Web page. You can specify one of 16 predefined colors or specify a color from the hexadecimal color palette. You can also use the `color` property to change other Web page elements, such as tables, borders, and horizontal rules.

## Add Color to Text

**1** Click inside the tag declaration and type **color:** followed by a space.

**2** Type a color name or hexadecimal value for the color you want to assign.

**Note:** For more about HTML colors, see Chapter 4.

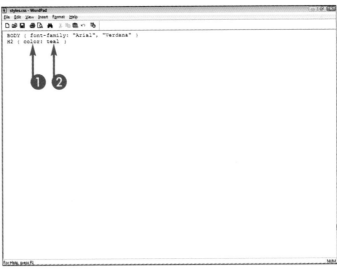

The Web browser uses the assigned color for the text to which the tag is applied.

● In this example, color is assigned to text within the `<H2>` tags.

You can use the `background` property to change the color that appears behind an element without changing the entire page's background.

**Use caution when assigning a background color to an element, making sure the color does not clash with the text color.**

Make sure the background color doesn't clash with the text color.

## Add a Background Color to an Element

① Click inside the tag declaration and type `background:` and a space.

② Type a color name or hexadecimal value for the color you want to assign.

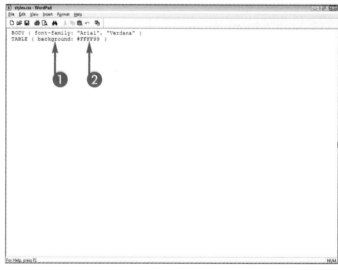

The Web browser assigns the background color to the content.

● In this example, background color is added to the `<TABLE>` element, which encloses several links.

*Note: See Chapter 7 to learn how to add tables.*

# Add a Background Image to an Element

You can add a background image to an element using a style sheet rule. To specify a background image, you must know the name and location of the image file. If the image is small, the browser repeats, or *tiles*, it to fill the background area. You can control the repeat using the repeat values.

**Be careful when assigning a background image; make sure any overlying text is legible over the background. You may need to change the text color. See the section "Add Color to Text" to learn more.**

**1** Click inside the tag declaration and type **background:** and a space.

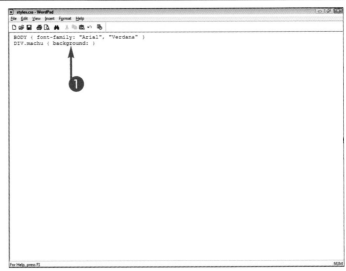

**2** Type **url("?")** and a space, replacing *?* with the location and name of the image file you want to use as a background.

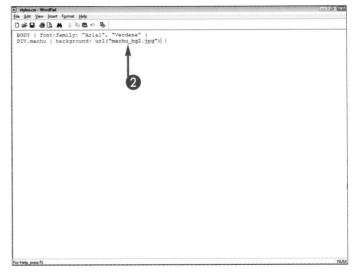

③ Type a repeat option for the image:

**repeat** repeats the image to fill the background (default).

**repeat-x** tiles the image horizontally.

**repeat-y** tiles the image vertically.

**no-repeat** prevents a background image from repeating.

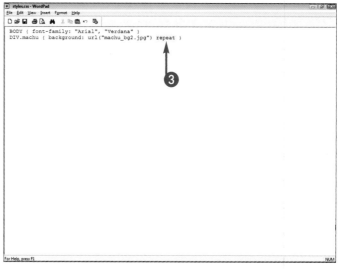

The Web browser displays the background image as designated in the style rule.

● In this example, a background image is added to a DIV tag surrounding one of the sections of content.

*Note: For more about applying styles with a DIV tag, see Chapter 10.*

**TIPS**

**Where can I find background images to use with my Web pages?**

If you do not have images to use as backgrounds, you can try finding free ones on the Web. Many sites offer texture images, such as marble backgrounds and water. For example, BackgroundCity.com (www.backgroundcity.com) and Free-Backgrounds.com (www.free-backgrounds.com) are good places to start. Try conducting a Web search on the keywords "free background images."

**If users have images turned off in their browsers, can they see the background image for an element?**

No. However, you can insert both a background color and a background image. While the image downloads, the browser displays the background color. If the users have images turned off, they still see the background color. Be sure to type the color property before the URL.

# Add a Border

You can add a border to a Web page element using the border property. A border can help separate the element from other Web page objects. You can specify a thickness value in pixels or using one of three descriptive values: thin, medium, or thick.

**You can assign a color value to a border. For more about HTML colors, see Chapter 4.**

## Add a Border

1 Click inside the tag declaration and type **border:** followed by a space.

2 Type a thickness value in pixels or by descriptive value (**thin**, **medium**, or **thick**).

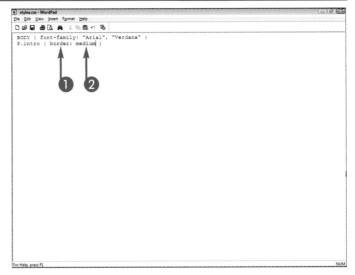

3 Type a space and then a border style (**solid, double, groove, ridge, inset, outset, dotted,** or **dashed**).

***Note:*** *If you do not set a border style with the* border *property, the browser will not display a border.*

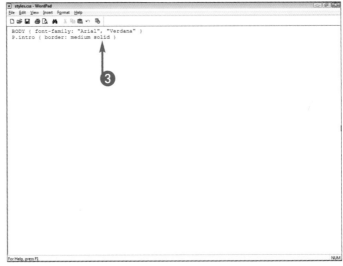

chapter **11**

④ Type a space and then a color value.

**Note:** *To see a list of color values, see Chapter 4.*

● In many instances, you will need to add some padding between the content and the border; you can use the `padding` property to do so.

Be sure to separate multiple style declarations in a rule with semicolons (;).

**Note:** *See Chapter 12 to learn more about padding.*

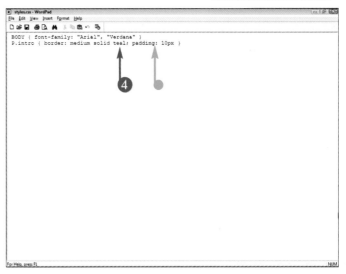

The Web browser assigns a border to the content.

● In this example, a border is added to the introductory paragraph using a style-sheet class.

**Note:** *See Chapter 10 to learn more about creating classes in your style sheets.*

**Can I add a border to certain sides of an element instead of the entire element?**

Yes. You can use the `border-left`, `border-right`, `border-top`, and `border-bottom` properties to designate on which sides you want to add a border. Your code may look like this:

```
H3 {border-left: double 5px;
border-right: double 5px}
```

In this example, a double border is added to the left and right sides of the heading.

**Is there a way to remove all the borders on my page?**

Yes. To remove borders, such as those that appear by default around linked images, you can use the `border` property and set the value to none. Your code may look like this:

```
IMG {border: none}
```

# Change Link Colors

You can control the appearance of links throughout your Web pages using a style rule. You can change the color of unvisited, visited, and active links. You can also remove the default underlining that normally appears beneath a link.

## Change Link Colors

① Type **A:?{}** to identify the link tag, replacing *?* with the type of link you want to change (**link**, **visited**, or **active**).

*Note: To learn more about writing style sheets and rules, see Chapter 10.*

```
BODY { font-family: "Arial", "Verdana" }
A:link {}
```

② Click between the { } and type **color:** and a space.

③ Type the color name or hexadecimal code you want to assign.

*Note: To see a list of color values, see Chapter 4.*

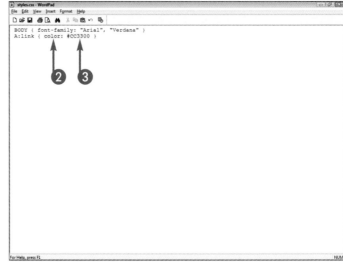

```
BODY { font-family: "Arial", "Verdana" }
A:link { color: #CC3300 }
```

④ Type a semicolon (;) followed by a space.

⑤ Type **text-decoration: none** to remove the link underline.

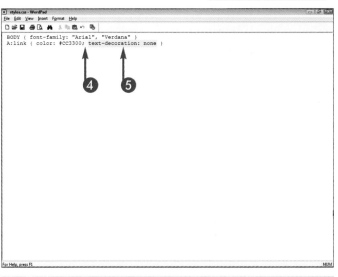

The Web browser displays the link in the style you specified.

● In this example, the style is assigned to the navigation links.

TIPS

**What other style sheet properties can I apply to links?**

You can use the background and font-family properties to control the appearance of your links. Here is an example of a style rule with other properties assigned:

A:link {background: yellow; font-family: "Arial"}

Anytime you type more than one declaration in a style rule, be sure to separate them with semicolons.

**Do I need to use style sheets to change the link color?**

If you just want to change the link color, you don't have to use style sheets. You can use regular HTML. The LINK, VLINK, and ALINK attributes for the BODY tag allow you to set the colors for regular links, visited links, and active links, respectively. See Chapter 6 for more information.

# Change Link Hover Effects

You can use a style rule to control how link text appears when the mouse pointer hovers over it. For example, you can change the font style of the text, add a border, or change the background color. If you have created another rule that removes the underlining from your links, you can use a hover style to make the underlining reappear.

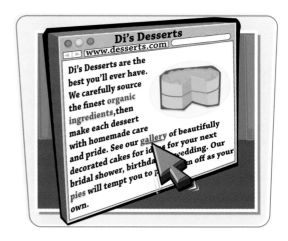

① Type **A:hover {}** to define the hover style selector.

*Note: To learn more about writing style sheets and rules, see Chapter 10.*

② Click between the { } and type one or more declarations that will be applied when the mouse pointer hovers over a link.

In this example, bold and border styles are defined.

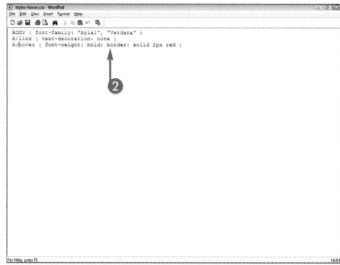

③ To add underlining, type **text-decoration: underline**.

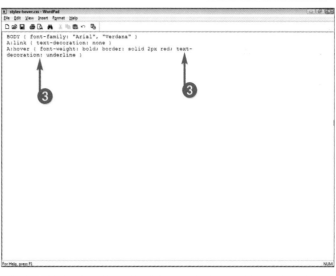

● The Web browser changes the link's style when the mouse pointer hovers over it.

**TIPS**

**Can I add other line decorations besides underline for my hover styles?**

In addition to assigning the underline value to the text-decoration property, you can assign overline to place a line over the link text or line-through to place a line through the link text. You can also use these decorations to style regular, non-link text.

**Why might I want to add a hover style using CSS?**

With style sheets, you can customize your links so that they look more like regular text. You can do this by changing their color and removing the underlining usually associated with text links. This may be stylistically appealing, but it can also hide the fact that elements on a page are hyperlinks. A hover style can give a user visual feedback that certain words on a page are clickable links.

# Change Bullet or Number Styles

You can use the `list-style` property to change the bullet or number style for your unordered or ordered lists. You can choose from three bullet styles and five number styles.

Bullets come in three styles: **circle, disc,** and **square.** Disc is the default bullet style. Numbers can be `decimal` **(1, 2, 3),** `lower-alpha` **(a,b,c),** `upper-alpha` **(A, B, C),** `lower-roman` **(i, ii, iii),** and `upper-roman` **(I, II, III).** The default number style is `decimal`.

## CHANGE THE BULLET STYLE

① Click inside the UL tag declaration and type **list-style:** followed by a space.

② Type the bullet style you want to apply (**circle**, **disc**, or **square**).

**Note:** *To learn more about creating lists, see Chapter 3.*

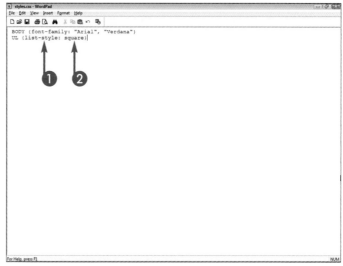

The Web browser displays the bullet style you specified in the style rule.

● In this example, the bulleted list has square bullets.

**CHANGE THE NUMBER STYLE**

1. Click inside the OL tag declaration and type **list-style:** followed by a space.

2. Type the number style you want to apply (**decimal**, **lower-alpha**, **upper-alpha**, **lower-roman**, or **upper-roman**).

*Note:* To learn more about creating lists, see Chapter 3.

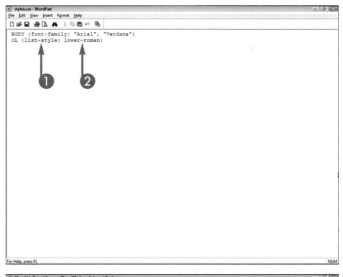

The Web browser uses the number style you specified in the style rule.

● In this example, the numbered list shows lowercase Roman numerals.

**TIPS**

**Can I use an image for a bullet?**

Yes. To use an image as a bullet, you must include the url value to designate the location and name of the image. Your style rule may look similar to this:

```
UL {list-style: url("images/
flower1.gif") circle}
```

You can find numerous bullet images on the Web. The W3 Schools site (www.w3schools.com/graphics/) and Stylegala (www.stylegala.com/features/bulletmadness/) are two such sites.

**Can I control the position of bullets or numbers in my lists?**

Yes. You can use the inside or outside value to position bullets or numbers in your lists. You can use the inside value to wrap text beneath the bullet or number marker. The outside value indents all the text to line up neatly to the inside of the markers. Here is an example of the inside value applied in a style rule:

```
OL {list-style: decimal; inside}
```

# Customize Form Elements

You can use style sheets to customize the elements in your HTML forms. You can enlarge text fields to give them more prominence on your pages. You can also change the color of form buttons to make them match the other colors on your pages.

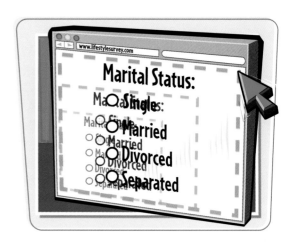

## CUTOMIZE A TEXT FIELD

1️⃣ In your style sheet, type **INPUT.?** **{}**, replacing ? with a unique name for your `text-box` class.

**Note:** For more details about creating a CSS class, see Chapter 10.

2️⃣ Type a `height` declaration to set the height of the text box.

3️⃣ Type a `font-size` declaration to set the size of the font inside the text box.

4️⃣ Inside the INPUT tag for the text box, type **CLASS="?"**, replacing ? with the class name.

● The Web browser applies the new style to the form text box.

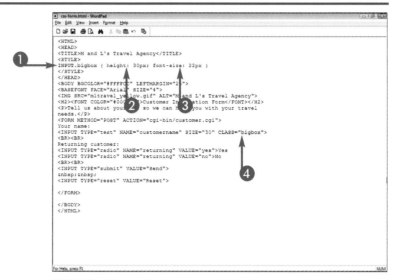

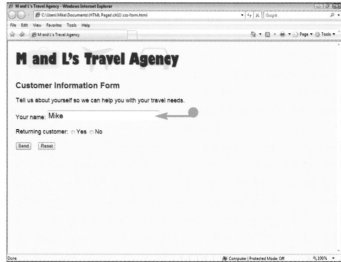

## CUSTOMIZE A BUTTON

**1** In your style sheet, type **INPUT.?** **{}**, replacing *?* with a unique name for your button class.

***Note:*** *For more details about creating a CSS class, see Chapter 10.*

**2** Type a `color` declaration to set the color of the button label.

**3** Type a `background` declaration to set the background color of the button.

**4** Inside the `INPUT` tag for the button, type **CLASS="?"**, replacing *?* with the class name.

● The Web browser applies the new style to the form button.

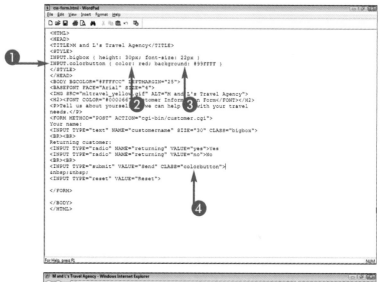

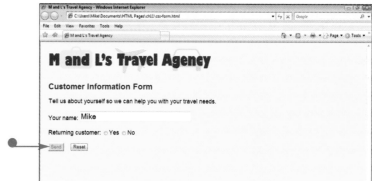

**TIP**

### Can I customize a form menu using style sheets?

Yes. You can customize menus in your HTML forms similar to how you customize text fields.

**1** In your style sheet, type **SELECT.? {}**, replacing *?* with a unique name for your menu class.

**2** Inside the **{}**, type a `height` declaration to set the height of the menu.

**3** Inside the **{}**, type a `font-size` declaration to set the size of the font in the menu options.

**4** Inside the `SELECT` tag for the menu, type **CLASS="?"**, replacing *?* with the class name.

● The Web browser applies the new style to the form menu.

# 12

# Controlling Layout with Style Sheets

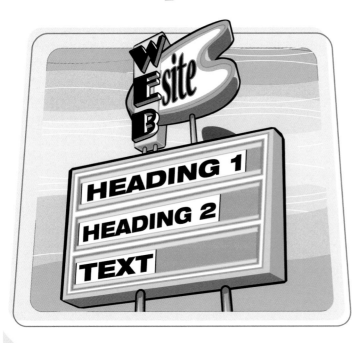

Want to create complex layouts on your Web pages beyond what is possible using HTML alone? This chapter shows you how to use style sheets to precisely position text, images, and other elements on your pages. You can also control the spacing around those elements and even overlap them.

# Control Layout

You can use cascading style sheets, or CSS, to organize text, images, and other elements on your Web page in precise ways. This enables you to create layouts that are more complicated than those you can create with HTML. Style sheets allow you to specify where in a page to put different types of content by defining coordinates within the browser window. You can also precisely control the space around different elements and even overlap content on your pages.

**By combining layout techniques with other CSS features covered in Chapter 11, you can produce pages that look like they were created using a page layout program.**

## Box Model

The key to understanding layout using style sheets is the *box model* of Web page layout, where each element on a page exists in its own rectangular box. Style sheets let you control the dimensions of the box using `height` and `width` properties, where the box is placed on the Web page, and how the box aligns or overlaps with other boxes on the page.

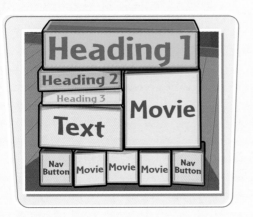

## HTML Block Tags

You define boxes for your content using block-level HTML tags. Block-level tags place new lines before and after the content they enclose. The `<P>`, `<H1>`, and `<TABLE>` tags are examples of block-level tags. The `<DIV>` is a generic block-level tag that is commonly placed around other tags to organize content when using style sheets to determine layout.

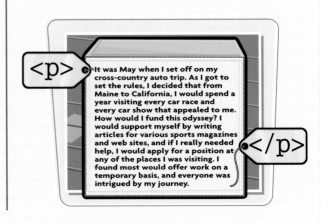

## Positioning Content

You can use different types of positioning to place the boxes of content on your pages. *Relative* positioning places content on the page relative to the normal flow of the other content on the page. *Absolute* positioning places content on absolute points on the page relative to the containing block. *Fixed* positioning places content relative to the browser window and keeps it fixed as a user scrolls.

## Offsetting Content

You can offset content on your Web page from its normal position using the `top`, `left`, `right`, and `bottom` style sheet properties. This allows you to place content in a precise position within the browser window. You can even place content completely outside of the browser window by using a large or negative offset value. You can also overlap content in the browser window by placing an element at the same window coordinates as another element.

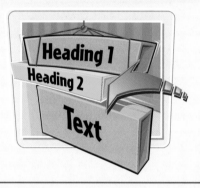

## Padding and Margins

You can control the space that surrounds content inside each box on your page. Space outside the edge of the box is known as *margin*, while space inside the edge of the box is called *padding*. Style sheets let you control space on the top, left, right, and bottom of the boxes independently. You can also turn on borders, which appear where the margin and padding meet.

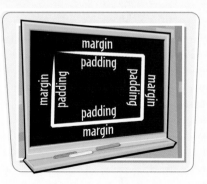

## Floating Content

The `float` CSS property takes a box out of the normal flow of your page and moves it to the right or left side of the enclosing box. Content that follows then wraps around the floated element. Floating allows you to align images, paragraphs, tables, and other content, similar to how you can align images using the `ALIGN` attribute in HTML.

# Set Width and Height for an Element

You can use the `width` and `height` properties in your style sheet to set the dimensions of your Web page elements. For example, if you want a specific paragraph to take up a certain amount of space in your page flow, you can apply a style rule using the ID attribute. See Chapter 10 to learn more about the ID attribute.

**You can also specify a size based on a percentage.**

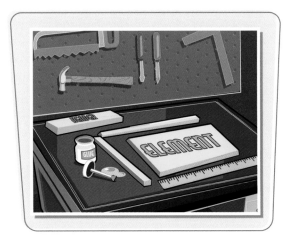

**DEFINE AN ABSOLUTE SIZE**

① Click inside the tag declaration and type **width: ?; height: ?**, replacing ? with absolute sizes for the width and height.

You can specify values in points (pt), pixels (px), millimeters (mm), centimeters (cm), inches (in), picas (pc), x-height (ex), or em.

● In this example, the size is applied by assigning a style to an ID attribute inside a DIV tag.

**Note:** For more about using ID attributes, see Chapter 10.

② Type **ID="?"** inside the HTML tag, replacing ? with the ID name.

● The Web browser displays the element with an absolute width and height.

In this example, borders are turned on to show the dimensions of the content boxes.

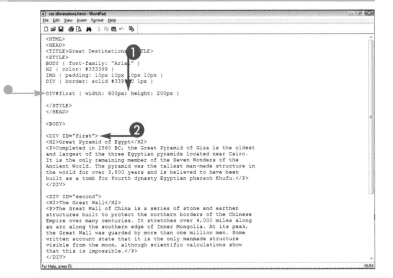

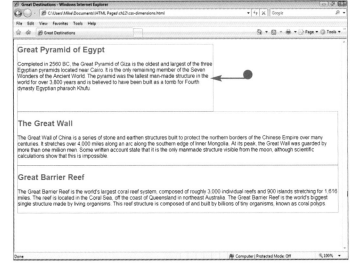

## DEFINE A RELATIVE SIZE

1 Click inside the tag declaration and type **width: ?, height: ?**, replacing *?* with percentage sizes for the width and height.

2 Type **ID="?"** inside the HTML tag, replacing *?* with the ID name.

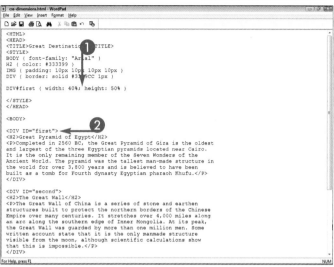

● The Web browser displays the element with a width and height that are relative to the size of the enclosing box.

In this case, the enclosing box is the `<BODY>` tag, so the content is resized based on the browser window dimensions.

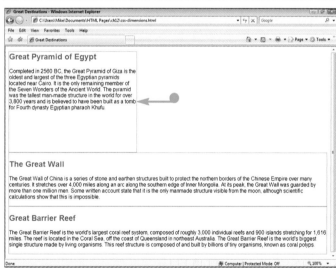

---

**TIPS**

### What are the em and ex style-sheet measures?

The em and ex measures allow you to define sizes on your pages based on the size of the surrounding text. The concept comes from typography, where em represents the width of the capital letter *M* and ex represents the height of the lowercase *x*. If you set a style sheet measurement to 2em, text will be twice the size of the normal font. If viewers adjust the font size of their browser, the content sized on your page using em also adjusts. The ex measure works similarly but on a smaller scale.

### How do I control what happens to text that extends outside a CSS box?

You can control how text outside a box is handled using the `overflow` property. Setting the property to `visible` causes the text to be rendered outside the box. A `hidden` value hides the text that is outside the box. Both `scroll` and `auto` values display scroll bars for viewing the content, if needed.

# Use Relative Positioning

You can apply *relative* positioning to elements on your Web page to place content relative to other content on the page. If you offset a relatively positioned element using the top, left, right, or bottom property, the element is offset relative to the point where it would normally begin.

**Relative is the default setting for the position style property.**

Use Relative Positioning

## APPLY RELATIVE POSITIONING

1 Click inside the tag declaration and type **position: relative**.

● In this example, the positioning is applied to all the paragraphs on a page by defining a style for the <P> tag.

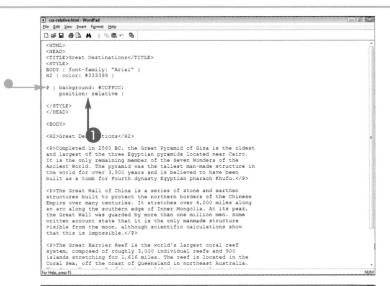

● The Web browser displays the elements with relative positioning, one after the other.

In this example, a background color is applied to the paragraphs to show the dimensions of the content boxes.

**APPLY AN OFFSET**

① Click inside the tag declaration and type **top: ?;**, replacing *?* with the amount you want to offset the elements from the top of the normal page flow.

② Click inside the tag declaration and type **left: ?**, replacing *?* with the amount you want to offset the element from the left of the normal page flow.

You can specify values in points (pt), pixels (px), millimeters (mm), centimeters (cm), inches (in), picas (pc), x-height (ex), or em.

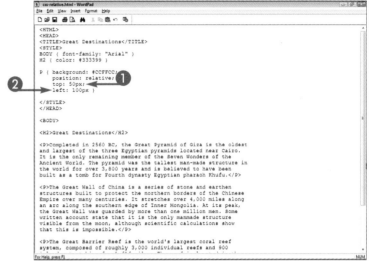

● The Web browser displays elements with offsets applied.

In this example, the paragraphs are offset relative to their normal position in the page flow.

You can narrow elements on your page so that they appear within the browser window by setting their dimensions. See the section "Set Width and Height for an Element" for details.

**Can I offset content from the bottom or the right?**

Yes, but note that offsetting from the bottom may obscure the page content that is above the positioned element. Use the following steps:

① Click inside the tag declaration and type **bottom: ?;**, replacing *?* with the amount of offset from the bottom.

② Click inside the tag declaration and type **right: ?**, replacing *?* with the amount of offset from the right.

The Web browser offsets the page content 100 pixels from the bottom and 50 pixels from the right.

# Use Absolute Positioning

You can apply *absolute* positioning to place an element at exact coordinates on a page, independent of elements that came before it. The coordinates are determined relative to the box that encloses it. This allows you to precisely fit together boxes of text, images, and other content on a page, like a jigsaw puzzle.

**Absolute positioning removes an object from the normal flow of page content. Its size and position have no effect on the position of content that follows it.**

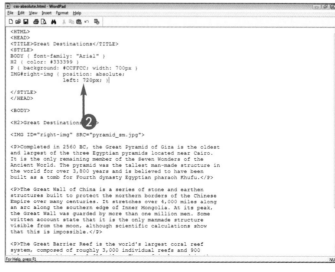

① Click inside the tag declaration and type **position: absolute**.

In this example, absolute positioning is applied to an image using an ID attribute. For more about using the ID attribute, see Chapter 10.

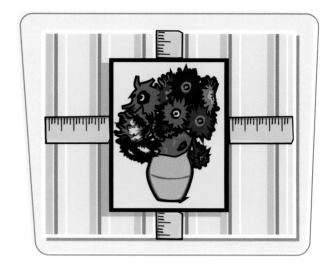

② Click inside the tag declaration and type **left: ?**, replacing *?* with the amount you want to offset the element from the left.

In this example, the image is offset to the left of several paragraphs of text.

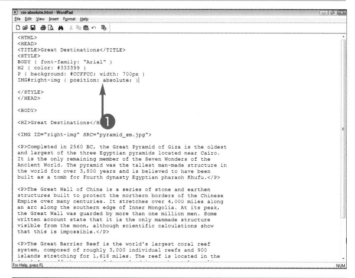

③ Click inside the tag declaration and type **top: ?**, replacing *?* with the amount you want to offset the element from the top.

④ Type **ID="?"** inside the HTML tag to apply the style, replacing *?* with the ID name.

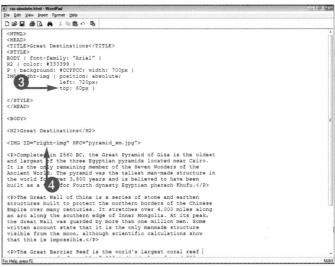

● The Web browser displays the element with offsets applied.

The element is offset relative to the enclosing box, which in this example is the browser window.

In this example, the paragraphs are narrowed using a width style to make space for the image on the right.

 **TIP**

**How can I apply absolute positioning to an image and a caption?**
You can apply absolute positioning to both an image and caption text by surrounding the content with DIV tags. Use the following steps:

① Define the custom style for the DIV tag.

*Note: For details, see Chapter 10.*

② Type the HTML for the image and the caption.

③ Before the image and caption, type **<DIV ID="?">**, replacing *?* with the ID name.

④ Following the image and caption text, type **</DIV>**.

# Use Fixed Positioning

You can apply *fixed* positioning to place an element at exact coordinates on a page and have it remain fixed while a viewer scrolls. This is one way to keep navigation links visible as visitors view content on a long page.

**You can also fix content on your Web pages by putting it in a frame. See Chapter 8 for more about frames.**

Use Fixed Positioning

① Click inside the tag declaration and type **position: fixed**.

In this example, fixed positioning is applied to a box of navigation links using a DIV tag and an ID attribute.

**Note:** *For more about using the DIV tag and ID attribute, see Chapter 10.*

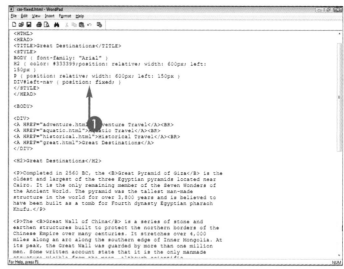

Click inside the tag declaration and type **left: ?**, replacing *?* with the amount you want to offset the element from the left.

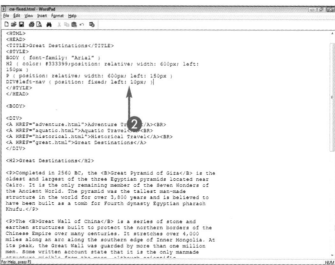

236

③ Click inside the tag declaration and type **top: ?**, replacing *?* with the amount you want to offset the element from the top.

④ Type **ID="?"** inside the HTML tag to apply the style, replacing *?* with the ID name.

In this example, navigation links are fixed to the left of several paragraphs of text. The paragraphs are shifted to the right using relative positioning.

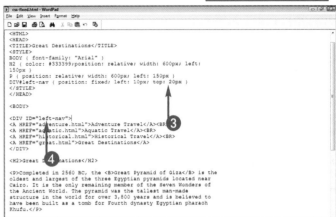

The Web browser displays the element with offsets applied.

The element is offset relative to the enclosing box, which in this example is the browser window.

⑤ Click and drag the scroll bar to scroll down the page.

● The fixed content stays in the same place while the rest of the page content moves.

**TIP**

**How can I ensure that as many browsers as possible display my fixed content correctly?**

Some earlier versions of Web browsers, such as Internet Explorer 6, do not support fixed positioning. Later versions of Internet Explorer support it, but only if the page has a document type set to strict. Use the following steps to set the document type:

① Insert a new line before the <HTML> tag.

② Type the HTML strict document type:

```
<!DOCTYPE HTML PUBLIC "-//W3C//DTD HTML 4.01 Strict//EN"
"http://www.w3.org/TR/REC-html4/strict.dtd">
```

# Set Margins

You can control the margins of your Web page elements using the `margin` properties. You can set margin values for the top, bottom, left, and right margins around a Web page element.

You can set margin sizing using points (pt), pixels (px), millimeters (mm), centimeters (cm), inches (in), picas (pc), x-height (ex), or em.

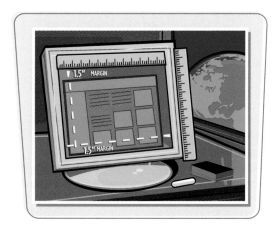

## Set Margins

① Click inside the tag declaration and type **margin-?:** and a space, replacing *?* with the margin you want to adjust (top, bottom, left, or right).

② Type a value for the margin spacing.

Typing **margin:** and then a spacing value adds that spacing around all sides of an element.

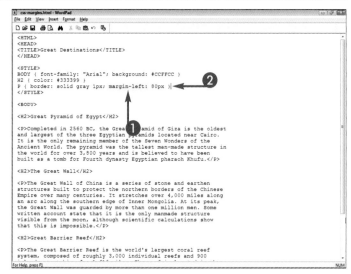

The Web browser assigns margins to the Web page element.

● In this example, margins are assigned to the paragraphs on a page.

In this example, borders are turned on. Margin spacing exists outside an element's border.

**Note:** See the section "Add Padding" to learn how to add spacing inside borders.

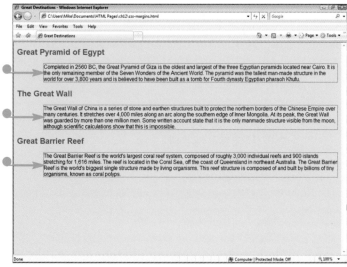

You can use the `padding` property to add space around a Web page element. Adding padding can be useful for making text elements readable when they abut one another in a page layout.

**You can specify padding in points (pt), pixels (px), millimeters (mm), centimeters (cm), inches (in), picas (pc), x-height (ex), or em.**

### Add Padding

**1** Click inside the tag declaration and type **padding:** and a space.

**2** Type a value for the spacing.

To add padding to just one side, you can type **padding-?:**, replacing *?* with `top`, `bottom`, `left`, or `right`.

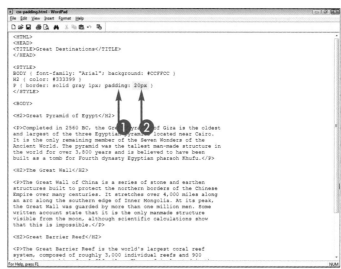

The Web browser uses the assigned padding for the element to which the tag is applied.

In this example, padding is assigned to the paragraphs on a page.

In this example, borders are turned on. Padding spacing exists inside an element's border.

***Note:*** *See the section "Set Margins" to learn how to add spacing outside borders.*

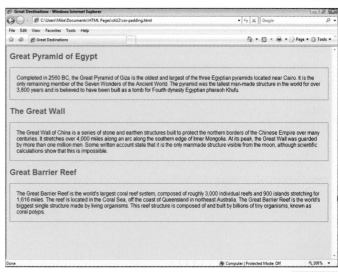

# Wrap Text around Elements

You can use the `float` property to control how text wraps around the elements on your Web page. The left value controls the left side of an element, and the right value controls the right side of an element. To ensure proper text wrapping, place the floating element right before the text you want to wrap.

**The `float` property does not work with elements for which you have assigned an absolute or fixed position.**

① Click inside the tag declaration you want to control and type **float:** and a space.

② Type **left** to set the element to the left side of the text, or type **right** to set the element to the right side of the text.

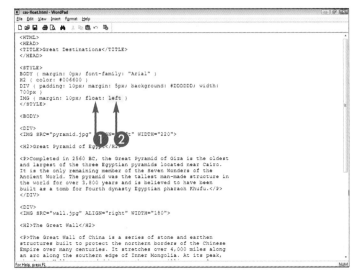

The Web browser floats the element as directed.

● In this example, the `<IMG>` elements float to the right of the headings and paragraphs.

Margins have been added to the `<IMG>` elements to separate them from the text.

*Note: See the section "Add Margins" for details about setting margins.*

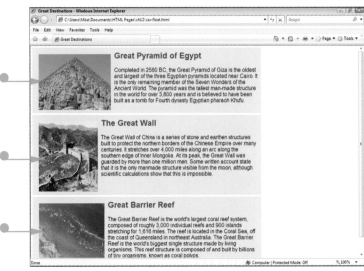

# Change Vertical Alignment

You can control the vertical positioning of elements on your page using the vertical-align property. You can choose from six vertical alignments: baseline, text-top, text-bottom, middle, top, and bottom.

① Click inside the tag declaration and type **vertical-align: ?**, replacing ? with the vertical alignment option you want to assign (**baseline**, **text-top**, **text-bottom**, **middle**, **top**, or **bottom**).

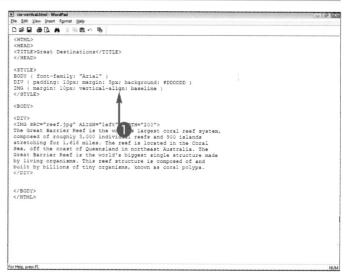

The Web browser displays the element using the assigned vertical alignment.

● In this example, an image is vertically aligned so that it sits at the baseline of the text.

**Note:** Learn how to add images in Chapter 5.

# Create a Centered Layout

You can use style-sheet rules to create a fixed-width layout that is centered in the browser window. The layout places equal spacing on the left and right sides of the content.

Create a Centered Layout

1 In the declaration for the BODY tag, type **text-align: center**.

2 Create an ID style for a DIV tag by typing **DIV#? {}**, replacing ? with a unique name.

**Note:** For more about creating ID styles, see Chapter 10.

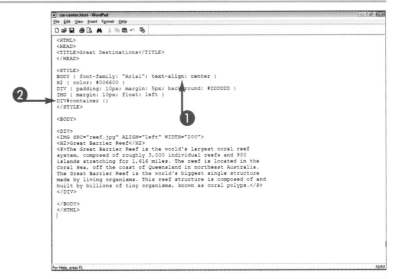

3 Inside the ID style declaration, type **margin: 0 auto;**. This centers the page content.

4 Type **text-align: left;**.

5 Type **width: ?**, replacing ? with a measurement value. This sets the width of your page content.

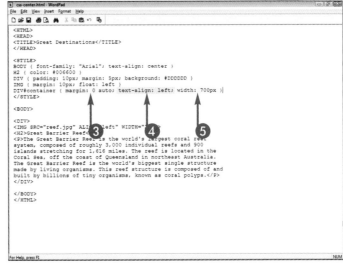

⑥ After the `<BODY>` tag in your HTML document and before the main page content, type **<DIV>**.

⑦ Inside the `<DIV>` tag, type the attribute **ID="?"**, replacing *?* with the ID style name from step **2**.

⑧ After the main page content and before the `</BODY>` tag, type **</DIV>**.

The Web browser displays the content in a fixed-width style in the center of the window.

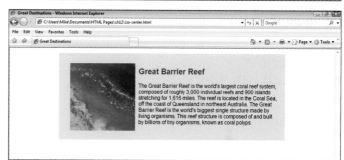

TIP

**How can I make my page content flush with the edges of the browser window using CSS?**
By default, Web browsers add some space between page content and the edge of the browser window. To remove this space using style sheets, follow these steps:

① Create a style declaration for the BODY tag.

② Add the style rule **margin: 0px** to the declaration.

The Web browser removes the space between the page content and the edges of the browser window.

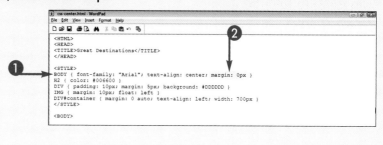

# Control the Overlap of Elements

You can use style sheets to overlap elements on your pages by positioning them at similar coordinates. You can then control the stack order of those elements by adjusting the z-index property for each element. An element with a higher z-index value appears above an element with a lower z-index value.

**See the section "Use Absolute Positioning" for more about setting the coordinates of a page element.**

① Create ID styles for the overlapping elements.

② Use absolute positioning to arrange the elements on the page.

③ Apply the ID styles to the elements by typing **ID="?"** inside the HTML tags, replacing ? with the ID names.

In this example, two images are overlapped.

**Note:** For more about creating ID styles, see Chapter 10. For more about absolute positioning, see the section "Use Absolute Positioning."

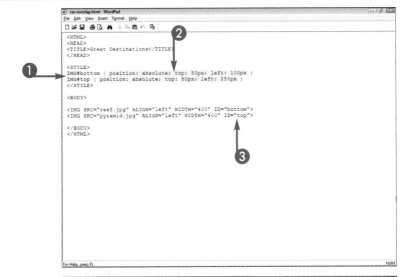

④ Inside the ID style declaration for the element you want on the bottom, type **z-index: ?**, replacing ? with a number.

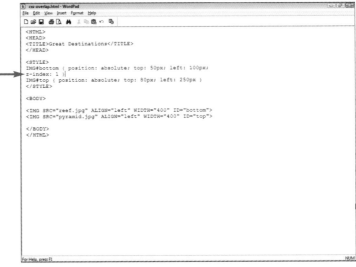

⑤ Inside the ID style declaration for the element you want on top, type **z-index: ?**, replacing *?* with a number greater than the number in step **4**.

The Web browser displays content in the stack order determined by the z-index values.

● In this example, the image with the z-index of 1 is on the bottom.

● The image with the z-index of 2 is on top.

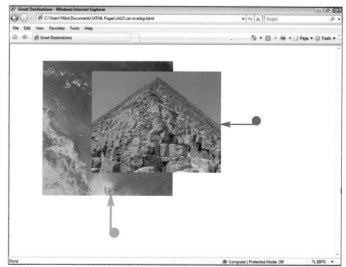

**TIPS**

### How can I make an element transparent so that elements below it show through?

You can make content on your Web page transparent by changing its opacity. Note that different browsers recognize different style sheet commands for changing opacity. Use the following steps:

① Create a style rule for the element you want to make transparent.

② Type **filter: alpha(opacity=?)**, replacing *?* with a value from 0 to 100. The `filter` property works in Internet Explorer.

③ Type **opacity: ?**, replacing *?* with a fractional number from 0.0 to 1.0. The `opacity` property works in other popular browsers.

The Web browser turns the element transparent, allowing elements below it to show through.

# Hide an Element

You can use the display property in your CSS to determine whether or not an element in your HTML is displayed on the page. When the display property is set to none, the Web browser hides the element and takes it out of the flow of the Web page.

**Generally this feature is used in conjunction with JavaScript code, which can make an element appear in response to a user action such as a hyperlink click. JavaScript can turn on an element by dynamically changing the value of the display property. See Chapter 13 for details.**

## Hide an Element

1 Type the HTML for the element you want to hide.

In this example, one of three photos on a page will be hidden.

2 Type **IMG#? { }**, replacing ? with a name for the style that will hide the element.

**Note:** *For more about creating ID styles, see Chapter 10.*

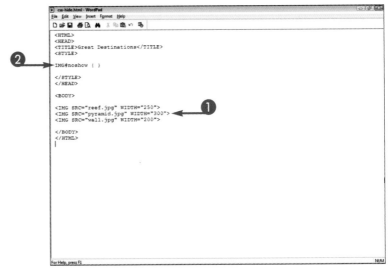

3 Inside the CSS brackets, type **display: none**.

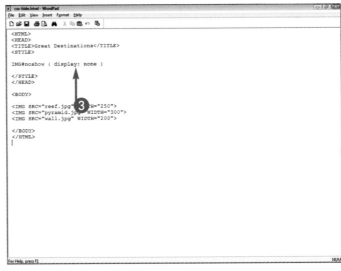

chapter 12

④ Type the attribute **ID="?"** for the element you want to hide, replacing *?* with the style name from step **2**.

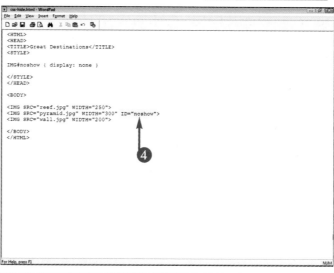

The Web browser hides the element.

**TIPS**

**What other values does the display property accept?**

The display property can accept a number of values, but only two are commonly supported across all of the currently popular browsers. A block value creates a block-level element, which means the element is added to the page with line breaks above and below it. An inline value creates an element that can sit within the text of a sentence, similar to how a SPAN tag works. For more about the SPAN tag, see Chapter 10.

**What is the visibility property?**

The visibility property is similar to the display property in that it renders an element invisible. However, the visibility property does not remove the area that would normally be occupied by the element. For example, hiding an image using the visibility property leaves a blank rectangular area on the page.

# Customize a Background Image

You can place an image as a background on your Web page and control how the image repeats using style sheets. You can make it repeat horizontally to create a border across the top of your page, or you can make it repeat vertically to create a border down the left side.

**A background image normally repeats both horizontally and vertically to fill the entire page.**

## Customize a Background Image

① Place the image you want to use as your background in the same directory as your HTML file.

② Type **BODY { }** to create a style rule for the BODY HTML tag.

*Note: For more about creating ID styles, see Chapter 10. For more about absolute positioning, see the section "Use Absolute Positioning."*

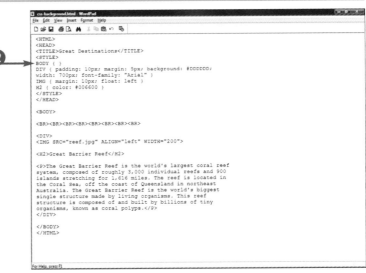

③ To insert the image as a background, type **background-image: url('?');**, replacing ? with the image file name.

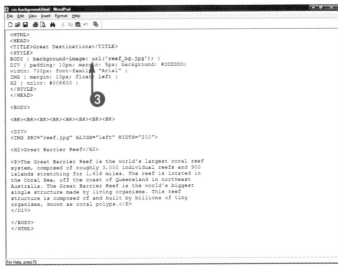

④ To control how the image repeats, type **background-repeat: ?**, replacing ? with **repeat**, **repeat-x**, **repeat-y**, or **no-repeat**.

The repeat-x value tiles the image horizontally, while repeat-y tiles the image vertically.

The repeat value, which is the default, tiles the image in both directions.

The no-repeat value displays the image once.

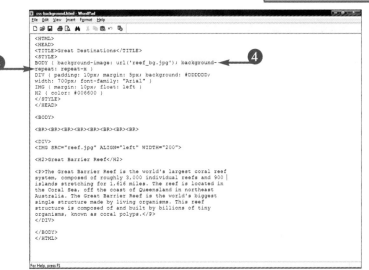

● The Web browser displays the image as a background with the specified repeat style.

**Note:** To add a background image using HTML, see Chapter 5.

## TIPS

### How do I create a background image that appears once in the center of my page?

You can assign a no-repeat value to the background-repeat property to place the image once in the background. Then you can specify the location of the image using the background-position property. A center center value places the image in the center of the Web page. You can use percentage values to place the image relative to the entire height and width of the window or numeric values to place it at pixel coordinates. The first value is always the horizontal position, while the second value is the vertical.

### How do I keep a background image from scrolling with the page?

To control whether or not your background image scrolls with the page content, you can assign a background-attachment property. Assigning the scroll value, which is the default, allows the background image to scroll, while fixed keeps the background image fixed as the page content moves. This feature works with the different repeat and positioning settings described in this task.

# Working with JavaScript

Make your Web site more exciting and interactive!!

Looking for ways to add action and interest to your Web site? JavaScript can help you add interactivity to your HTML documents. This chapter shows you how to use JavaScript code to make your pages more interesting to people who visit your Web site.

# Understanding JavaScript

You can use snippets of code written in JavaScript to add dynamic effects to your Web pages. Such scripts can help turn a static HTML page into a more exciting, interactive experience. You can use JavaScript to display message boxes, change images when a user rolls a mouse over an area of the page, validate form information, and more.

## How Scripts Work

Scripts are short programs you can write to add interactivity to Web pages. Scripting instructions can be activated when an event occurs, such as when a user clicks a link or moves the mouse pointer over an image. Scripts can also be activated automatically when the user downloads your page. Because scripts are written in programming languages, you need to know a little bit about programming if you want to write your own scripts. To learn more about writing scripts, visit www.htmlgoodies.com/primers/jsp.

## JavaScript

Most Web page scripts are written in the JavaScript language, which nearly all Web browsers support. Because JavaScript code is executed by Web browsers, also known as *clients*, JavaScript is known as a *client-side* scripting language. Other scripting languages, such as PHP and Perl, run on Web servers and are known as *server-side* scripting languages.

## Adding Scripts to Your Pages

JavaScript code can be embedded within the HTML of your page or in a separate file. If you put JavaScript inside an HTML page, you need to bracket it with opening and closing <SCRIPT> tags. If you put your JavaScript in a separate file, you need to end the file name with a .js extension. To use code from an external file, you need to link to the file in your page using <SCRIPT> tags and an SRC attribute. JavaScript is case-sensitive and requires careful placement of semicolons, single quotes, double quotes, and other punctuation, so use care when typing your scripts.

## Scripting Tools

You can create your own scripts using an HTML editor. Many editors, such as Adobe Dreamweaver, offer built-in toolsets to help you create your own scripts without needing to know a lot about programming. You can also easily incorporate scripts that other users have written.

## Finding Prewritten Scripts

Many Internet sites offer JavaScripts that you can use in your own Web pages. Be sure to ask permission, if needed. For example, Java-Scripts.net (www.java-scripts.net), JavaScript City (www.javascriptcity.com), and The JavaScript Source (javascript.internet.com) offer free JavaScripts for Web pages.

## Scripting Tips

Some users turn off the JavaScript function in their browsers for security reasons. You can use the <NOSCRIPT> tag to include alternative text about the script. For example, you might include a simple message like "Your browser does not support this script." It is also good policy to note the scripting language in your HTML document, using the <META> tag. The remaining sections of this chapter show you a few JavaScript features you can try out on your own pages.

# Understanding Script Events and Handlers

When you use JavaScript to add interactivity to your pages, it helps to understand when and why a script executes. Some scripts run as soon as the page downloads, while others require an action on the part of the Web page visitor. As the Web site developer, you decide when and how a script executes. You can use events and event handlers to control your scripts.

## Script Events

*Script events* are any actions taken by a Web page visitor, such as clicking on an area of the page. The browser can also cause an event, such as loading a page, to occur. For example, mouse events are actions a user performs with a mouse, such as clicking, moving the mouse pointer over an object, and releasing the mouse button after clicking it. Keyboard events include key presses on a keyboard.

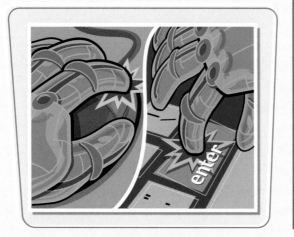

## Event Handlers

You can determine what happens after an action by specifying an *event handler*. Event handlers associate an object or Web page element with an event. For example, you can use the ONCLICK event handler to associate a Web page button with a mouse click. Event handlers are not added using the <SCRIPT> tags but, rather, appear within HTML element tags.

| Scriptable Events | |
|---|---|
| *Event* | *Trigger* |
| LOAD | Triggers when the page is loaded |
| UNLOAD | Triggers when the page is unloaded |
| MOUSEOVER | Triggers when the mouse moves over an object or area on the page |
| MOUSEOUT | Triggers when the mouse is no longer over an object or area on the page |
| MOUSEDOWN | Triggers when the mouse is clicked on an object |
| MOUSEUP | Triggers when the mouse button is released after being clicked |
| CLICK | Triggers when the mouse button is clicked and released |
| KEYPRESS | Triggers when a keyboard key is pressed and released |
| KEYDOWN | Triggers when a keyboard key is pressed |
| KEYUP | Triggers when a keyboard key is released |
| SUBMIT | Triggers when a form button is clicked |
| RESET | Triggers when a reset form button is clicked |
| **Event Handlers** | |
| *Event Handler* | *Action* |
| ONLOAD | Browser loads a page |
| ONUNLOAD | Browser unloads a page |
| ONMOUSEOVER | User positions the mouse over an element |
| ONMOUSEDOWN | User presses the mouse button |
| ONMOUSEUP | User releases the mouse button |
| ONMOUSEMOVE | User moves the mouse |
| ONMOUSEOUT | User moves the mouse away from an element |
| ONCLICK | User clicks an element |
| ONDBLCLICK | User double-clicks element |
| ONKEYPRESS | User presses and releases a keyboard key |
| ONKEYDOWN | User presses a key |
| ONKEYUP | User releases a key |
| ONSUBMIT | User clicks a Submit button |

# Add JavaScript to a Web Page

JavaScripts are a great way to add interactivity to your Web pages. You can use the <SCRIPT> and </SCRIPT> tags to add JavaScript to your HTML document. The browser reads anything between the two tags as a script.

**To learn more about writing your own JavaScripts, try one of these books: JavaScript for Dummies, Beginning JavaScript, or JavaScript Visual Blueprint, all from Wiley Publishing.**

## Add JavaScript to a Web Page

① Type **<SCRIPT LANGUAGE="javascript">** where you want to insert the script on the page.

② Type the code for the script you want to add.

In this example, the script tells the user the size of the monitor screen.

③ Type **</SCRIPT>** at the end of the script.

- If you are using Internet Explorer, you may have to click here and then click **Allow Blocked Content** to allow scripts to run in your browser.

- The Web browser runs the script when the user views your page.

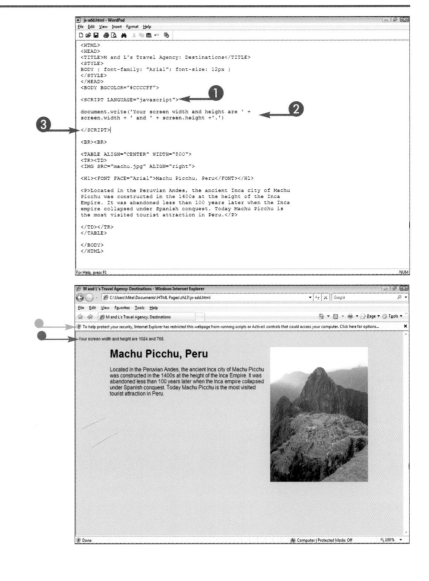

# Create a JavaScript File

Many developers prefer to save their scripts in a separate text file and link the file to the Web page. Storing your scripts in a separate file can free up your HTML document to focus on Web page content. When saving a JavaScript file, use the .js file extension.

**When you upload your Web pages to a server, be sure to include the linked JavaScript file. See Chapter 15 to learn more about publishing Web pages.**

## Create a JavaScript File

1 Create a new document in your text editor.

2 Type your JavaScript code.

*Note: You can find many free JavaScript programs on the Internet. See the section "Understanding JavaScript" to learn more.*

3 Save the file using the .js file extension.

*Note: See Chapter 2 to learn how to create and save documents.*

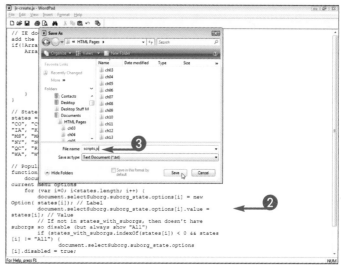

4 In your Web page document, click where you want to insert the code and type **<SCRIPT TYPE="text/javascript"**.

5 Type a space and **SRC="?">**, replacing ? with the location and name of the JavaScript file.

6 Type **</SCRIPT>**.

The JavaScript file is now linked to the Web page.

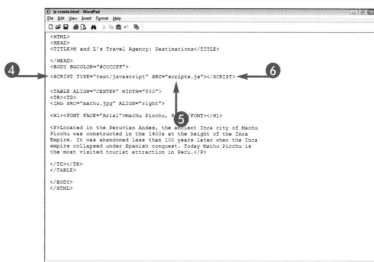

# Hide
# JavaScript

You can hide your JavaScript coding from older Web browsers. Ordinarily, if a browser does not support JavaScript, it displays your script coding on the Web page instead of activating the script. To prevent this from happening, you can hide the script using the comment tags.

## Hide JavaScript

① Type **<!- -** directly after the opening **<SCRIPT>** tag.

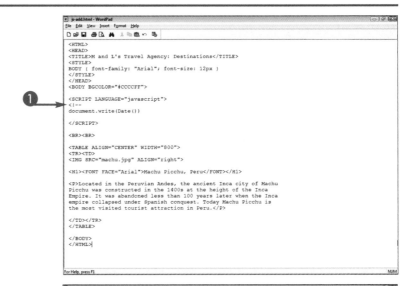

② Type **//- ->** directly before the closing **</SCRIPT>** tag.

If an older browser that does not read scripts encounters your page, it does not display the script coding on the page.

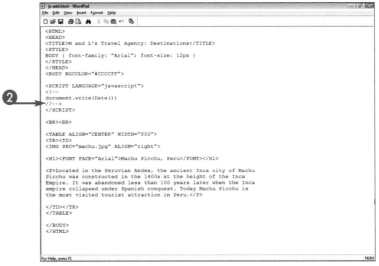

# Add Alternative Text

Some users turn off JavaScript in their Web browsers for security reasons. You can provide alternative text to describe what the user is missing or to remind users that their scripting feature is turned off.

## Add Alternative Text

**1** Type **<NOSCRIPT>** below the </SCRIPT> tag.

**2** Type your alternative text message.

**3** Type **</NOSCRIPT>**.

*Note: You can format the alternative text. See Chapter 3 to learn how to add formatting to HTML text.*

● If the browser's script feature is turned off, the browser displays your alternative text.

# Insert the Current Date and Time

You can use JavaScript to insert the current date and time on your Web page. This can help your page seem current and up to date.

① Click where you want to insert the date and time on the page and add a new line.

② Type **<SCRIPT TYPE="text/javascript">**.

③ Type **document.write(Date())**.

④ Type **</SCRIPT>**.

You can keep your script on one line or break it onto multiple lines to make it easier to read.

● The Web browser displays the current date and time.

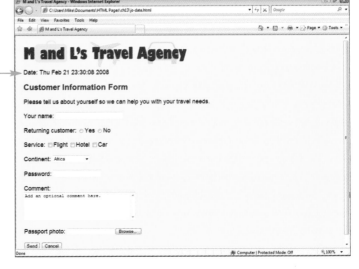

# Display an Alert Message Box

You can use JavaScript to display an alert message box on your Web page. For example, you might use alert messages to provide special instructions about your site or to alert the user to any important information. After reading the message, the user can close the box.

## Display an Alert Message Box

1. Type **<SCRIPT TYPE="text/javascript">**.

2. Type **alert('?')**, replacing ? with the message text you want to appear in the box.

3. Type **</SCRIPT>** to end the JavaScript code.

   The placement of your script on the page determines when it appears during the page download.

   Place the script at the top to load first or at the bottom to load last.

   When the user displays your page in a browser, the alert message box appears.

● The user can click here to close the box.

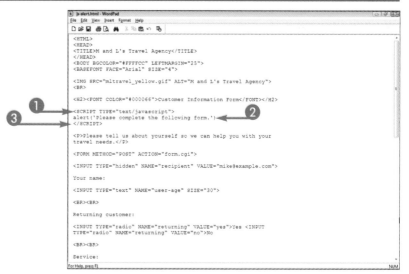

# Display a Pop-Up Window

You can use JavaScript to display a pop-up window on your Web page. Pop-up windows are a great way of alerting your Web site visitors to important news about your site, announcing a sale, or describing an upcoming event. The message that appears in the window is actually another Web page created just for the pop-up window.

**The pop-up window references a separate HTML file. You need to create the file before writing the JavaScript. See Chapter 2 to learn more about building HTML documents.**

## Display a Pop-Up Window

① Within the `<BODY>` tag, type **ONLOAD="javascript:window. open('?',**.

② Replace *?* with the location and name of the Web page you want to appear in the pop-up box.

③ Type **'?'**, replacing *?* with a name for the window.

④ Type **'HEIGHT=?, WIDTH=?')"**, replacing *?* with a height and width, measured in pixels, for the pop-up window.

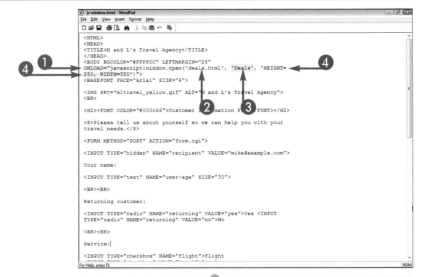

When the user displays the page in a browser, the pop-up window appears.

● The user can click here to close the window.

***Note:*** *Be careful about the punctuation you type in your JavaScript code. A missed comma or quote can cause an error in your script.*

Ordinarily, when the user moves the mouse pointer over a link on your page, the browser's status bar displays the address of the link. You can customize the text that appears in the status bar for a link. For example, you might shorten a complex address to something simpler or create your own text message to appear instead.

**Always be careful about typing single quotes and double quotes in JavaScript code. Do not inadvertently leave any spaces unless the code requires it. A mistake can cause problems with your script.**

### Customize the Status Bar Message for a Link

① Within the `<A>` tag for the link you want to change, type **ONMOUSEOVER="window. status=**.

② Type **'** followed by the status bar message text, ending with **'**.

Anything you type between the single quotes will appear in the status bar.

③ Type **; return true"**.

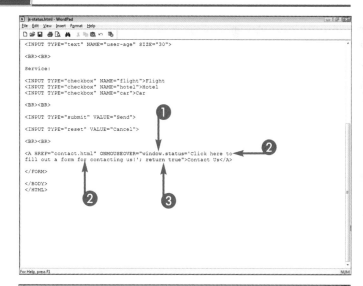

● When the user moves the mouse pointer (⇱) over the link, the status bar displays your custom text.

# Create an Image Rollover Effect

You can use JavaScript to create an image rollover effect. When the user moves the mouse pointer over the image on the Web page, the image is replaced with a different one. When the user moves the mouse pointer off the image, the original image returns.

**To create an image rollover, you must add two mouse event handlers to a hyperlink tag. The effect works best if the images have the same dimensions. You can resize your images using an image-editing program.**

## Create an Image Rollover Effect

① Add an image to your page by typing **<IMG SRC="?"**, replacing *?* with the file name and location of the image.

② Type a space and then **NAME="?">**, replacing *?* with an identifier.

③ Before the <IMG> tag, type **<A HREF="?">**, replacing *?* with a destination for the link.

④ After the <IMG> tag, type **</A>**.

**Note:** For more about adding images, see Chapter 5. For more about links, see Chapter 6.

⑤ Within the <A> tag, type **ONMOUSEOVER="document.?**, replacing *?* with the identifier from step **2**.

⑥ Type **.src='?'"**, replacing *?* with the name and location of the image that will replace the existing image when the user rolls over the picture.

**Note:** Be careful not to leave out any single quotes in the script.

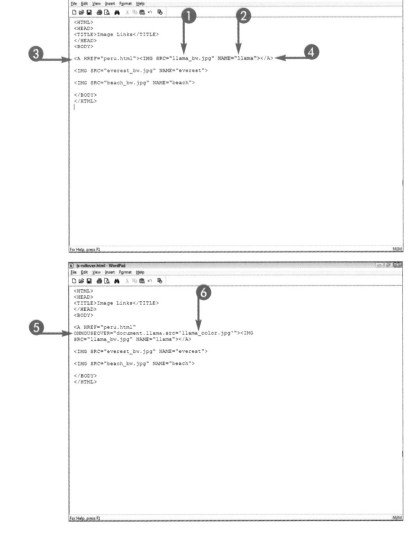

7 Type a space and then
**ONMOUSEOUT="document.?,**
replacing *?* with the name of the
original image.

8 Type a space and then **.src='?'"**,
replacing *?* with the name and
location of the original image.

```
js-rollover.html - WordPad
File  Edit  View  Insert  Format  Help

<HTML>
<HEAD>
<TITLE>Image Links</TITLE>
</HEAD>
<BODY>

<A HREF="peru.html"
ONMOUSEOVER="document.llama.src='llama_color.jpg'"
ONMOUSEOUT="document.llama.src='llama_bw.jpg'"><IMG
SRC="llama_bw.jpg" NAME="llama"></A>

<IMG SRC="everest_bw.jpg" NAME="everest">

<IMG SRC="beach_bw.jpg" NAME="beach">

</BODY>
</HTML>
```

● When the user moves the mouse
pointer over the image, the Web
browser replaces the original
image with the rollover image.

---

**How can I make my rollover effects more immediate?**

You can instruct the browser to preload the
rollover image using JavaScript. This way, the
browser doesn't have to download the rollover
image when the mouse pointer rolls over the
original image. You can preload an image by adding
the following script inside the <HEAD> tags of your
HTML:

`<SCRIPT>?=new Image(h,w)?.SRC="image.url"</SCRIPT>`

Replace *?* with an identifier for the image, replace *h,w* with height
and width values for the image, and replace `image.url` with the
location and file name of the image.

**How do I add multiple rollover images to my page?**

Follow the
previous steps
for each image,
but remember to
assign a different
NAME identifier to each image in
step **2**. If you specify the same
identifier for more than one of
the images, some browsers will
not display the rollover effect
correctly.

# Validate Form Data

You can use JavaScript to check the values of a Web page form after the form is submitted. If the values are invalid, the script can prompt users to enter correct ones. Form validation can help ensure that only valid information is submitted with your Web page forms.

**To learn more about creating Web page forms, see Chapter 9.**

Please type numbers, not letters.

Enter your ZIP Code:
24368
Enter

click

## Validate Form Data

**VALIDATE INPUT CHARACTERS**

1 In the <INPUT> or <TEXTAREA> tag you want to validate, type **ONCHANGE="var pattern=/[?]/;**, replacing *?* with the characters the user is not allowed to type into the form.

2 Type a space and **if (pattern.test(this.value)) alert('?')"**, replacing *?* with the error message text you want to display.

In this example, the value prevents users from typing numbers into the form field.

● If the user types the wrong data, the validation prompt box appears.

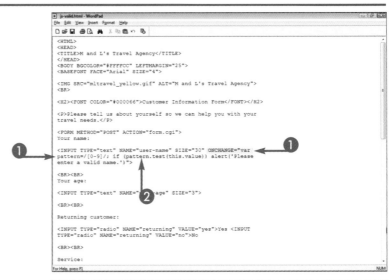

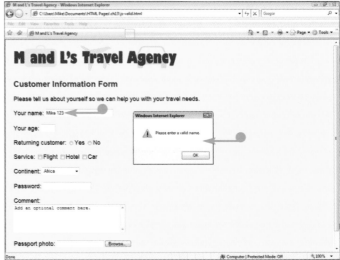

**VALIDATE MINIMUM LENGTH**

1 In the `<INPUT>` or `<TEXTAREA>`
tag you want to validate, type
**ONCHANGE="if (this.value.length>?)**,
replacing *?* with the maximum number of
characters allowed for the form field.

To set a minimum number, type **<?**,
replacing *?* with the minimum number
of characters allowed.

2 Type a space and **alert('?')"**, replacing *?*
with the error message text you want to
display.

● If the user exceeds the maximum or types
fewer than the minimum number of
characters allowed, the validation prompt
box appears.

**TIPS**

**What characters can I control in my form validations?**

You can control whether a user is allowed to type upper- or lowercase letters, numbers, and spacing. For example, if you want the user to type only numbers into a field, you can specify characters in the pattern value in step **1** on the facing page. If you want to limit both upper- and lowercase letters, you must type the values separately; for example, **/[A-Za-z]/**. The following table shows the correct characters for form fields:

| Value | Users Cannot Enter |
|---|---|
| A–Z | Uppercase letters |
| a–z | Lowercase letters |
| 0–9 | Any number |
| \d | Any number |
| \s | Any spacing |
| \w | Any letters, any numbers, or the underscore character |

**Where can I find more data validation scripts?**

You can find more JavaScripts for validating form data at the following Web sites: javascript.internet.com, www.javascripts.com, www.houseofscripts.com, and www.free-javascripts.com.

# Show a Hidden Element

You can use JavaScript to show an HTML element that has been hidden on a page. You can hide an element by setting the CSS display property to none. With JavaScript, you can change that property to block or span, which exposes the element on the page.

**To learn more about hiding elements using CSS, see Chapter 12.**

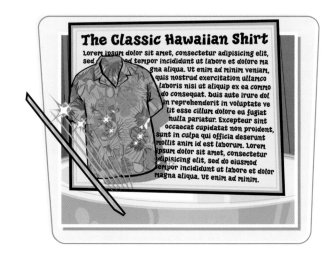

## Show a Hidden Element

1. Add the HTML element that you want to hide or display to your Web page. In this example, an <IMG> element is added.

**Note:** *For more about adding images, see Chapter 5.*

2. Inside the element tag, type the attribute **STYLE="display: none"** to hide the element.

**Note:** *For more about using the STYLE attribute, see Chapter 10.*

3. Type **NAME="?"** to identify the element, replacing *?* with a descriptive name. This allows JavaScript code to reference the element and change its style.

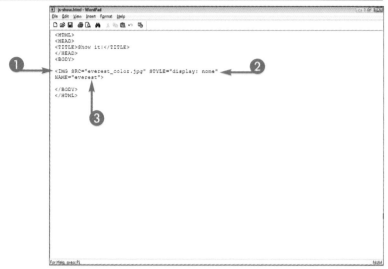

4. Type some text to serve as a hyperlink. The user clicks the link to show the element.

5. Before the text, type **<A HREF="javascript:void(0)">** .

6. After the text, type **</A>**.

This creates a nonfunctional hyperlink. Clicking the link does not take the user to a new page.

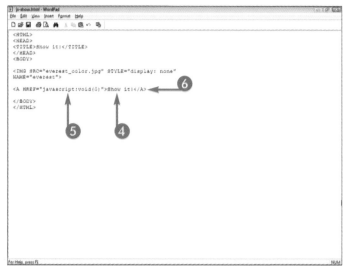

⑦ Inside the `<A>` tag, type **ONCLICK="document.?**, replacing *?* with the identifier created in step **3**.

⑧ Type **.style.display='?';"**, replacing *?* with **inline** or **block**.

The `inline` value shows the element within the flow of any surrounding text.

The `block` value shows the element on its own line with space above and below.

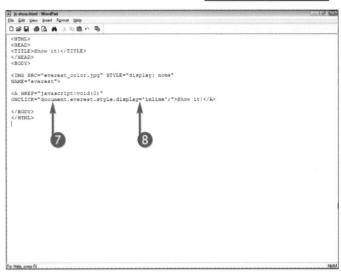

⑨ Click the link on the Web page.

● The element appears.

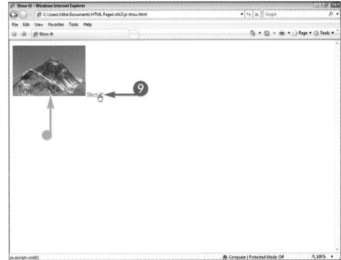

**How can I hide an element on a page using JavaScript?**
Use the technique just described, but set the `display` property of the element to `inline` or `block`. Then use JavaScript to change the `display` property to `none`. You can create separate links on a page to both show and hide an element.

**How can I hide an element when the mouse pointer rolls over a hyperlink?**
Instead of using the `ONCLICK` event handler, as shown previously, use the `ONMOUSEOVER` event handler. This causes the element to appear when the user mouses over the link. You can add an `ONMOUSEOFF` event handler to the same link to change the `display` property back to `none`, so the element disappears again when the user moves the mouse off the link.

# 14

# Adding Multimedia and Extra Touches

Do you want to add multimedia and other extra touches to your Web pages? This chapter shows you how to use HTML to integrate audio, video, Java, and more to enliven your pages and attract visitors.

# Understanding Multimedia Elements

The term *multimedia* encompasses all kinds of dynamic visual and audio data, including graphics, sound, animation, and movies. You can incorporate multimedia elements into your own HTML pages, but first it is useful to understand how such elements work on the Web.

## Ways to Use Multimedia

You can use media files in a variety of ways on your Web page. Media can create an ambiance for the site, enhance your site's message, illustrate a product or service, or simply entertain. When choosing a media file and format to add to your page, always consider the main target audience for your pages. Be sure to include information about the multimedia elements on your page in case the user needs to install special programs or plug-ins to view them.

## Delivering Media Files

You can deliver multimedia files to your Web site visitors in several ways. You can link to an external media file, embed the file into your page, or stream the file. The method you choose depends on how you want the user to interact with the file. Regardless of the method, you must specify the location of the file—either on your Web server, where the multimedia files are stored with your HTML, or on an external host such as YouTube.

## External Media Files

One way to incorporate a multimedia element into your page is to supply a link to an external media file. For example, you might allow a visitor to click a link and download a slide show of your vacation pictures or a music file of your latest song. If the user decides to access the file, the browser helps him or her determine how to download it and where to store it. After downloading the file, the user can play the file in a separate window using the appropriate media player or program.

## Embedded Files

You can integrate a multimedia file directly onto your page by embedding the file. When the user accesses the page, the file plays as part of the page content. For example, you might embed a video file to play in an area on the Web page. Depending on the file type and setup, the file may play immediately when the user displays the page or when the user activates a button or other feature on the page.

## Streaming Media

With streaming media, the user can immediately start viewing or hearing the file as the rest of it continues to download. The data starts downloading into a buffer and then the media player begins playing the file. Adding streaming media to your page is similar to linking or embedding a file, but instead of referencing the actual file, you define a metafile that contains information about the target file's location.

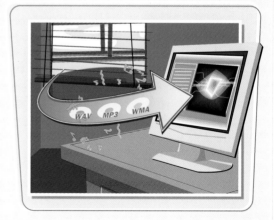

# Understanding Plug-Ins and Players

A wide variety of media formats exist on the Internet, but to play these formats the user needs a plug-in or media player. When determining what type of media file to include with your page, think about how your target audience will interact with the file. Do they need a special plug-in or player program to play the file? If so, you need to add information about those requirements to your page, along with access to the actual media file.

## Plug-ins

Plug-ins are specialized applications that work with the browser to play media files, typically focusing on a particular file format. If users do not have the right plug-in to play your file, they can easily download it, install it, and use it as part of their Web browser. First introduced by Netscape, plug-ins are now popular among all the browsers. For example, you can install a Flash Player plug-in to allow your browser to play Flash multimedia files.

## Media Players

Media players are separate programs designed to handle many types of media files. Often called *all-in-one players*, media players can work both separately and alongside browsers to play multimedia files encountered on and off the Web. Popular media players include Microsoft's Windows Media Player, Apple's QuickTime player, and RealNetworks' RealPlayer. Users can download copies of these popular media players from the Internet. You can help your users by providing links to download locations.

## Dueling HTML Elements

Establishing standards for Web page development is an ongoing task for the World Wide Web Consortium (W3C). Currently, two popular elements exist for showing multimedia files on Web pages: EMBED and OBJECT. Netscape created the nonstandard EMBED element, while the W3C introduced the standard OBJECT element. Microsoft has added ActiveX controls to the OBJECT element. Today's browser versions support them to varying degrees. For the widest support, many developers combine the OBJECT element with the nonstandard EMBED element. See the section "Embed an Audio File" for details.

## Embed with ActiveX Controls

Another way you can embed video clips into your pages is using ActiveX controls along with the OBJECT element. ActiveX uses a CLASSID attribute control number to define which data type the browser loads for playback. The CLASSID attribute for QuickTime, for example, is different from that for Windows Media Player. After you define the proper player, you can set the parameters for the clip's playback. For an example, see the section "Embed a Flash Movie."

## Finding Media Players and Plug-ins

| Player | Web Site |
|---|---|
| Windows Media Player | www.microsoft.com/downloads |
| QuickTime | www.apple.com/quicktime |
| Adobe Flash Player | www.adobe.com/flashplayer |
| Adobe Shockwave Player | www.adobe.com/shockwave/download |
| Adobe Reader | www.adobe.com/products/acrobat |
| RealPlayer | www.real.com |

# Link to Audio or Video Files

You can insert links on your Web page that, when clicked, download and play an audio or video file. When you link to a file, the file may open within the Web browser or in a separate application window, depending on the configuration of your computer. Linking is the least complicated way to deliver multimedia files to your Web page visitors.

**When publishing your HTML page to a Web server, make sure you upload the audio or video file along with the HTML document.**

## Link to Audio or Video Files

1. Type the text you want to use as a link.

2. Type **<A HREF="?">** in front of the link text, replacing *?* with the location and name of the audio or video file to which you want to link.

*Note: See Chapter 6 to learn more about creating HTML links.*

3. Type **</A>** at the end of the link text.

● You can optionally describe the multimedia file. You can include the file format and file size.

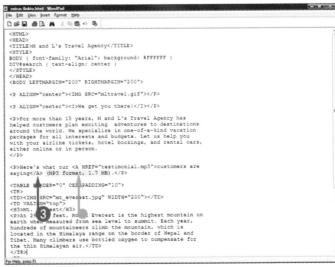

276

When you open the HTML document, the Web browser displays the link on the page.

● When the user clicks the link, the Web browser attempts to play the audio or video file.

*Note: See Chapter 2 to learn more about viewing your HTML document as an offline Web page.*

In this example, a QuickTime player is displayed within the Web browser to play the audio file.

④ Click the Play button (▶) to play the file.

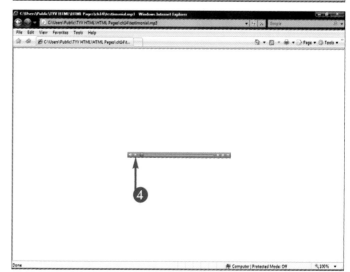

**TIPS**

**Does my page need to include information about the file that is available for downloading?**

It is always good practice to give your Web page visitors all the information they need to know to download and view any type of multimedia file. For example, you can include a brief description of the file, list the file format and size, and provide a link to any plug-ins or media players the user might need to play the file.

**How can I add background music to my page?**

You can assign an audio clip to play in the background while users visit your page using the BGSOUND tag. The tag is not part of the official HTML standard; it works in Internet Explorer but does not work in some other browsers such as Firefox. You reference the audio file using the SRC attribute, such as <BGSOUND SRC="audio.mp3">.

# Embed a Video File

You can use the `<EMBED>` tag to add an embedded video clip to your HTML page. Embedded videos play directly on your page. Playback controls also appear on the page, allowing the user to start and stop the video.

**You can control the size of the window in which an embedded video file appears.**

① Type **`<EMBED SRC="?">`** where you want to insert the video window on the page, replacing *?* with the location and name of the video file.

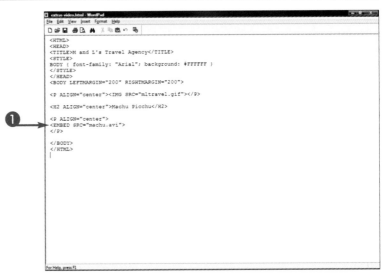

② Within the `<EMBED>` tag, type **`WIDTH="?" HEIGHT="?"`**, replacing *?* in both attributes with width and height values for the size of the window.

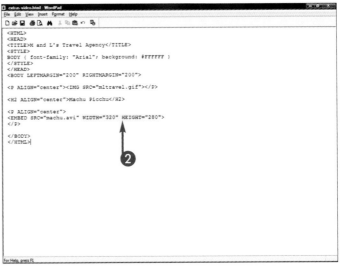

- If you want the video to play immediately when the page loads, type **AUTOSTART="true"** in the EMBED tag.

- If you want the video to play continuously, type **LOOP="true"** in the EMBED tag.

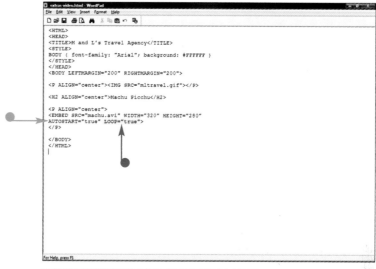

When you open the HTML document, the Web browser displays the embedded video window and playback controls on the page.

- The embedded controls enable you to play, pause, stop, rewind, and fast-forward the video.

**TIP**

**What video file formats are commonly found on the Web?**
Here is a list of common video formats supported by many browsers, plug-ins, and media players:

| Video Formats | |
| Format | File Extension |
| --- | --- |
| AVI (Audio/Video Interleaved) | .avi |
| QT (Apple QuickTime) | .qt |
| MOV (QuickTime) | .mov |
| MPG (Motion Picture Experts Group) | .mpg |
| RV (Real Video) | .rv |
| DCR (Macromedia Director) | .dcr |

# Embed an Audio File

You can add an embedded sound to your HTML page using the <EMBED> tag. You can surround the <EMBED> tag with <OBJECT> tags to make your code compatible with more Web browsers.

You can adjust the space in which the sound controls appear in the page.

① Type **<EMBED SRC="?">** where you want to insert sound controls on the page, replacing *?* with the location and name of the audio file.

② Within the <EMBED> tag, type **WIDTH="?" HEIGHT="?"**, replacing *?* in both attributes with width and height values for the size of the movie and controls.

You can experiment with the values to make the controls the right size for your page.

③ Before the EMBED tag, type **<OBJECT CLASSID="clsid: ?"**, replacing *?* with the class ID for a multimedia plug-in.

In this example, the QuickTime plug-in is specified with a class ID of 02BF25D5-8C17-4B23-BC80-D3488ABDDC6B.

You can perform a Web search to find the class IDs for other popular plug-ins.

④ Type **WIDTH="?" HEIGHT="?">**, replacing *?* in both attributes with width and height values.

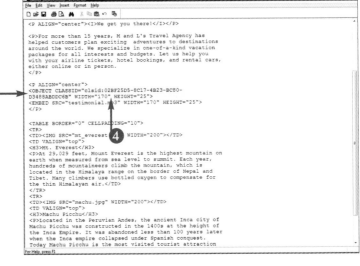

⑤ Type **<PARAM NAME="src" VALUE="?"/>**, substituting the audio file name for *?*.

⑥ Type a closing **</OBJECT>** tag after the EMBED tag.

When you open the HTML document, the Web browser displays the sound controls on the page.

● The user can click ▶ to start the sound.

The embedded sound controls allow you to play, pause, and stop the sound as well as control the volume.

**TIP**

**What audio file formats are common on the Web?**

Audio file formats come in several flavors, but some are more popular on the Web than others. Here is a list of common audio formats supported by most browsers, plug-ins, and media players:

| Audio Formats | |
|---|---|
| **Format** | **File Extension** |
| MP3 (MPEG-1, Layer III) | .mp3 |
| MIDI (Musical Instrument Digital Interface) | .mid |
| AIFF (Audio Interchange File Format) | .aif |
| WAV (RIFF WAVE) | .wav |
| WMA (Windows Media Audio) | .wma |
| RA (RealAudio) | .ra |

## Embed a Flash Movie

You can add a Flash animation to your Web page. Using an ActiveX control number along with the OBJECT element, you can instruct the browser to load and play the Flash file.

### Embed a Flash Movie

① Type **<OBJECT classid= "clsid:D27CDB6E-AE6D-11cf- 96B8-4445535 40000"**.

② Type **CODEBASE="http:// download.macromedia.com/pub /shockwave/cabs/flash/swflash. cab#version=6,0,29,0"**.

③ Type **WIDTH="?" HEIGHT="?">**, replacing ? with width and height values.

④ Type **<PARAM NAME="movie" VALUE="?">**, substituting the Flash file name for ?.

⑤ Type a closing **</OBJECT>**.

When the browser displays your page, the embedded Flash movie plays.

You can use Java applets in your Web pages to add animation and interactivity. Java applets are programs written in the Java programming language.

**Many Java applets are available for downloading on the Web. The Java Boutique (www.javaboutique.internet.com) and JavaShareware.com (www.javashareware.com) are good places to start. You can also conduct a Web search to find more free Java applets.**

## Add a Java Applet

① Click where you want to insert the applet and type **<APPLET CODE="?">**, replacing *?* with the location and name of the applet.

● Optionally, to control the size of the applet window, type **WIDTH="?" HEIGHT="?"** within the <APPLET> tag, replacing *?* with width and height values.

● You can also add alternative text for browsers that do not run Java applets.

② Type **</APPLET>**.

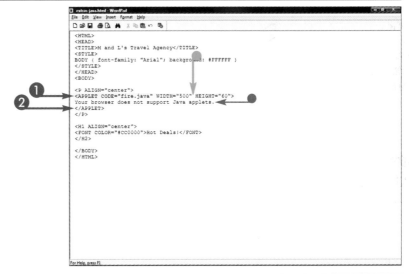

● The Web browser runs the Java applet when the user views your page.

# Embed a Video Clip from YouTube

You can embed a video that is stored on a hosting service such as YouTube by inserting HTML into your Web page. The video appears on the page the same way as a video that is stored locally with your HTML files.

**To host images at YouTube, you can sign up for a free account at www.youtube.com and use the service's uploading tool.**

## Embed a Video Clip from YouTube

① Open your Web browser to the YouTube video you want to add to your Web page.

You can visit YouTube at www.youtube.com.

② Click the **Embed** field.

The HTML is selected.

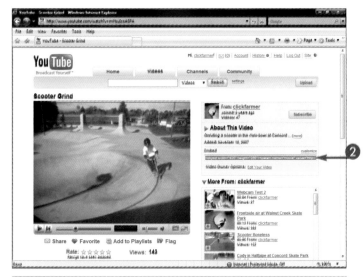

③ In your Web browser, click **Edit**.

④ Click **Copy**.

5️⃣ Open the HTML document in which you want to embed the video.

6️⃣ In your HTML, click where you want to insert the video.

7️⃣ Click **Edit**.

8️⃣ Click **Paste**.

The video HTML is inserted.

9️⃣ Save your HTML document

🔟 Open the document in a browser.

The video clip appears on the page with controls for playing the video.

---

**TIPS**

**Can I embed any YouTube video in my page?**

When you put a video on YouTube, you can control whether that video can be embedded on other pages. The embed feature only works for videos that have the embedded setting turned on.

**How do I change the dimensions of the video?**

You can change the dimensions of an embedded video by changing the WIDTH and HEIGHT attributes in the embedded code. For compatibility with the most browsers, remember to change the WIDTH and HEIGHT attributes in both the OBJECT tag and the EMBED tag.

# Embed an Image from Flickr

You can insert an image that is stored on a hosting service such as Flickr on your Web page. After you locate the hosted image's URL, you can insert the URL into an IMG tag on your page. The image appears on the page the same way as an image that is stored locally with your HTML files.

**To host images at Flickr, you can sign up for a free account at www.flickr.com and use the service's uploading tools.**

## Embed an Image from Flickr

**①** Open your Web browser to the Flickr image you want to add to your Web page.

You can visit Flickr at www.flickr.com.

**②** Click **All Sizes**.

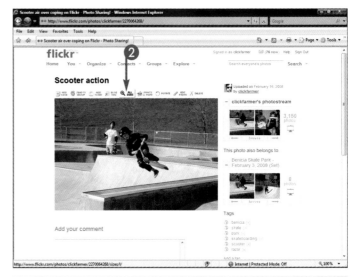

The picture appears with links to different sizes.

● You can click a different size to view a larger or smaller version.

**③** Scroll down to the bottom of the page.

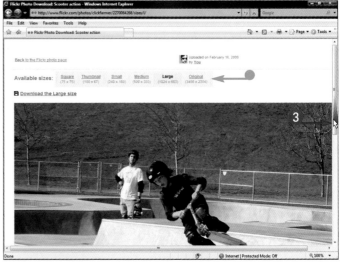

④ Click inside the text box to select the URL for the image.

● You can also click here to select HTML for inserting a linked image.

⑤ In your Web browser, click **Edit**.

⑥ Click **Copy**.

⑦ In your HTML, type **<IMG SRC="">**.

**Note:** *For more about adding images, see Chapter 5.*

⑧ Click inside the quotes.

⑨ Click **Edit**.

⑩ Click **Paste**.

The URL is added to the IMG tag.

After you save the page, you can open it to view the inserted image.

---

**TIPS**

### How can I customize the Flickr image on my page?
You can customize your embedded Flickr photos using IMG attributes just as you would any other photo on your page. You can use the ALIGN attribute to align the photo to the left or right of the text on your page. You can resize your image using the WIDTH and HEIGHT attributes. For more about customizing images, see Chapter 5.

### What other image hosting services are available?
In addition to Flickr, there are many other free hosting services such as ImageBucket (www.imagebucket.com), Picasa (www.picasa.com), and WebShots (www.webshots.com). Many of these services make it easy to embed the hosted images on your own Web site.

# Add a Google Search Box to Your Page

You can make it easy for your visitors to perform searches from your Web page by adding a Google search box. When a user types keywords into the box and clicks a Submit button, a Google results page appears. You can customize the search box to display results from your Web site only.

**To add a search box, you use some of the form tags described in Chapter 9.**

**1** Where you want to add the search box in your HTML, type **<FORM METHOD="get" ACTION="http://www.google.com/search">**.

**2** Type a label for the search form.

**3** Type **<INPUT TYPE="text" NAME="q" SIZE="?" VALUE="">**, replacing *?* with a character width. This creates a search box.

④ Type **<input type="submit" value="?">**, replacing *?* with a button label. This creates a Submit button.

⑤ Type **</FORM>** to complete the form.

⑥ Save the page and open it in a browser.

● The Google search box appears.

To find out how to create a more advanced Google search box, visit www.google.com/coop/cse/.

To find out how to create a Yahoo! search box, visit http://builder.search. yahoo.com.

**TIP**

**How do I give visitors the option of searching for content on my Web site only?**
If your Web site has its own custom Internet domain name, you can let users specify whether Google returns results from the Web or only from that domain. Follow these steps:

① Inside the <FORM> tags, type **<input type="radio" name="sitesearch" value="?">**, replacing *?* with the name of your domain.

This creates a radio button for searching your site only.

② Type a space and then a label for the radio button.

③ Type **<input type="radio" name="sitesearch" value="">**.

This creates a radio button for searching the Web.

④ Type a space and then a label for the radio button.

# Add a Digg Link to Your Page

You can add a Digg link to your page to allow viewers to recommend the page to readers of Digg, which is a social recommendation site. Pages that get a high number of recommendations get exposure on the Digg Web site (www.digg.com), which can result in increased traffic to your pages.

**You create a Digg link by adding JavaScript code to a page. For more about JavaScript, see Chapter 13.**

① Click where you want to embed the link.

② Type **<SCRIPT TYPE="text/javascript">**.

③ Type **digg_url = "?";**, replacing ? with the absolute URL of your Web page.

An absolute URL includes http:// and your domain name; for example, http://www.example.com/page.html.

④ Type **</SCRIPT>**.

5. Type **<script src="http://digg.com/tools/diggthis.js"**.

6. Type a space and then **type="text/javascript">**.

7. Type **</script>**.

8. Save the page and open it in a browser.

● The Digg link appears on the page. The graphic that appears is served from a Digg Web server.

Users can click the link to submit the Web page to Digg.

**TIP**

**How do I add a del.icio.us hyperlink to my Web page?**

Follow these steps to add the Web site del.icio.us.

1. Where you want to add the link, type **<A HREF="http://del.icio.us/post?url=?**, replacing *?* with the URL of your Web page. Be sure to include the http:// in the URL.

2. Type **&title=?**, replacing the second *?* with the title of your Web page.

3. Type **">Add to del.icio.us</a>** to complete the hyperlink.

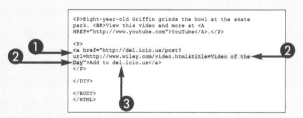

# Automatically Load another Web Page

You can automatically load a new Web page in the browser after a certain amount of time has passed. You might use this technique on a placeholder page that informs visitors that your Web page has moved.

① Add a new line between the `<HEAD>` and `</HEAD>` tags.

② Type **`<META HTTP-EQUIV= "Refresh"`**.

③ Type a space and **`CONTENT="?;`**, replacing *?* with the number of seconds you want to elapse before the new page appears.

④ Type a space and **URL=?">**, replacing *?* with the location and name of the page you want to appear.

⑤ Save and then open your HTML page.

The Web browser displays the first page. After the allotted time has elapsed, the second page loads.

**TIP**

### Can I load one page right after another to create a slide show?

Yes. You can use the <META> tag you used for loading pages to set up an automatic Web slide show of your pages. The pages progress from one to another, each staying on-screen for a designated time. Follow these steps:

① Add a new line between the <HEAD> and </HEAD> tags for the start page of your show.

② Type **<META HTTP-EQUIV="Refresh" CONTENT="?;**, replacing *?* with the number of seconds you want the current page to appear on-screen.

③ Type a space and then **URL=?"/>**, replacing *?* with the URL of the next page you want to appear.

④ Repeat steps **1** to **3** in each page you want to appear in the slide show. On each page, reference the page you want to follow.

For the last page, reference the first page again so the slide show loops.

# Create an Image Map

You can create an image map that links users to different pages based on where they click on the image. For example, you might use an image map as a navigational tool for your Web site. The key to creating a good image map is finding an image with distinct areas to click.

You can define each clickable area on the map using three shape values: rect (for rectangle), circle (for circle), and poly (for polygon, or an irregular shape).

TO DO LIST:
✓ MAKE IMAGE MAP
– CLEAN TOOL BENCH

## Create an Image Map

① Click where you want to insert an image map.

② Type **<IMG SRC="?"**, replacing *?* with the location and name of the image file.

③ Type a space and then **USEMAP="#?">**, replacing *?* with a name for the image map.

④ Click where you want to insert the map information and type **<MAP NAME="?">**, replacing *?* with the map name you assigned in step **3**.

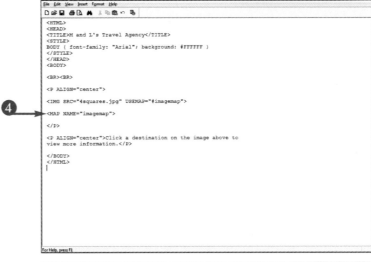

⑤ Type **<AREA** and a space.

⑥ Type **SHAPE="?"** followed by a space, replacing *?* with the shape of the area (rect, circle, or poly).

Choose a shape that best fits the clickable area you want to create.

## TIPS

**What is the difference between client-side image maps and server-side image maps?**

There are two kinds of image maps: client-side and server-side. Client-side maps are interpreted by the browser, so the response time is much faster. The user clicks a map area, and the page loads. With server-side maps, each mouse click must be sent to the server using a CGI script before the linked page appears. Most Web developers create client-side image maps for use with less-complex Web sites.

**How do I prepare an image to be an image map?**

You can use a photograph as an image map or, design your own graphic image map. You can use a drawing program to create a simple image map of several shapes with labels over the shapes. For example, you can take a large shape and divide it into smaller shapes, assigning each a different color and label corresponding to a Web page or content on your site. Regardless of how you create an image map, it should have logical areas to click.

# Create an Image Map *(continued)*

You use the <AREA> tag to define each clickable part of your image map. This information includes the shape of the clickable area and the corresponding coordinates on the image. You must also specify which Web page you want to open when each area is clicked on the map.

⑦ Type the coordinates for the clickable shape:

For a rectangle, type **COORDS="x1,y1,x2,y2"**, replacing *x1,y1* with the coordinates for the top-left corner and *x2,y2* with the coordinates for the bottom-right corner.

For a circle, type **COORDS="x,y,r"**, replacing *x,y* with the coordinates for the center of the circle and *r* with the radius.

For a polygon, type **COORDS= "x1,y1,x2,y2,x3 . . . "**, replacing each pair with the coordinates for each point on the polygon.

⑧ Type a blank space and **HREF="?">,** replacing *?* with the name and location of the Web page you want to appear when the area is clicked.

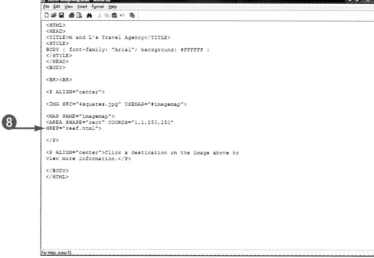

**⑨** Repeat steps **5** to **8** for each area of the image map.

**⑩** Type **</MAP>**.

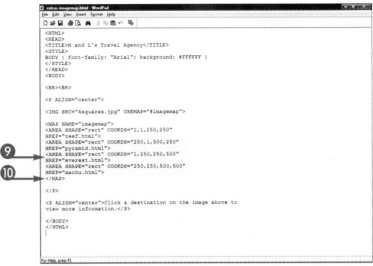

The Web browser displays the image map.

● When a user clicks an area on the map, the corresponding Web page opens.

**TIPS**

**How do I determine the coordinates for an area on my image map?**

You can use an image map editor to create image maps. You can also use an image map editor to determine the coordinates necessary to define the clickable areas within the map. One of the most popular image map editors is Mapedit. You can find it at www.boutell.com/mapedit. You can also conduct a Web search for free image map editors. If your graphics editing program has a graph feature, you might use it to figure out the map coordinates as well.

**What happens if my clickable areas overlap?**

If you accidentally overlap two areas with your coordinates, the Web browser treats the second area as part of the first. If you type coordinates that extend past the image area, the Web browser ignores them.

# CHAPTER

# 15

# Publishing Your Web Pages

Are you ready to place your HTML documents on the Web so others can view your pages? This chapter shows you how to find a Web host and transfer your files to a server.

# Understanding Web Page Publishing

The final phase of creating a Web site is publishing your pages. In the realm of HTML, the term *publishing* refers to all the necessary steps you must take to make your HTML documents available to others. This includes finding a Web host.

### Web Hosts

To make your pages available on the Web, you need a Web server — an Internet-connected computer specifically set up to store and manage Web pages. Commonly called *hosts*, Web servers allow you to transfer and store files, including HTML documents, images, and multimedia files. Unless you have your own Web server, you need to find a server to host your pages.

### Determine Your Needs

Before you start looking for a Web host, first determine what features and services you need. For example, how much storage space do you anticipate using for your Web site? Will you be serving multimedia content that uses a lot of space? Does your site require e-commerce features, such as an online shopping cart, or a secure server for handling confidential information? Do you need to keep track of Web statistics, such as who visits your site and how often? Knowing your needs beforehand can help you find the right host.

## Web Hosting Scenarios

Numerous companies around the world provide Web site hosting. Some do so for free, in exchange for placing advertising on your site, while others charge a monthly fee. Many Internet service providers (ISPs) and commercial online services offer their members a certain amount of storage space free. If you expect your site to generate a lot of traffic, you can use a dedicated Web presence provider — a company that specializes in helping others establish and maintain a presence on the Web. Web presence providers generally offer more features and support than ISPs.

## Search for a Web Host

The best place to start looking for a host is your own ISP or commercial service. If it does not offer hosting services, you can look for Web hosting services on the Internet. For example, the Web Hosting Ratings site (www.webhostingratings.com) can help you start your search. Also, consider asking friends and family for recommendations.

## Features to Consider

When considering a Web host, take some time to compare features and services as well as fees. Find out how much disk space the host allows. Although HTML documents are generally small, images and multimedia files included with Web pages can consume large amounts of space. Also find out the host's Internet connection speed and what advanced features and software it supports, such as CGI scripts, PHP, and database access. Ask whether it offers technical support, registers domain names, or provides Web hit statistics to track visitors to your site.

continued

After you find a host for your Web site and establish a domain name, if needed, the next step in publishing your Web page is to transfer the HTML documents from your computer to the Web server.

Ordinarily, when you publish your pages to a Web host, your Web address is the name of the host's domain followed by the path to your files. If you want a more unique address, you may want to obtain your own domain name. A domain name is a high-level address for a Web site, such as wiley.com (owned by the publisher of this book). To acquire a domain name, you must register and pay for it.

### Acquire Your Own Domain Name

You can register for a domain name through VeriSign (www.netsol.com), which manages the infrastructure for the .com and .net domain names. Dozens of other domain name registrars can help you register these and other types of domain names. Your Web hosting service may also offer a registration service for domain names, for a reduced fee. After you acquire a domain name, you can ask your Web host to create a virtual domain for your site on the host's server. This allows you to use your unique domain name rather than the provider's server name in your URL.

### Transfer Files

After you set up an account with a Web host, you can transfer your HTML files to the server and set up your Web site. Transferring files from your computer to a Web server is called *uploading*. Depending on your server, you can transfer files using FTP (File Transfer Protocol) or a Web interface provided by your hosting service. More often than not, you use FTP to upload your files.

### FTP Programs

FTP is the standard for file transfer on the Internet. To transfer files with FTP, you need an FTP program, also called a *client*. You can find free and shareware FTP clients on the Internet. Popular FTP programs include WS_FTP for Windows (www.ipswitch.com/Products/WS_FTP/) and CuteFTP (www.globalscape.com/products/cuteFTP). Also, check your Web host to see what FTP clients or file upload tools it offers. See the section "Transfer Files to a Web Server with WS_FTP" for more information.

### Maintain Your Site

After you upload your pages, you can view and test your site. One of your chores as a Web developer is to maintain your Web site. It is up to you to keep your information and links current. It is good practice to regularly test your site for broken links. See the section "Troubleshoot Your Web Pages" to learn more about fixing page problems. Although some sites need more updating than others do, it is also good practice to update your content on a regular basis or give it a fresh look from time to time. Stale data can keep visitors from returning to your site.

### Publicize Your Site

After you publish your Web site, you can look for ways to attract visitors. You can add descriptions and keywords in <META> tags and useful page titles to gain the attention of search engines. See Chapter 2 for more information. You can also advertise your pages on other sites, through e-mails, and offline. See the section "Promote Your Web Site" for more information.

# Transfer Files to a Web Server with WS_FTP

You can transfer your Web page files to a Web server using FTP software. FTP stands for *File Transfer Protocol*, which is a method for moving files on the Internet. In this section, you learn how to transfer files using Ipswitch WS_FTP, a popular program for transferring Web files. If you use another FTP program, your steps may differ.

## SET UP YOUR CONNECTION

**1** Open the WS_FTP program window.

The first time you use the program, the Connection Wizard appears to help you set up your server connection.

***Note:*** *To download and install the program, visit www.ipswitch.com. This example uses the Home version of WS_FTP.*

**2** Type a name for your connection. This can be the name of your Web site.

**3** Click **Next**.

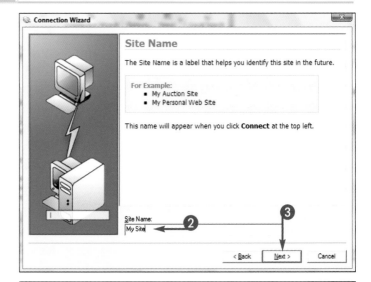

**4** Select a connection type.

The default and most common type for transferring files is FTP.

**5** Click **Next**.

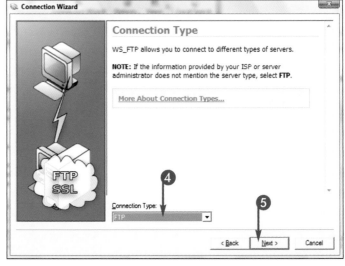

⑥ Type your server address.

If you do not know the server address, contact your service provider for more information.

Typically, you receive this information when you sign up for an account.

⑦ Click **Next**.

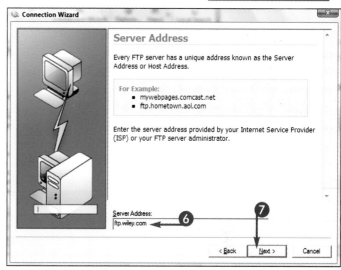

⑧ Type your user name.

⑨ Type your password.

If you do not know your user name or password, contact your service provider.

Again, you typically receive this information when you sign up for an account.

⑩ Click **Next**.

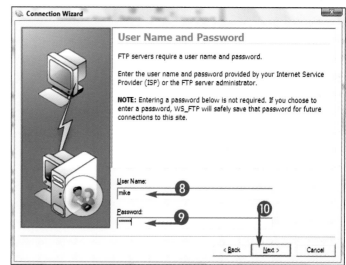

**Where can I find an FTP program?**
You can find numerous FTP programs on the Internet, including freeware and shareware programs. Download.com (www.download.com) is a popular site for obtaining such programs. Many programs offer a free trial version you can experiment with to see if you want to purchase the full version. You can find a trial version of Ipswitch WS_FTP at www.ipswitch.com.

**What information do I need to set up an account with an FTP program?**
Most servers ask you for a server address, a user name, and a password. When you create an account with a Web host provider, you are assigned this information, including a destination folder on the server's directory. You can use this folder to store your HTML files, along with any image and multimedia files you include with your Web page.

continued

After you establish your server connection, you can start transferring files. The WS_FTP program window shows two panes, one displaying the files on your computer and the other displaying files on your server. You can move files between the two by clicking the Upload and Download buttons.

**You can upload a single file or multiple files. Anytime you need to update your site, you must transfer more files to the server.**

Transfer Files to a Web Server with WS_FTP *(continued)*

● You can select this option if you want to open your connection immediately upon completing the Connection Wizard.

⑪ Click **Finish**.

Your connection information is saved, and the program window remains open and ready for any file transfer activities you want to perform.

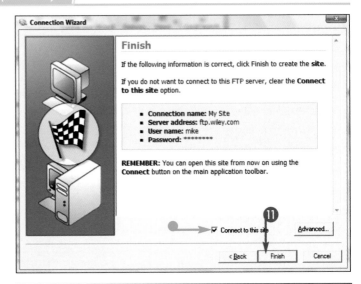

**TRANSFER FILES**

① If you have not connected to your server, click **Connect**.

**Note:** *You must connect to the Internet before transferring files.*

The Site Manager dialog box appears.

② Select your connection name from the list.

③ Click **Connect**.

WS_FTP connects your computer to the server.

4 Navigate to the folder on your computer that contains your HTML and other site files.

● You may need to navigate to a special folder on the server where Web site files are stored. Check with your service provider for details.

5 Click the files you want to transfer.

To select multiple files, press and hold **Shift** shift while clicking file names.

6 Click the **Upload** button (●).

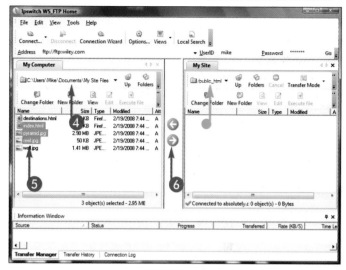

● WS_FTP shows status messages as it transfers the files.

Depending on the file size, the transfer may take several minutes.

● The transferred files appear in the list of server files.

7 Click the **Close** button (✕) to exit the program when you finish transferring files.

You can now use your browser to view the pages.

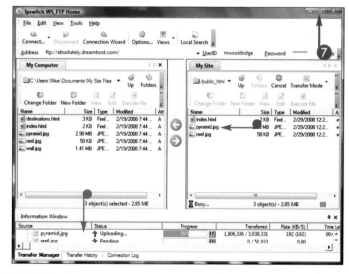

**TIPS**

**How do I remove a file from my Web site?**

Open your connection to the server, select the file you want to delete from the left pane, and press **Delete** (Delete). A prompt box appears asking if you really want to remove the file. Click **Yes** to remove your file from the server.

**Can I transfer a new version of a file that is already on the server?**

Yes. You can overwrite existing files. WS_FTP prompts you if it finds the same file on the server. You then have the option of overwriting the existing file with the new file. Simply click **Overwrite** in the prompt box. If you prefer to wait and check the file later, click **Skip** and WS_FTP leaves the original file on the server.

# Troubleshoot Your Web Pages

No matter how carefully you create your pages, errors can creep in. If your Web page does not display properly in a browser, you must track down the problem. In most situations, you can trace the problem to a common coding error. If you cannot find the error even after a thorough check, try showing your document to another Web developer for feedback.

## Typing Errors

Typing errors are the most common mistakes in HTML documents. Web browsers ignore tags they do not recognize, so always start your troubleshooting process with a careful proofread of your document. Read each line in your document, paying close attention to tags and attributes. One mistyped character, quotation mark, or bracket can cause a browser to display broken content. Many Web editors color-code HTML tags to help you find such errors.

## Invalid Paths

Typing the wrong path to a file can cause an error on your pages. This can occur in hyperlinks, image and multimedia tags, and references to JavaScript and CSS. If a server cannot locate a file on the Web host, it cannot access or display the corresponding content. When page content does not appear as expected, double-check your text for the correct paths. It is also essential to use the correct file extensions when specifying files.

## Broken Links

Even if the paths to your links are syntactically correct, that doesn't guarantee that the file on the corresponding server is still there. Nothing is more frustrating to Web page visitors than clicking a nonfunctioning link, so test your links on a regular basis. Because pages come and go on the Web, make it a regular practice to check your links.

## Missing Image Files

If the Web browser cannot display your images, you may have typed the wrong file name. Verify your image name, making sure you typed the correct upper- and lowercase letters for the file name. It is also common to type the wrong file extension for an image file, such as GIF instead of JPG. Remember, not all browsers support all kinds of image files. Be sure to stick with formats commonly found on the Web. See Chapter 5 to learn more.

## HTML Code Appears

If the browser displays your HTML code instead of the Web page, you probably saved the document as a TXT file instead of an HTML file. Also double-check to see if your <HTML> tag appears at the top of the page. If this tag is missing, the browser may not read your page as an HTML document.

## HTML Validators

After you upload your pages, you can access an HTML validator and have it automatically download and process your page content. Because most validators reference the official HTML specification, they can point out syntax errors and tell you if you are coding to the latest official standard. The W3C, which maintains HTML specifications, offers a validation service at http://validator.w3.org.

After you publish your site, it is available for others to view on the Web. There are several ways you can bring attention to your Web site. You can advertise it offline by adding your URL to business cards, stationery, and other products you distribute to others. You can advertise your site online by adding your URL to your e-mail message signature. You can also enlist the help of search engines to index your site.

### Search Engines

Search engines collect information about pages encountered on the Web and then make that information easily searchable. They do this by cataloging URLs, keywords, page titles, and text from HTML documents. When someone performs a search for keywords, the search engine compares the request with the information gathered in its database and displays matching results as links, listing what it determines to be the most relevant links first.

### Submit Your Site

To help bring attention to your site, you can register it with search engines. Some search engines offer an online form you can fill out to register your URL. Popular search engines to contact include Google (www.google.com/addurl.html) and Yahoo (docs.yahoo.com/info/suggest/). Even if you do not register your site with search engines, they will often do a good job of finding your site by following links from other sites.

## Add Keywords

When users look for Web sites, they type keywords into a search engine. You can add keywords to your page to help users find your site. You can add keywords to your metadata information, as well as use them in your title and headers. Keywords should honestly reflect your content. Take time to think about keywords users might type to find your page, and then add them to your metadata tag. See Chapter 2 to learn how to insert metadata on your page.

## Write Good Page Titles

Because search engines give greater weight to page titles when analyzing Web pages, adding descriptive titles can help draw users to your site. Search engine results pages typically list page titles, so a well-written title can tell a potential visitor whether your site is relevant or not. When writing titles, keep your text descriptive but concise. See Chapter 2 to learn how to add title text to your page.

## Linking with Others

Another good way to publicize your site is through links. You can contact sites with similar content to see if they will link to your site. You can then link to those sites in exchange. You can also join Web rings of similar sites. A Web ring is a group of sites focusing on a related topic, all linking to each other.

## Advertising

You can advertise your Web site on other pages. Some free link-exchange networks can help you promote your site by allowing you to exchange links with similar sites. Search for "link exchange" on your favorite search engine to find them. Advertising networks such as Adbrite (www.adbrite.com) and Google AdWords (http://adwords.google.com) allow you to promote your site's services on other Web sites for a fee.

# HTML Tags

## Basic Tags/Attributes

| Tag/Attribute | Description |
|---|---|
| <!--> | Inserts a comment |
| <!DOCTYPE> | Indicates what version of HTML is used |
| <BODY> | Identifies content on a Web page |
| <BR> | Creates a new line |
| <H1>, <H2>, <H3>, <H4>, <H5>, <H6> | Creates heading levels |
| <HEAD> | Contains information about a Web page title, style sheets, and search engine keywords |
| <HTML> | Identifies an HTML document |
| <META> | Contains extra information about the Web page |
| CONTENT | Specifies custom information about a page |
| NAME | Adds description or copyright information to a Web page |
| <P> | Starts a new paragraph |
| ALIGN | Aligns a paragraph |
| <TITLE> | Creates a title for a Web page |

## Text Formatting Tags/Attributes

| Tag/Attribute | Description |
|---|---|
| <B> | Bolds text |
| <BASEFONT> | Specifies a default font for the entire page |
| COLOR | Specifies default text color |
| FACE | Specifies default font |
| SIZE | Specifies default text size |
| <BIG> | Makes text larger than surrounding text |
| <BLINK> | Makes text blink |
| <BLOCKQUOTE> | Separates text from the main text for attention |
| <BODY> | |
| BGCOLOR | Sets a background color for a page |
| BOTTOMMARGIN | Changes the bottom margin |
| LEFTMARGIN | Changes the left margin |
| MARGINHEIGHT | Changes the top and bottom margins |

| Tag/Attribute | Description |
| --- | --- |
| MARGINWIDTH | Changes the left and right margins |
| RIGHTMARGIN | Changes the right margin |
| TEXT | Specifies a color for all the text on the page |
| TOPMARGIN | Changes the top margin |
| <CENTER> | Centers information on the page |
| <FONT> | Changes the appearance of text |
| COLOR | Changes the text color |
| FACE | Changes the font |
| SIZE | Changes the text size |
| <I> | Italicizes text |
| <NOBR> | Keeps all the text on one line, without breaks |
| <PRE> | Retains preformatted spacing for text |
| <Q> | Adds quotes to text |
| <SMALL> | Makes the text smaller than surrounding text |
| <STRIKE> | Adds a strikethrough line to text |
| <SUB> | Places text slightly below the baseline |
| <SUP> | Places text slightly above the baseline |
| <TT> | Creates typewriter text |
| <U> | Underlines text |

| List Tags/Attributes | |
| --- | --- |
| **Tag/Attribute** | **Description** |
| <DD> | Identifies a definition in a definition list |
| <DL> | Creates a definition list of terms |
| <DT> | Identifies a term in a definition list |
| <LI> | Identifies an item in an ordered or unordered list |
| <OL> | Creates an ordered list |
| START | Specifies a start number for an ordered list |
| TYPE | Specifies a number style for an ordered list |
| <UL> | Creates an unordered list |
| TYPE | Specifies a bullet style for an unordered list |

## HTML Tags

| Table Tags/Attributes | |
|---|---|
| **Tag/Attribute** | **Description** |
| <CAPTION> | Adds a caption to a table |
| <CENTER> | Center aligns a table on a page |
| <COL> | Defines special columns in a column group |
| ALIGN | Aligns column content |
| SPAN | Specifies the number of columns to format |
| WIDTH | Specifies the default width for columns |
| <COLGROUP> | Defines a column group |
| ALIGN | Aligns column content |
| SPAN | Specifies the number of columns |
| WIDTH | Specifies the default width for columns |
| <TABLE> | Creates a table |
| ALIGN | Controls table alignment |
| BACKGROUND | Inserts a background image into a table |
| BGCOLOR | Changes the table background color |
| BORDER | Adds a border to a table |
| CELLPADDING | Changes the amount of space around cell contents |
| CELLSPACING | Changes the amount of space between cells |
| HEIGHT | Controls the height of a table |
| WIDTH | Controls the width of a table |
| <TD> | Creates a data cell in a table |
| ALIGN | Aligns data in a cell |
| BGCOLOR | Changes the cell background color |
| COLSPAN | Combines two or more cells across columns |
| HEIGHT | Controls the height of a table cell |
| NOWRAP | Keeps text in a cell on one line |
| ROWSPAN | Combines two or more cells down rows |
| VALIGN | Aligns data vertically in a cell |
| WIDTH | Controls the width of a table cell |
| <TH> | Creates a header cell |
| ALIGN | Aligns data in a header cell |
| BGCOLOR | Adds background color to a header cell |
| COLSPAN | Combines two or more header cells across columns |
| HEIGHT | Controls the height of a header cell |

| Tag/Attribute | Description |
| --- | --- |
| NOWRAP | Keeps text in a header cell on one line |
| ROWSPAN | Combines two or more header cells down rows |
| WIDTH | Controls the width of a header cell |
| VALIGN | Aligns data vertically in a header cell |
| <TR> | Creates a new row in a table |
| ALIGN | Aligns data horizontally in a table |
| BGCOLOR | Changes the background color of a row |
| VALIGN | Aligns data vertically in a table |

| Image Tags/Attributes | |
| --- | --- |
| **Tag/Attribute** | **Description** |
| <BODY> | |
| BACKGROUND | Inserts a background image on the page |
| <BR> | |
| CLEAR | Stops text from wrapping around an image |
| <CENTER> | Center aligns an image |
| <HR> | Adds a horizontal rule |
| ALIGN | Aligns a horizontal rule |
| NOSHADE | Displays rule without shading |
| SIZE | Changes the thickness of a horizontal rule |
| WIDTH | Changes the width of a horizontal rule |
| <IMG> | Inserts an image on a page |
| ALIGN | Aligns an image on the page |
| ALT | Displays alternative text when an image does not download |
| BORDER | Adds a border to an image |
| HEIGHT | Controls the height of an image |
| HSPACE | Adds space to the left and right sides of an image |
| SRC | Specifies the image location or path |
| VSPACE | Adds space above and below an image |
| WIDTH | Controls the width of an image |

# HTML Tags

## Links Tags/Attributes

| Tag/Attribute | Description |
| --- | --- |
| <A> | Creates a link |
| HREF | Specifies the path and location of a linked page or other resource |
| NAME | Names a Web page area for referencing by a link |
| TARGET | Specifies where linked information appears |
| <BODY> | |
| ALINK | Changes the color of a link as the user clicks it |
| LINK | Changes the color of an unvisited link |
| VLINK | Changes the color of a visited link |

## Image Map Tags/Attributes

| Tag/Attribute | Description |
| --- | --- |
| <AREA> | Specifies an image area |
| COORDS | Specifies all the coordinates for an image area |
| HREF | Specifies the location of a Web page linked to an image area |
| NOHREF | Excludes an area from an image map |
| SHAPE | Controls the shape of an image area |
| TARGET | Specifies a window or frame that a link should display in |
| <IMG> | Adds an image to a page |
| USEMAP | Identifies an image map for an image |
| <MAP> | Creates an image map |
| NAME | Names an image map |

## Multimedia Tags/Attributes

| Tag/Attribute | Description |
| --- | --- |
| <A> | |
| HREF | Specifies the path and location of a linked sound or video |
| <BGSOUND> | Specifies a background audio clip for a Web page |
| LOOP | Controls how often an audio clip plays |
| SRC | Specifies the path and location of the audio clip |

| Tag/Attribute | Description |
|---|---|
| <EMBED> | Adds an audio or video clip to a Web page |
| AUTOSTART | Plays a multimedia clip automatically |
| CONTROLS | Adds control buttons for the multimedia element |
| HEIGHT | Controls the height of a multimedia element |
| LOOP | Plays a multimedia clip continuously |
| SRC | Specifies the path and location of a multimedia clip |
| WIDTH | Specifies the width of a multimedia element |
| <OBJECT> | Adds a multimedia object to a Web page |
| ALIGN | Aligns objects |
| BORDER | Adds a border to an object |
| CLASSID | Identifies the kind of object being embedded |
| CODEBASE | Defines the base URL of the source object |
| DATA | Identifies the source of the multimedia file |
| HEIGHT | Controls the height of an object |
| HSPACE | Adds space to the sides of the object |
| NAME | Identifies the object |
| STANDBY | Displays a message as the object is loading |
| TYPE | Identifies the object's MIME type |
| VSPACE | Adds space to the top and bottom of the object |
| WIDTH | Controls the width of an object |

| Java and JavaScript Tags/Attributes | |
|---|---|
| Tag/Attribute | Description |
| <APPLET> | Adds a Java applet to a Web page |
| CODE | Specifies the location of a Java applet |
| HEIGHT | Specifies the height of a Java applet |
| WIDTH | Specifies the width of a Java applet |
| <NOSCRIPT> | Displays alternative text when a JavaScript does not run |
| <SCRIPT> | Adds JavaScript code to a Web page |
| SRC | Specifies the path and location of JavaScript code |
| TYPE | Identifies the script as JavaScript |

## Frame Tags/Attributes

| Tag/Attribute | Description |
|---|---|
| <A> | |
| HREF | Specifies the location of a linked Web page to appear in a frame |
| TARGET | Specifies the frame where a linked Web page will appear |
| <BASE> | Specifies the information about links on a page |
| TARGET | Specifies the frame where linked Web pages appear |
| <FRAME> | Specifies information for a frame |
| MARGINHEIGHT | Changes the top and bottom margins of a frame |
| MARGINWIDTH | Changes the left and right margins of a frame |
| NAME | Names a frame |
| NORESIZE | Prevents users from resizing a frame |
| SCROLLING | Hides or displays scroll bars for a frame |
| SRC | Specifies the location of a Web page to appear in a frame |
| <FRAMESET> | Specifies a structure for frames |
| BORDER | Specifies a border thickness for a frame |
| COLS | Creates frames in columns |
| ROWS | Creates frames in rows |
| <NOFRAMES> | Displays alternative text for frames that do not appear |

## Form Tags/Attributes

| Tag/Attribute | Description |
|---|---|
| <FORM> | Creates a form |
| ACTION | Specifies the location of a CGI script for a form |
| METHOD | Specifies how form information is sent to a Web server |
| <INPUT> | Creates an input item on a form |
| CHECKED | Automatically selects a radio button or check box |
| ENCTYPE | Specifies file transfer for form data over the Internet |

| Tag/Attribute | Description |
|---|---|
| MAXLENGTH | Specifies the maximum number of characters for a form entry |
| NAME | Identifies the name of a form item for a server |
| SIZE | Specifies the form item size |
| TYPE | Specifies the form item type |
| VALUE | Identifies the value of a form item for a server |
| <LABEL> | Labels a form element |
| FOR | Specifies which form element the label belongs to |
| <OPTION> | Creates a menu option for a form |
| SELECTED | Specifies which menu option is selected by default |
| VALUE | Identifies a form item for a server |
| <SELECT> | Creates a menu item on a form |
| NAME | Identifies a form menu for a server |
| SIZE | Specifies the number of menu options displayed at a time |
| <TEXTAREA> | Creates a large text area on a form |
| COLS | Specifies a width of a large text area |
| NAME | Identifies the name of a text area for a server |
| ROWS | Specifies a height of a large text area |
| WRAP | Wraps text within a large text area |

| Style Sheet Tags/Attributes | |
|---|---|
| **Tag/Attribute** | **Description** |
| CLASS | Assigns a style rule to an HTML tag |
| ID | Assigns a style rule to an HTML tag |
| STYLE | Assigns a style declaration to an HTML tag |
| <DIV> | Assigns a style to a specific area of a page |
| CLASS | Assigns a style rule |

*continued*

## Style Sheet Tags/Attributes *(continued)*

| Tag/Attribute | Description |
|---|---|
| <LINK> | Links a Web page to an external style sheet |
|    HREF | Specifies the path and location of an external style sheet |
|    REL | Specifies a link to a style sheet, whether the sheet is primary or alternative |
|    TYPE | Specifies the format of a style sheet |
| <STYLE> | Creates a style sheet |

## Style Sheet Characteristics

| Characteristic | Description |
|---|---|
| background | Specifies a background color or image |
| background-color | Specifies a background color of an element |
| border | Specifies a border |
| border-color | Specifies a border color |
| border-spacing | Controls the amount of space between borders in a table |
| border-style | Specifies a border style |
| border-width | Specifies a line thickness for a border |
| color | Specifies a color |
| float | Aligns and wraps text on a page |
| font-family | Specifies a font |
| font-size | Specifies a font size |
| font-style | Italicizes text |
| font-weight | Bolds text |
| height | Specifies the height of an element |
| line-height | Specifies line spacing |
| list-style | Specifies a bullet or number style for lists |
| margin | Sets a margin of an element |
| padding | Specifies the space between content and borders |
| text-align | Aligns text |
| text-decoration | Adds underlining to text |
| text-indent | Indents the first line of text |
| text-transform | Specifies a text case |
| width | Specifies the width of an element |

## Sixteen Named Colors

| Color | Name |
|---|---|
| | Black (#000000) |
| | Silver (#C0C0C0) |
| | Gray (#808080) |
| | White (#FFFFFF) |
| | Maroon (#800000) |
| | Red (#FF0000) |
| | Purple (#800080) |
| | Fuchsia (#FF00FF) |
| | Green (#008000) |
| | Lime (#00FF00) |
| | Olive (#808000) |
| | Yellow (#FFFF00) |
| | Navy (#000080) |
| | Blue (#0000FF) |
| | Teal (#008080) |
| | Aqua (#00FFFF) |

# Index

# Index

# Index

# Index

line breaks, 36, 45, 137
line spacing, `line-height` property, 210
linear structure, Web site layout, 15
`line-height` property, leading, 210
lines, horizontal rule, 62–63
`LINK` attribute, link colors, 102–103, 219
link exchanges, Web site promotion, 311
links
    absolute, 89
    anchor tags `<A>` and `</A>`, 89
    another place/same Web page, 96–97
    another Web page, 92–93
    another Web page/same Web site, 93
    area names, 96–97
    audio/video file, 276–277
    borders, 93
    colors, 88, 102–103, 218–219
    Digg, 290–291
    e-mail address, 100–101
    external style sheets, 187
    external Web pages, 88
    file type, 98–99
    frames, 152–153
    hover effects, 220–221
    image maps, 294–297
    images, 88
    internal Web pages, 89
    media file delivery method, 272, 276–277
    new browser window, 94–95
    online bookmarking tools, 291
    plain-text files, 99
    pointing hand cursor, 88
    relative, 89
    same page, 89
    status bar message, 263
    style sheets, 190
    text, 88
    troubleshooting, 309
    underline removal, 103
    underlined text, 88
    URL (Uniform Resource Locator), 5, 90–91
    Web page navigation uses, 97
    Web site promotion, 311
lists
    `ALIGN` attribute, 35
    body content, 19, 22
    bulleted (unordered), 44–45
    definition, 47
    form element, 161, 174–175
    `<LI>` and `</LI>` tags, 42–43
    `list-style` property, 222–223
    nested, 46
    numbered (ordered), 42–43
`list-style` property, 222–223
logos, GIF format, 67
lowercase letters, 10, 21, 208

## M

Macintosh, 8–9
MAILTO prefix, 90, 100–101
`<MAP>` and `</MAP>` tags, 296–297
Mapedit, image map editor, 297
`MARGIN` attribute, 60
`margin` property, 238
`MARGINHEIGHT` attribute, 148
margins, 60, 148, 229, 238
`MARGINWIDTH` attribute, frame margins, 148
`MAXLENGTH` attribute, form text box, 166–167
Mbps. *See* megabits per second (Mbps)
measurement units, 204–205, 231, 239
media players, multimedia playback method, 274–275
megabits per second (Mbps), Internet connection speeds, 4
menus, form element, 161, 174–175, 225
merging cells, 126–127
message boxes, JavaScript, 261
`<META>` tag, 30–31, 293
metadata, 19, 30–31
Microsoft Expression, HTML editor, 9
Microsoft Internet Explorer, 5. *See also* Internet Explorer
Microsoft Windows Vista, 8–9, 12–13
Microsoft Word, HTML editor uses, 9
MIME. *See* Multi-purpose Internet Mail Extensions (MIME)
minimum length, JavaScript form data validation, 267
minus (-) character, relative font sizing, 57
modems, Internet connection type, 4
monitors, image sizing issues, 73
monospace, supported font style, 55
mouse pointer, 88, 220–221, 264–265, 269
Mozilla Firefox, 5, 8. *See also* Firefox
multimedia
    ActiveX controls, 275
    background music, 277
    Digg link, 290–291
    EMBED element, 275
    embedded media types, 272, 273
    embedding a Flash movie, 282
    embedding files, 278–281
    external media files, 273
    file delivery methods, 272
    Flickr images, 286–287
    Google search box, 288–289
    Java applets, 283

# Index

# Index

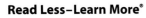

**Read Less–Learn More®**

# There's a Visual book for every learning level...

## Simplified®

**The place to start if you're new to computers. Full color.**

- Computers
- Creating Web Pages
- Mac OS
- Office
- Windows

## Teach Yourself VISUALLY™

**Get beginning to intermediate-level training in a variety of topics. Full color.**

- Access
- Bridge
- Chess
- Computers
- Crocheting
- Digital Photography
- Dog training
- Dreamweaver
- Excel
- Flash
- Golf
- Guitar
- Handspinning
- HTML
- Jewelry Making & Beading
- Knitting
- Mac OS
- Office
- Photoshop
- Photoshop Elements
- Piano
- Poker
- PowerPoint
- Quilting
- Scrapbooking
- Sewing
- Windows
- Wireless Networking
- Word

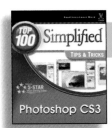

## Top 100 Simplified® Tips & Tricks

**Tips and techniques to take your skills beyond the basics. Full color.**

- Digital Photography
- eBay
- Excel
- Google
- Internet
- Mac OS
- Office
- Photoshop
- Photoshop Elements
- PowerPoint
- Windows

# ...all designed for visual learners—just like you!

## Master VISUALLY®

**Your complete visual reference. Two-color interior.**

- 3ds Max
- Creating Web Pages
- Dreamweaver and Flash
- Excel
- Excel VBA Programming
- iPod and iTunes
- Mac OS
- Office
- Optimizing PC Performance
- Photoshop Elements
- QuickBooks
- Quicken
- Windows
- Windows Mobile
- Windows Server

## Visual Blueprint™

**Where to go for professional-level programming instruction. Two-color interior.**

- Ajax
- ASP.NET 2.0
- Excel Data Analysis
- Excel Pivot Tables
- Excel Programming
- HTML
- JavaScript
- Mambo
- PHP & MySQL
- SEO
- Vista Sidebar
- Visual Basic
- XML

## Visual Encyclopedia™

**Your A to Z reference of tools and techniques. Full color.**

- Dreamweaver
- Excel
- Mac OS
- Photoshop
- Windows

## Visual Quick Tips

**Shortcuts, tricks, and techniques for getting more done in less time. Full color.**

- Crochet
- Digital Photography
- Excel
- iPod & iTunes
- Knitting
- MySpace
- Office
- PowerPoint
- Windows
- Wireless Networking